Rugby League Nostalgia

Dave Jones

London League Publications Ltd

Rugby League Nostalgia
© Dave Jones
Foreword © Gary Hetherington

The moral right of Dave Jones to be identified as the author has been asserted.

Front & back cover design @ Stephen McCarthy.

All photographs are as credited to the photographer or provider of the photo. No copyright has been intentionally breached; please contact London League Publications Ltd if you believe there has been a breach of copyright.

Front cover photos: Whitehaven versus Bradford Northern (Courtesy *Rugby League Journal*) and Tommy Smales in action for Bradford Northern versus Hull KR (Courtesy *Rugby League Journal*)

Back cover photos: Vince Karalius (Courtesy Alex Service)

This book is copyright under the Berne Convention. All rights are reserved. It is sold subject to the condition that it shall not, by way of trade or otherwise, be lent, resold, hired out or otherwise circulated without the publisher's prior consent in any form of binding or cover other than that in which it is published and without a similar condition being imposed on the subsequent purchaser.

A CIP catalogue record for this book is available from the British Library.

Published in October 2024 by London League Publications Ltd, PO Box 65784, London NW2 9NS

ISBN: 978-1-909885-38-7

Cover design by Stephen McCarthy Graphic Design
46, Clarence Road, London N15 5BB.

Editing and layout by Peter Lush

Printed and bound in Great Britain by CPI Group (UK) Ltd, Croydon CR0 4YY

To the one who makes me look forward to the future,
As well as looking to the past –
For my Heather
Who is my anchor and my harbour.

Dave Jones

Foreword

I first met Dave Jones almost 20 years ago when he came to Headingley to lead a teacher training session for the Leeds Rhinos Foundation. He had produced some educational resources to help teachers to use the values of the game to inspire personal and moral development amongst children in schools across the city. His passion for the game was immediately apparent and he has a strong and continued commitment to highlighting the heritage of rugby league.

Rugby League Nostalgia is an unashamed celebration of the way we were. Dave has drawn on his love for the game he has followed for several decades to compile this important contribution to the recorded history of our sport. In its pages he draws attention to the exploits of the great players and characters who have graced the game since the founding fathers broke the shackles from the union code in 1895. He highlights the epic Ashes clashes and Wembley finals as well as drawing on his own personal recollections of his boyhood heroes. Nor does he neglect to pay homage to the organisations and individuals without whom our sport would not exist. Those who form the very bedrock of the grass roots community game receive their place alongside the great and the good in this book which will delight all those fans who wish to keep alive their love for the game we all cherish.

Gary Hetherington
Leeds Rhinos Chief Executive

Gary Hetherington is a dyed-in-the-wool rugby league man. A son of Castleford, Gary hails from coal mining stock. As a player he played for Wakefield Trinity, York, Leeds, Kent Invicta and Huddersfield. Primarily a hooker, Gary was always interested in coaching. He says that the reason for his nomadic career was his strong views on tactics. His entrepreneurial spirit was typified in the way he established the Sheffield Eagles club in 1984 in a soccer-mad city. Gary coached the club for 11 seasons and was assistant coach for Great Britain in two tests. He enabled the Eagles to become part of the fabric of the city before moving in 1996 to become chief executive at Headingley. During his tenure, the club – which had often flattered to deceive – built a successful dynasty of players who became and remain household names. As well as being a visionary for the future, Gary is a champion of the heritage of rugby league and Headingley has become a beacon of celebration of the game's past and a shrine to the history of the club and the sport in general.

About the author

Dave Jones is a retired primary school Headteacher who was awarded the National College for School Leadership Headteacher of the Year Award for the North of England, having served as a Head for some 20 years. Shortly before his retirement, he was invited as an expert witness to give evidence to the Parliamentary Sub-Committee on Education at the House of Commons on the achievement of working class pupils. Prior to embarking on his teaching career, Dave attended university in Wales before becoming a youth worker in the East End of London. He believes passionately in the transformative power of sport to enrich and enhance the life chances of young people. For many years he played an active role in Bradford Schools Rugby League. He was introduced to the sport by his father, a Welsh coal miner, who took him to Odsal Stadium in 1964 to see the resurgent Bradford Northern. Ever since that experience, he has remained a keen student of the history of 'the greatest game'. Dave is a regular contributor to *Rugby League Journal* which celebrates the heritage of the XIII-a-side code.

Introduction

In his sequel travelogue to *Notes from a Small Island* entitled *The Road to Little Dribbling*, Bill Bryson expresses the view that everyone should be permitted a dozen dislikes which they should not be required to justify or explain. His list included colour names like taupe or teal which mean nothing and Harry Redknapp. This set me thinking about my own aversions to features of our modern game. My wife sometimes points out that I have an increased tendency to grumpiness and that this is often most apparent when I am watching a game on television. I argue that the development of a curmudgeonly gene is entirely natural like the increased tendency to grow nasal hair and that it is a healthy outlet for the spleen. Here then are a list of my own 'reflex loathings' as Bryson calls them, regarding rugby league in the current era. There are 13 of them.

1. Calling **Rugby** League **Super** League.
2. Ridiculous kit designs which resemble Hawaiian shirts for a lads' weekend in Magaluf and which bear no resemblance to club's traditional colours – an issue which really comes to a head on 'Magic Weekend'.
3. Pundits whose jackets are two sizes too small. (Take note Brian Carney, fine winger though you were).
4. Interminable delays caused by sending decisions 'upstairs.'
5. Players' boots in every conceivable pastel shade from bright pink to luminous apricot to banana yellow – anything but black.
6. Modern references to positional play or combinations such as spines, edges or middles as opposed to those with some traditional meaning like forwards, backs etc.
7. The play-the-ball area becoming 'the ruck'.
8. Referees who ignore players' flagrant refusal to involve their foot in the process of playing the ball.
9. Clubs who jump into bed with dubious sponsors like betting companies and money lenders who feed off working class communities which our game purports to serve.
10. 'Golden Point'. Draws denote a good close game with honours shared evenly.
11. 'Spelling' – not in an orthographic sense – but rather the practice of substituting 'the middles' every 10 minutes to remove any meaningful attritional contest which merely benefits those with the bigger and better resourced squads.
12. The use of the Australianism "real" when the coach or pundit really means "really", as in "real tough", "real close" etc.
13. Pre-match, on-field wrestling warm-ups. It's like going to the theatre and seeing all those actors rehearsing on stage prior to curtain up. Talk about puncturing the fourth wall. It kills the drama of the gladiatorial entry and really lets smoke in on the magic.

Now let me be clear from the outset that I admire many aspects of the modern game. The players who entertain us at the highest level are tremendous athletes. When you meet them, they are still humble and grounded and do tremendous work in their communities. Rob Burrow, who sadly passed away while this book was being written, and Kevin Sinfield have become national treasures and they epitomise the quality of people that our game grows. The modern game is fast and furious and the collisions are fierce. Matchdays are full of razzmatazz for kids to enjoy. I took my youngest grandson to a World Cup game at Headingley and he was mesmerised by the whole affair, particularly the bee mascot. I am not like 'the old gits' played by Harry Enfield and Paul Whitehouse no matter what my wife may think.

All that I would ask is that we do not fall into the trap of believing that the game only began with the advent of Super League and summer rugby. I merely make a plea not to jettison our heritage. I am firmly of the belief that it's hard to know where you're going if you are unsure of where you've been. There is no need to blow out the candle of our past to make the present seem that bit brighter.

This book is unashamedly nostalgic for a game I have loved for some 60 years. I fear that some modern fans have a rather jaundiced view of 'the bad old days' as an era where pot-bellied, muddied oafs played a moribund brand of football egged on by flat capped, wheezing old men, puffing on pipes and Woodbines. Rugby league 'back in the day' is depicted in some quarters as slow and ponderous, played out on windswept winter days in a dour, turgid slog. But these lazy stereotyped views of the game back in those seemingly grim and grotty times is simply not fair.

Those of us who followed the game back then know what pleasure we derived from supporting our favoured team. Some 20 years ago, I attended a lunch at Headingley in honour of former players who had represented Leeds and the city's other clubs, Bramley and Hunslet. The former opponents and teammates mingled over a few pints and a pleasant meal, sharing stories and re-cementing old friendships.

I chatted to Keith Hepworth who had a wonderful half-back partnership with Alan Hardisty for Cas, Leeds and Great Britain in the 1960s and 1970s. I explained to him as best I could, what their efforts meant to us mere mortals on the terraces. I told him how their heroic deeds every weekend lifted our workaday lives. They elevated us to new highs as we were released from the weekly drudgery at a time when work was hard and money was at a premium in most working-class homes. Like many players at clubs like Castleford, my old man worked as a miner and spent a large proportion of his life toiling in the dark.

But on the weekend he was freed from his cares and he would beam as we stood together watching rugby royalty like 'Heppy' and his mates work their magic. I summed up by saying, "I just hope you know what a difference you made to us." Gary Hetherington had overheard our conversation and he handed me a microphone. "Please Dave," he said, "would you tell the rest of them that, too." Gary is an unapologetic rugby league nostalgic. He is also a successful innovator and advocate for the modern game. He is one of that rare breed who recognise that these two positions can be held simultaneously and are not mutually exclusive.

I suppose this miscellany of writings is a way of paying homage to those who have given such pleasure over so many years, for "all those still here and those just around the corner" as my dear old dad would say in his Christmas dinner toast. It is a love letter to the past and a celebration of the people, places and events which make up the rich tapestry of our beloved game of rugby league. It is a 'Remembrancer' and a homage to a heritage which we must celebrate and preserve, for as one Vietnamese proverb goes, "When eating fruit, remember the one who planted the tree."

Through personal recollections and accounts of the game's great events and the stars and characters who illuminated its history, this book honours the past and reminds today's management consultants and administrators, to paraphrase W B Yeats, to tread softly because you tread on our dreams.

Dave Jones
June 2024

Bibliography

Collins, T. (2009), *Inside Rugby League's Hidden History*, Scratching Shed Publishing, (ISBN: 9780956007599)
Sellar, W.C and Yeatman, R.J (1998), *1066 And All That*, Methuen, (ISBN:9780413772701)
Chalkley, G. (2006), *Rugby League Back o' t 'Wall*, London League Publications Ltd, (ISBN:9781903659281)
Gate, R. (2005), *Neil Fox - Rugby League's Greatest Points Scorer*, London League Publications Ltd, (ISBN:9781903659243)
Hornby, N. (1998), *Fever Pitch*, (ISBN:9780241980118)
Thompson, C. (1995), *Born On The Wrong Side*, Pentland Press, (ISBN:1858213398)
Maconie, S. (2018), *Long Road From Jarrow*, Ebury Publishing, (ISBN:9781785030543)
Howard, P. (2010), *Braver Than All the Rest*, London League Publications Ltd, (ISBN:9781903659526)
Chester, R. (2014), *The Glory and the Dream*, London League Publications Ltd, (ISBN:9781909885035)
Berry, C. (2019), *Tough Season*, Great Northern Books, (ISBN:9781912101986)
Malley, F. (2017), *Simply the Best - The Inside Story of How Wigan Became Rugby League's Greatest Cup Team and Won Eight in a Row*, Pitch Publishing, (ISBN:9781785312816)
Aspinall, P. (2019), *Two Weeks to Live*, Troubadour Publishing, (ISBN:9781789018523)
Mason, K. (2019), *Rugby Blood (A Graphic Novel)*, Markosia Enterprises, (ISBN:1912700735)
Light, R (2010), *No Sand Dunes in Featherstone - Memories of West Yorkshire Rugby League*, London League Publications Ltd, (ISBN:9781903659533)
Smith, E. (2009), *What Sport Tells Us About Life*, Penguin, (ISBN:9780141031859)
Hardcastle, A. (2013), *In Full Bloem*, London League Publications Ltd, (ISBN:9781903659656)
Williams, G. (2017), *70 Years of Reaching Forward: Shaw Cross Rugby League Club*, London League Publications, (ISBN:1909885142)
Lindley, J. (1973), *100 Years of Rugby*, Wakefield Trinity Centenary Committee
Lush, P. (2022), *Ahead of his Time: Roy Francis and Rugby League*, London League Publications Ltd, (ISBN:9781909885295)
Bell, S. (2020), *The Man of All Talents*, Pitch Publishing, (ISBN:9781785316821)
Gate, R. (2010), *Billy Boston – Rugby League Footballer*, London League Publications Ltd, (ISBN:9781903659502)
Mather, T. (2021), *The Rorke's Drift Rugby League Test Fiasco*, self- Published, (ISBN:9798747883093)
Woodworth, B. (2020), *Backs to the Wall*, self-published, (ISBN:9798650027676)
Holmes, P & Holmes, P. (2010), *Reluctant Hero - The John Holmes Story*, Scratching Shed Publishing, (ISBN:9780956478702)
Gate, R. (1986), *Gone North (Welshmen in Rugby League) (Vol.1)*, self- published, (ISBN:0951119001)
Gate, R. (1988), *Gone North (Welshmen in Rugby League) (Vol.2)*, self-published, (ISBN:0951119036)
Melling, P. & Collins, T.(eds) (2004), *The Glory of Their Times*, Vertical Editions, (ISBN:9781904091073)
Lush, P. & Bamford, M. (2013), *Big Jim: Jim Mills – A Rugby Giant*, London League Publications Ltd, (ISBN:9781909885011)
Roberts, J & Roberts, C. (2018), *The Greatest Sacrifice - Fallen Heroes of the Northern Union*, Scratching Shed Publishing, (ISBN:9780995586161)
Gate, R. (2004), *100 Great Thrum Hallers: Halifax Heroes 1945-1998*, The History Press, (ISBN:9780752432113)
McCrery, N. (2018), *The Final Scrum – International Rugby Players Killed in the Second World War*, Pen and Sword Books, (ISBN:9781473894501)
Breverton, T. (2022), *The Greatest Sporting Family in History – The Blue and Black Brothers*, Glyndwr Publishing, (ISBN:9781903529317)
Whitcombe, M. & Richards, H. (2024), *The Indomitables*, Ashley Drake Publishing, (ISBN:9781902719702)
Thomson, C. (2009), *The Indomitables: The 1946 Rugby League Tour of Australia and New Zealand*, London League Publications Ltd, (ISBN:9781903659441)

Contents

1	In the beginning	1
2	1964 and all that	6
3	Sharlston	9
4	Hull – a divided city	13
5	Cec Thompson	18
6	Headingley Heritage	21
7	Vince Karalius	26
8	Rugby league in film, fiction and drama	30
9	The tragic death of John Davies	34
10	Tommy Smales – just like the Lone Ranger	37
11	The Goldthorpes of Stourton	41
12	South Africans in English rugby league	44
13	Modern scrums	50
14	Alex Murphy OBE	53
15	Shaw Cross	58
16	Statues and memorials	62
17	Harry Pinner's socks	67
18	The Arkwrights of St Helens	71
19	Roger Millward MBE	74
20	The Rorke's Drift test	78
21	Wally Lewis is coming!	82
22	Lance Todd	86
23	Phil and John Holmes – Brothers in Arms	90
24	Billy Thompson MBE	96
25	The road most travelled – Geoff Clarkson	100
26	Cross-code conversions	104
27	Tom and Ralph Winnard	111
28	Retiring to Blackpool	115
29	Seeing double – twins in rugby league	120
30	Roy Kinnear	124
31	The 'Dad's Army' test	127
32	Alf Meakin and Berwyn Jones	130
33	Geoff Fletcher	133
34	Remembrance	138
35	Jimmy Birts and Keith Mumby	142
36	Alex Givvons	145
37	Featherstone Rovers – 1983 The last hurrah	148
38	Rugby league in the Second World War	153
39	The Indomitables	160
40	Mr Dudley Hill – Andy Harland	165
41	1969 – "I was there!"	169

Rugby League Journal

We would like to thank Harry Edgar and *Rugby League Journal* for their support for this book. The following pieces were originally published in *Rugby League Journal*:

1964 and All That - *Issue 79 Summer 2022*
Remembrance (World War I) - *Issue 81 Winter 2022*
Tommy Smales - I*ssue 82 Spring 2023*
Harry Pinner's Socks - *Issue 83 Summer 2023*
Tom and Ralph Winnard - *Issue 84 Autumn 2023*
Keith Mumby and Jimmy Birts - *Issue 86 Spring 2024*
Berwyn Jones and Alf Meakin - *Issue 87 Summer 2024*
The tragic death of John Davies – *Issue 88 Autumn 2024*

Thank you

London League Publications Ltd and Dave Jones would like to thank Steve McCarthy for designing the cover and the staff at CPI Antony Rowe for printing the book. Thanks to everyone who supplied photos, especially Harry Edgar (*Rugby League Journal*) and Alex Service.

This plaque in Featherstone shows the relationship between mining and rugby league.
(Photo: Peter Lush)

1. In the beginning

I had a huge stroke of luck when I was at secondary school. By chance, the period of history which was selected as the syllabus for History 'O' Level for the 1972 cohort of pupils was 'The Industrial Revolution'. Our year group was not to be condemned to some tedious exploration of Tudors and Stuarts or the politics of pre-revolutionary France.

We were to study our own history. We would learn about our forebearers and how they contributed to the fortunes of this island race. We were to learn the story of how we became who we are and how the north became 'the workshop of the world'. We would explore how the combined ingredients of economics, mass migration, human ingenuity and social upheaval shaped the topography, demography and geography of our region. As a kid brought up in a home where politics was a staple of family discussion, I relished the opportunity to learn how workers fought against the iron heel of capitalism to gain their rights to decent working conditions, education and social and political representation. In short, this was literally and figuratively, right up my street.

Our studies revealed how the coming of the steam engine and the resultant demand for 'King Coal' shaped our northern landscapes as huge masses of humanity flocked to the sprawling new, unplanned conurbations. Hunger, disease and poverty were the lot of the vast majority of the urban poor. We learned how Irish migrants, who were fortunate not to join the millions who died in the potato famine of the 1840s, as the powers that be at Westminster looked on, flooded into industrial towns where they lived in indescribable squalor. We studied accounts given by six-year-old children to the commission on child labour and learned of the cruelty of the Poor Laws which condemned the sick, unemployed and elderly to the brutalising and inhumane conditions of the dreaded workhouses. These prison-like institutions cast a long shadow and served to remind workers of the consequences of idleness or ill fortune.

Eventually, thanks to a combination of collective action by workers themselves, allied with informed philanthropy and government legislation, conditions for the urban masses improved. While universal suffrage was still a distant dream, elementary education was made compulsory after the 1870 Education Act. Child employment was restricted, though the 'Half-time' system did persist in the textile industry in west Yorkshire for many years to come, as children spent half their time at school and the other half in the mill. While working conditions for adults would appear brutal by modern standards, one concession was eventually granted which would have massive social ramifications. Workers were released from the drudgery of labour on Saturday afternoons. Men who grafted throughout the week in mines, mills and factories now sought an outlet for their energies in this brief respite from hard manual toil. Athletic activity spiralled in all northern communities as workers participated in, and spectated at, the sporting events which were established to meet this growing demand for access to physical recreation.

Most organised athletic pursuits originated in the Public Schools of England. The offspring of the new upper classes learned to become 'muscular Christians' as they 'benefited' from the privations of bullying or 'fagging' and cold showers as they emerged as young gentlemen fit to become the leaders their birthright dictated they would be in the years ahead. At Rugby

School, Thomas Arnold was a visionary headmaster who encouraged his charges to expend their youthful passions and energies in sporting activity rather than in any other forms of 'ghastly beastliness'. It was at this august educational institution, so the story goes, that the game of rugby originated. All students of both forms of the sport are told how an otherwise unremarkable pupil of the school by the name of William Webb Ellis picked up the ball to the amazed bafflement of his peers, and ran with it, contrary to the rules of football at the time. Sadly, this romantic story is just that. A story.

The true origins of rugby are less spontaneous and rather more evolutionary. The game owes its birth to football and the disagreements regarding two features of the sport, 'handling' and 'hacking'. Those schools who wished to outlaw these practices developed the game of association football. The institutions which wished to preserve these aspects of the sport eventually formed the Rugby Football Union.

While rugby continued to flourish in the elite schools which served the privileged classes in the south of the country, the newly freed workers were also embracing opportunities to play the game in the industrial centres in the north of England. The first signs of tensions between these two disparate groups can be traced to the start of the Yorkshire Cup in 1877. The notion of competition and the attendant risk of gambling on the outcome of matches was anathema to the ruling powers. They believed that participation, not victory, should be the object of the exercise. The first skirmishes in what would eventually break out into open warfare had been fought as the authorities expressed their hostility to 'this sort of thing.'

I have had the good fortune to meet the eminent sports historian Professor Tony Collins on a few occasions. He wears his encyclopaedic knowledge of the origins and development of all forms of football very lightly but he is fascinating to talk to about the history of our sport. In an excellent article entitled *Myth and Reality in the 1895 Rugby Split*, he debunks some widely held myths about how the 'Great Schism' unfolded. An understanding of the actual circumstances which contributed to the great divide which resulted from the meeting at the George Hotel is vital to our understanding of how and why we came to be.

The first myth that Collins explodes is that relating to the view that amateurism was adhered to by the purists in the south of England while the pressure for payments to players came from the northern clubs. He points out that payment was not the issue but rather *who* could be paid. 'Gentlemen' who were out of pocket could claim 'expenses'. He cites the case of the England captain of both the country's rugby and cricket teams, Andrew Stoddart, to highlight the point. In 1888, Stoddart received £200 for a rugby tour with Shaw and Shrewsbury to Australia (a staggering £32,000 in today's values)! Furthermore, Collins points out that the Corinthians, the club often held up for their pure 'Corinthian values', charged opponents £150 to play against them.

At the same time as this was going on, Harry Garnett, a prominent member of the Yorkshire committee expressed the view regarding working class players that "if they cannot afford to play, they should go without the game." The Professor explains, "For the RFU, it was not payment to players which was an issue, but payments to working class players." The level of upper-class hypocrisy is quite staggering! The second myth which Collins lays bare is in regard to the north-south nature of the split.

Festival of Rugby League at Rugby School prior to the 2000 World Cup.
Trevor Foster, Billy Boston, Neil Fox and Sir Rodney Walker join officials from Rugby Council.
(Photo: Courtesy Simon Foster)

Rugby versus Wolverhampton in the Rugby League Conference at Rugby School.
(Photo: Peter Lush)

The received wisdom is it was the northern representatives who wanted to sanction payments while their southern counterparts stuck to the strict amateur party line. This view ignores the reality that there were many prominent Yorkshire representatives at the RFU top table. Some of these men were the main drivers of the witch hunts to wheedle out the 'veiled professionals' who were hiding in plain sight among the ranks of northern players. Furthermore, it was the Yorkshire Committee which unsuccessfully called for sanctions against Stoddart's Australian adventure.

Lancashire too came down hard on any perceived transgressions of the rules pertaining to amateurism. In 1894, they suspended Leigh, Salford and Wigan for breaches regarding payments to players, a move which contributed significantly to the eventual parting of the ways. Tony Collins reminds us that this is hardly surprising as the Yorkshire and Lancashire delegates who rose to positions of power and influence were "the northern bourgeoisie par excellence". They were not the type of mill owning northerners depicted in Monty Python like so many Oberdiers and Ebaneezers who had dragged themselves up by their boot laces. These were the sons of these captains of industry who, while their fathers themselves could not buy gentility with their tainted money sullied by the murky stain of industry, could gain respectability for their offspring. Northern they may have been but they were Public School men with an axe to grind! To summarise, Collins argues, it was *class* not *geography* which led to the great division.

The third and final misconception that Professor Collins challenges is that the split was caused by the insistence of the northern businessmen in forcing the issue of 'broken time'. The reaction of the RFU to the idea of players from working class backgrounds being paid compensation for loss of earnings was to force these players out of the game altogether. For clubs in the north, where most of their players and supporters were working men, this was not an acceptable proposition. It was the refusal of the RFU to compromise over the issue of 'broken time' that led the clubs to reluctantly take the action which they eventually did.

Nor should we assume a homogeneous response from members of the northern clubs. Their attitudes were largely dictated by their political allegiances. Those who supported the Conservatives tended to tow the strictly amateur line, whereas those of a Liberal persuasion were more sympathetic to change. The battle lines were drawn between those who wanted to introduce a little more 'free market' to the administration of the game and the die-hards who wished to maintain, in Collins's terms "a system of patronage and rigid class stratification". He identifies the Victorian ruling class's inability to come to terms with the reality of a newly emboldened, self-assertive working class as being the central feature which led to the game tearing itself asunder.

The fact is that on the evening of 29 August 1895, representatives of 21 clubs from Yorkshire and Lancashire met at the George Hotel in Huddersfield, selected as it was conveniently placed adjacent to the railway station, to discuss the possibility of breaking from the RFU. Subsequently the vote was carried by 20–1. Dewsbury was the only club not to agree, but who subsequently joined the group. Stockport were also accepted via the telephone. The new organisation adopted the name, the Northern Football Union and in 1922 this would become the Rugby Football League.

This whole dramatic, often traumatic birth has shaped the way we have come to see ourselves and our game. We are plucky underdogs who value solidarity and loyalty to our communities. We are a bit chippy in our attitudes to authority and to those who purport to be our betters. We are northern and proud of it by gum! Indeed, my own team in Bradford were proud to bear the title 'Northern' until clubs were encouraged to adopt ridiculous American suffixes like Bulls in the Super League revolution. Our game is steeped in our industrial past, though those industries have now all but vanished, along with their physical remnants as markers on our landscapes. But rugby league endures no matter how many times enemies within and without try to knock it down or change its essential characteristics to appeal to the modern palate. We have our memories to cherish.

The author's father, Gordon Jones, who introduced him to rugby league.
(Courtesy Dave Jones)

2. 1964 and all that

In 1930, WC Sellars and RJ Yeatman published their parody of school history text books, *1066 and All That.* Judging "good things" and "bad Kings", it reflected the tendency to view the Norman Conquest as the 'start' of our island's history. To Bradfordians of a certain vintage, 1964 marks a similar seminal significance in the city's sporting and civic life.

In 1964 I was seven years old. On 22 August of that year, my father and I joined over 13,540 other excited souls in the vast bowl which is Odsal Stadium to witness the rebirth of a club which had graced the game since 1907. Our opponents that day were Hull Kingston Rovers. Bradford Northern had last appeared here in December 1963 in front of a paltry crowd of 324. They were the remnants of the faithful, to witness their side's defeat at the hands of Barrow in what many feared were the Last Rites for the once mighty club. A friend of mine and future rugby and cricket teammate, Jimmy Collinson, was one of that not so happy few and he told me recently that Odsal felt like a ghost town on that sad afternoon. This was reflected by a cartoon in the local paper, the *Telegraph and Argus*, showing the vast terracing with barely a soul in sight as a spectator complains about someone in front blocking his view.

Ironically, in the visitor's ranks that day in 1963 was former Great Britain international centre Jim Challinor. He had also appeared at Odsal on that never to be repeated night of the Challenge Cup final replay in 1954. Over 102,000 people crammed in to see his Warrington team defeat Halifax with thousands more fans locked out. Consequently, Challinor had played in front of the highest and lowest ever crowds at Odsal Stadium!

So, on that sunny August afternoon in 1964, my dad introduced me to the world of rugby league. I was the youngest of five children born to parents who had met while serving in the forces in the Second World War. Mum was born in Barnsley, but the family moved to Bradford prior to her joining the ATS. After the War she and my father moved onto the Bierley Estate and mum worked in various mills in the district while the old man travelled on his motorbike to Netherton in Wakefield where he worked at Hartley Bank pit.

My elder siblings were all girls, so in those far off days of more clearly stratified, gender dictated activities, the old man must have considered I needed a masculine interest. This view had been brewing from the day he returned home from work some years previously when one of my sisters had dressed me like one of her dolls and was shoving little brother about in a pram! Dad was keen to rescue me from a future life devoted to crochet and flower arranging and he also felt rugby might provide us with a common bond. So it transpired and my fondest childhood memories are of going to home games together at Odsal and away trips on Wallace Arnold coaches to witness the highs and lows of following 't' Northern'.

Dad was a proud Welshman and had been a miner in South Wales before joining up at the start of hostilities. He was on a ship which was torpedoed and sunk in 1944 and he was a lucky survivor who ended up in a lifeboat which floated about in the Atlantic for days. Although his mother received a telegram pronouncing him "missing at sea presumed dead", dad was picked up by a Canadian ship and taken to hospital in Canada. He was told by the doctor that the frostbite he had suffered would have probably rendered him "barren". I believe that the Canadian medic is the person I should thank for my existence as the old man kept batting on to underline how wrong his prognosis had been!

Like many of his countrymen, dad was given to bouts of homesickness and this was certainly the case in his early days 'up north'. One of the saving graces for him was that Bradford Northern had several Welsh players in their ranks including Trevor Foster, Emlyn Walters and Willie Davies. Dad was particularly friendly with the huge Welsh prop Frank Whitcombe who sometimes visited our family home with a view to sampling some of my mum's home baking! Another factor which helped dad to settle was his involvement in the amateur game. At one point he had been a Physical Training Instructor in the army and he put his skills to good use in becoming coach of Dudley Hill ARLFC.

Many of the old man's mining colleagues in Wakefield were keen rugby league followers. Indeed, one of those at Hartley Bank was Albert Stephenson whose wife worked in the shoddy trade in Dewsbury. Mrs Stephenson would pull out any rugby jerseys which had been thrown away and recycled them my way. Consequently, I was never short of kit. Incidentally Albert's son Mike turned out to be not a bad player and we now know him as the same Mike 'Stevo' Stephenson, the former Sky pundit, who was a member of the Great Britain team who won the 1972 World Cup.

So back to Odsal on that August afternoon in 1964. It was thanks to another Welshman who had made Bradford his home that we were able to make our pilgrimage on that fateful day. Trevor Foster is a legend to generations of Bradford supporters. Whenever my father spoke of the former Newport man it was in almost reverential tones. Trevor was universally recognised as a true gentleman of our game. The long-serving Secretary of the RFL, John Wilson, described him as "a man who played the game in the true spirit of rugby, who did not consider that every knock that came his way was deliberate and intended and consequently never retaliated."

As a teenager I was fortunate to be coached by Trevor when selected for a Yorkshire Association of Boys Clubs side to play against a French touring team in a side including the future Northern great, Keith Mumby. Trevor was also a huge influence on the career of the young Brian Noble at the Police Boys' Club where he was a volunteer. He encouraged generations of children and I cringe to consider what he would think of the farcical state of the modern play the ball.

In 2005, I invited Trevor to come to speak to the children at Holybrook Primary school where I worked on Ravenscliffe Estate. We used sport to enrich the lives of the kids who often came from homes which did not enjoy the benefits of those from more affluent backgrounds. We gained lottery funding to construct a floodlit games area and named it in Trevor's honour as he epitomised the true spirit of sportsmanship. His humility is exemplified by the fact that he brought his MBE to show the children – in a Morrison's carrier bag.

One of my highest honours was to be asked to write Trevor's eulogy in the Bulls programme following his passing. I attended his funeral with several hundred other fans and as the players of the time, including Robbie Paul and Lesley Vainikolo, acted as pallbearers carrying Trevor from the church on their shoulders. There was a wonderfully poignant impromptu moment when an old chap in a gabardine coat with a hand knitted Northern scarf broke the silence as the coffin passed by saying, "Well played Trevor," and he began clapping. The whole congregation joined in the applause and Trevor was clapped off the field of play for one final time to the echoing refrain of, "Well played Trevor", and the cheers of his gathered admirers.

After the collapse of the club in 1963, Trevor, along with former New Zealand full-back Joe Phillips, who served the club throughout the 1950s, organised meetings across the city. Refusing to see the death of the club, they called a meeting at St George's Hall which 1,500 people attended. Over £1,000 was pledged to launch Bradford Northern (1964) Ltd. Before the meeting, another Welshman, Dai Rees, the former manager who guided the club to three consecutive Challenge Cup finals in the 1940s and who revolutionised the speed of the play the ball by using the scrum-half as dummy half, sent a message of encouragement. His telegram read, "It's a long way from Birch Lane to Wembley, it can be done again!"

The side that the new management assembled cost about £15,000 in total. Jack Wilkinson was the player-coach who had been released by Wakefield Trinity free of charge and this gesture typified the goodwill which the rugby league fraternity showed towards the new venture.

For the record, the teams that day were:

Bradford Northern: Williams; Levula, Lord, Todd, Walker; Brooke, Jones; Wilkinson, Ackerley, Tonkinson; Fisher, Ashton, Rae

Hull KR: Kellett; C. Young, Moore, Blackmore, Harris; Burwell, Hatch; Tyson, A. Holdstock, Taylor; Bonner, Palmer, Poole

My favourite player was the Fijian winger Joe Levula who, on a later date, when the pitch was a quagmire, carried me on his shoulders across the field to save my shoes getting caked with mud when I ran onto the pitch to get his autograph after a game. Sadly, many of the players that day are no longer with us but I remain grateful to them all for being part of my induction into the sport. It hardly seems to matter, but Bradford Northern lost that day 34–20, but my life had been transformed which, in Sellar & Yeatman's terms was "a good thing".

1965 Bradford Northern team. (Courtesy *Rugby League Journal*)

3. Sharlston

There is a long and well documented historical connection between the mining industry and the game of rugby league. The two have a good deal in common. Both involve hard physical toil and a reliance on your comrades to watch your back. They breed solidarity and an *esprit de corps* which bonds those involved in the activities in a way that outsiders fail to comprehend. Both rely on teamwork and shared endeavour. The hardships faced encourage banter and humour to lighten the load and lift the spirits. Men who toiled all week underground welcomed the opportunity to fill their lungs with God's good air on a Saturday afternoon and those who were good enough, would be remunerated with a few extra quid to supplement the family budget and to buy a couple of pints.

The village of Sharlston is a tightly knit, former pit village which lies more or less equidistant between Wakefield and Featherstone in west Yorkshire. It can trace its roots back to 1574 with the building of Old Sharlston Hall which still stands today. It has a population of around two and a half thousand people and in a visit there you would see various physical references to its mining heritage. The winding wheel from Sharlston Colliery's pit head gear has been mounted on a brick-built plinth as a permanent reminder of the area's reliance on the industry. The Parish Council's logo is emblazoned with two cross picks and a miner's lamp but the pit itself is no more.

In 1864, some 150 back-to-back houses were built for the miners and their families in the village and Sharlston Colliery opened for business in 1865. Delving into the records of the Durham Mining Museum's records, I discovered that while no disasters had occurred at Sharlston – in mining parlance meaning accidents resulting in five deaths in the same incident – there were over 90 deaths at the colliery over its existence. This is a sharp reminder of the price of coal.

Looking through old photos from the archives of Sharlston Colliery, I discovered a marvellous picture of the giant Featherstone prop Les Tonks. He is emerging from his shift underground with five other coal blackened workmates with his old butcher's aproned style 'Fev' shirt under his work jacket. Les towers above his colleagues and the simple caption on the photo reads Les Tonks RIP, as it was posted after his passing in 2017.

The mine closed in 1993, almost a decade after the bitter miner's strike which ripped communities asunder and set neighbour against neighbour, as Mrs Thatcher mobilised the resources of the state to defeat the miners and launch a pit closure programme which left communities across the north bereft of hope. Andy Wilson interviewed Graham Chalkley for the *Guardian* in 2004. Chalkley graduated from the Sharlston team to play in the professional game with Batley and Dewsbury and wrote the excellent history of the club, *Rugby League Back o' t' Wall* in 2006. He explained that the strike still cast a long shadow. "It were bad, family against family. The most difficult part about it was when we played other teams with a scab in – he would come in for some serious treatment. It's nothing like as bad now, but it's still there." Some wounds take a long time to heal and they leave scars.

In Sharlston though, the other twin mainspring of the community did not die. Sharlston Rovers ARLFC lives on and continues to provide a focal point in the lives of many in the area.

In memory of the miners who worked at Sharlston Colliery from 1865 to 1993. (Photo: Peter Lush)

Situated alongside the Sharlston Hotel, the recreation ground at which matches are played is known to all as 'Back o' t' Wall'.

The club has a rich tradition of success against professional clubs in the Challenge Cup which began in 1946. In that year the 38-year-old caretaker of the local school came out of rugby retirement to lead the amateur side to victory over Workington Town by 12–7. His six-year-old son watched his dad's team with pride. That boy was Neil Fox who we will return to presently. Fox Senior's opposite number that day was Ginger Hughes and he came off second best. He too fathered a famous son called Emlyn who became a Liverpool FC legend. Workington won the second leg, thus progressing in the competition, but the village could still rejoice in the giant-killing achievement. In 2004 Sharlston again lowered the colours of a professional outfit when they defeated Dewsbury to earn a fourth round tie against Oldham. Their player-manager in that victory was Martyn Wood who was a member of the Sheffield Eagles team which achieved the greatest ever Wembley upset with their defeat of Wigan in the final of 1998.

How many places of Sharlston's size can boast being home to two members of the Rugby League Hall of Fame and three winners of the Lance Todd Trophy Award? None, I would wager. But few places could compete with Sharlston's rugby pedigree.

Jonathan 'Jonty' Parkin was born in Sharlston on 'Bonfire Night' 1894 and he was to set the world of rugby league alight as one of the game's first superstars. He was one of the original nine inductees into the Rugby League Hall of Fame. He joined Wakefield Trinity in 1913 and gave 17 years service to the club, amassing a points total of 476 in 349 matches.

In 1930, at the age of 34, Jonty decided that he wanted to move on and he was transfer listed at £100. Hull Kingston Rovers expressed their interest, but couldn't afford the transfer fee. Parkin made the unprecedented move to 'buy his own contract' and paid the money, equivalent to about £8,000 today, and joined the Humberside club. Following this audacious action, the powers that be outlawed the practice so nobody could do this in the future. After a couple of seasons with Rovers, Jonty returned to Belle Vue where he served on the club's committee. At international level, Parkin gained 17 caps for Great Britain and played for England on 12 occasions. He toured Australia three times, twice as captain.

Cataloguing the achievements of Neil Fox MBE, who witnessed his dad's heroics against Workington Town as a six-year-old, would take a whole book. Thankfully Robert Gate has undertaken this task for posterity with his biography of the great man in 2005. Suffice to say that he is the greatest points scorer in the history of the game with 6,220 points. I recall in the early 1990s picking up a set of kit I had bought from Neil's sports company for my school team at Wyke and Neil gave my young son a kicking tee. I mused that with such aids and lighter balls on firmer ground how that amazing total might have swelled still further.

Born just four months before the outbreak of the Second World War, Neil Fox joined Wakefield as a 16-year-old. Given his tender age when turning professional with Trinity, he never turned out for the Sharlston senior team, a fact he records as a regret in his introduction to Graham Chalkley's book. His career at Belle Vue spanned the years of unprecedented success as the team beat Hull, 1959–60, Huddersfield, 1961–62 and Wigan 1962–63. in three Challenge Cup finals at Wembley. In the 1962 victory over Huddersfield by 12–6 Neil contributed a try and three drop goals earning him the Lance Todd Trophy.

In 1969 Neil Fox joined Bradford Northern, much to this young fan's delight. We already had a goalkicker in the form of Terry Price and the lack of opportunity to shoulder the kicking responsibilities led to his eventual return to Wakefield. The 1970s marked a rather nomadic phase in his career as the man who had now moved to the pack gave valuable service to Hull Kingston Rovers, York, Bramley, Huddersfield and Bradford again. He is a member of a very exclusive club, along with Alex Murphy, Billy Boston and Mark Forster, of players to have been rewarded with two testimonials – both times by Wakefield. In his international career, Fox gained 29 caps, twice contributing to Ashes victories. He was awarded an MBE for services to rugby league in 1983 and along with Jonty Parkin, became one of the original inductees to the Hall of Fame in 1989. In 2010 he was given the Freedom of the City and in 2017 the Wakefield Eastern Relief Road was renamed Neil Fox Way.

Neil was one of three famous sons of Sharlston. His other siblings, Don and Peter both left their mark on the game but in rather different ways. Don in an interview later in life rather lamented that if young people spotted the former player, they would say, "That's that old lad that missed that kick." He is alluding of course, to that infamous day at Wembley in 1968 when what has gone down in the annals of the game as 'the Watersplash Final' took place.

The heavens had opened before the kick off and there was an even greater deluge at half time. Wembley's usually immaculate surface was transformed into a series of huge puddles as players skidded around in comedic fashion. Some years later I spoke with Tony Crosby who was the Leeds hooker that day and he said that he seriously thought he would drown at the bottom of one collapsed scrum. In the dying seconds, Trinity's winger Ken Hirst slid onto a kick through when the ball stopped dead in one of the pools in the in-goal area giving Don Fox the opportunity to grab victory with the conversion from straight in front. Watching the old black and white footage is still painful as the saturated ball slips off the outside of Don Fox's boot, sailing wide as he sinks to his knees to the now legendary cries of Eddie Waring – "The poor lad!"

In an interview with Sky Television many years later, Neil, then the last surviving brother, spoke about that day. What people often forget, he points out, is that Don was awarded the Lance Todd trophy for his man-of-the-match performance. The award which is voted for by members of the press, is always announced a few minutes before the final whistle so in his brother's case it cannot be seen in any way as a 'sympathy award'. Graham Chalkley points out that the award was no consolation to Don for as David Coulman the iconic commentator told him he had won it in an interview in the Wembley tunnel he initially responded, "Stick it up thi arse, I don't want it." In a second take he accepted it apologetically.

Neil also admitted to feeling a little guilty as if he had not been injured prior to the final, it would have been he who would have borne responsibility for kicking that goal. Neil recalls in his biography that he was pressured to play in the Championship Final by his club the week before Wembley, and although he finished the game, his groin injury "went again" and he missed the Challenge Cup Final.

He also points out that had Don not knocked over his other kicks in the dreadful conditions, then Trinity wouldn't have been in striking distance anyway! Nevertheless, Neil did feel that that awful incident was an albatross which Don bore for the rest of his life.

This one incident should not overshadow what a good career Don Fox had. He joined Featherstone Rovers in 1953, initially as a scrum-half. He gave 13 years loyal service at Post Office Road and scored a record 162 tries for the club. He also kicked 503 goals and was capped while playing for the club. His sole international appearance was at Headingley in 1963, at loose-forward in Britain's 16–5 victory over the touring Kangaroos. He joined Neil at Belle Vue in 1965 and made 117 appearances in five years with Trinity.

A third former Sharlston Rovers player to join Neil and Don Fox as recipients of the Lance Todd Trophy was Carl Dooler. The Featherstone scrum-half toured Australia with Great Britain in 1966. In 1967, he won the award as his side beat Barrow 17–12 at Wembley.

Peter was the senior member of the Fox clan. He had 13 years as a player in the professional game. He began his career with Featherstone before plying his trade with Batley, Hull KR and Hunslet before being called out of retirement when he was helping with the 'A' team at Belle Vue in 1966. Peter made one appearance for Trinity at Swinton before being injured. Sadly, neither Neil nor Don played that day so the brothers missed the opportunity to play together. Peter hung up his boots after that single appearance for the club.

But the end of his playing days marked the start of the most successful part of the Sharlston man's career in the game. Peter Fox was a coach par-excellence and, more to the point, he was a winner! Following a successful three-year stint at Featherstone in which they won the Challenge Cup when his men totally out-foxed Albert Fearnley's Bradford Northern, he returned to coach Trinity, replacing his brother Neil. Finally, he ended up at Bradford via Bramley. He brought Championship success to a club which had spent years in the wilderness. He was one of the game's great motivators and knew which players could do a job for him. Many were lesser known or at a veteran stage of their careers. He led Yorkshire to six successive Wars of the Roses victories and he also coached the national team. He was famously in charge of Great Britain when his 1978 'Dads Army' side defeated the Australians at Odsal. This showed how Fox could get many a good tune out of some relatively old fiddles.

Sharlston has every right to be proud of its amazing contribution to the heritage of our game and to the achievements of these men who earned their stripes at 'Back o' t' Wall'.

4. Hull – a divided city

A police officer I once knew told me that he was always apprehensive when called to a domestic dispute lest the warring parties should pause their hostilities and turn their wrath on him for interfering in their business. As a Bradfordian, I feel a similar hesitancy in looking through the windows on a private row between the protagonists on Humberside, even though our cities experience similarities regarding poverty and urban decline which have caused some social commentators to call Hull, 'Bradford by the Sea'!

Hull is certainly a very interesting city. It is a singular sort of a place, with its unique cream coloured telephone boxes, its own telecommunication system and its distinct dialect which some linguists believe has been influenced by the Dutch - "Farv t' narn, werk", and all that. Its chip shops sell 'patties' which are unavailable anywhere else and these culinary delights are highly prized by local connoisseurs. A special feature of the city is its remoteness, at the far point of a seemingly never-ending cul-de-sac on the M62, which causes even adults to ask, "are we nearly there yet?" It also has a perennially outward gaze to the grey North Sea beyond its coastal boundary, as a stout rebuttal of its relationship to the inner rural lands of the Yorkshire Wolds.

People from Hull are justly proud of the amazing Humber Bridge, built in 1981, in its day the longest single-span suspension bridge in the world before being overtaken by several others, proving that imitation really is the sincerest form of flattery. It was home to the anti-slavery MP William Wilberforce and it was the city which locked out Charles I to kick off the English Civil War. It boasts a radical tradition of protest against injustice, as evidenced by the actions of Lillian Bilocca and her 'Headscarved Revolutionaries', who forced Harold Wilson's government to legislate to improve safety on trawlers following the tragic loss of 58 lives when three fishing boats sank within days of each other in the 1960s.

Hull is a plucky survivor of a history which has often dealt it a difficult hand. It was the second most bombed city in Britain outside London in the Second World War. In 82 raids on Hull, there were an estimated 1,200 deaths and 3,000 people were seriously injured. The devastation to housing and civic buildings was enormous. Furthermore, given wartime censorship, Hull's plight was made anonymous as it could only be referred to as a 'North East Coast Town'. It was not until *The Hull Daily Mail* brought the news of the Blitz on Hull to the nation's attention in 1947 that the impact was more widely appreciated. 'The Land of Green Ginger', as it is whimsically branded, took one for the proverbial Yorkshire team for, as Rosie Millard who had studied in the city explained in *The Telegraph* in November 2013, "It was even showered by bombs designed for *other* places; should the Luftwaffe fail to find Sheffield or Leeds, they would drop their deadly cargo on Hull on their way back home, almost as an afterthought." It was a German bomber's 'last chance saloon' if you will. Nevertheless, Hull survived and almost prospered, with its new(ish) Marina and Lottery funded 'Deep' aquarium and its successful bid for City of Culture in 2017, before Covid came along to arrest its development and that of all its northern neighbours.

For all this, Hull is a city divided. The social and geographical fault lines run east to west, rather than north to south. The demarcation point of the division is the River Hull. To the west lies the fishing industry, now largely gone but never forgotten. Its men went out to sea, returning home every few weeks with a collective thirst of epic proportions and wages burning holes in the pockets of their flash suits, earning them the title of "weekend millionaires". The womenfolk left on shore, back along the Hessle Road, were a fierce, independent bunch who could stand their own, whatever was thrown at them.

To the east lies the docks. Here there are large post war council estates which replaced those dwellings reduced to rubble by Goering's war machine. Some years ago, I did some work for Hull KR and was amazed by the sheer size of the Bransholme estate deemed to be the largest in Europe. Traditionally, the workforce from east of the river were more shore based and viewed the more nomadic men from the west with suspicion and disdain. In a similar scenario to their north eastern neighbours on Tyneside, where the demarcation between 'Mackems' and 'Tackems' reflects the industrial heritages of those major cities, so the historical roots of Hull's workforce have shaped its inhabitants' attitudes to their neighbours across the river.

In considering matters of social and geographical dislocation, I am reminded of a lesson I learned during my own career. I worked in a primary school which was seen to be doing well, on a council estate which was rather challenging due to the deprivation caused by the neglect of the authorities. We were asked to form a Federation with a school on a similar estate at the other side of an arterial road that separated us. It was the brainchild of the then Prime Minister Tony Blair, as a kind of BOGOF, where the Head would do a sort of two for the price of one deal. What I learnt very quickly was that ancient hostilities are often fuelled by proximity. Although the road between our two communities sometimes felt like the Grand Canyon, it was local suspicions, often the result of ignorance of 'the other', that held us apart. It's not Aston Villa that Man U fans hate, it's their noisy neighbours at City. Evertonians don't despise 'that lot' at Bournemouth, but their fellow Scousers across Stanley Park. People may sometimes love those people from two doors down – but they may also see them as the neighbours from hell. So it is with the two Hull clubs.

In an on-going study undertaken by Lincoln University, the researchers have conducted hundreds of interviews with people from the city. They conclude that, "The most tangible expression of the East-West divide is undoubtedly in sport, where club allegiances to rugby league teams Hull Kingston Rovers and Hull Football Club provides an important anchor for separating the city into two halves." As Mary Poppins would have it – "let's start at the very beginning – it's a very good place to start."

In the beginning, the Boulevard, traditionally deemed to be the spiritual abode of Hull FC, had been home to Rovers. At the end of the 19th century, Hull FC outbid Hull KR to become the new tenants and caused their gazumped neighbours to find a new ground which they duly did. Ironically, the two clubs had started out life on the opposite bank of the River Hull to the one on which they now reside. This inauspicious beginning would be fuel to fan the fans' flames for many a future flare-up. Imagine if your neighbours, who you may already have been a bit hacked off with, had you evicted and then moved in and painted your gaff in their own new colour scheme. Would you forgive and forget?

While hostilities in the long running dispute are mostly confined to good natured banter, such as FC supporters spurning the consumption of streaky bacon or Rovers fans refusing to own black and white cats, there have been less jovial manifestations. In 1981 at the Good Friday derby at the Boulevard, 13 arrests were made when violence and stone throwing erupted resulting in 40 people being injured. To be fair to the people of Hull, as one who frequented matches in rugby league in that era, it has to be said that the Humbersiders did not have a monopoly on anti-social behaviour. However, at the time when association football was making plenty of headlines of its own on the issue of hooliganism, the game's administrators largely turned a blind eye to maintain the top show of rugby league as wholesome entertainment for all the family.

When Rupert Murdock, Maurice Lindsay and Sky cuddled up together in the mid–1990s, they conjured up plans to merge clubs who had been the enemies of one another's blood since time immemorial. Skating over intractable differences, generational conflicts and ancient resentments, the unholy alliance was hell bent on bringing together sides like the two Hull teams under one unified umbrella. Perhaps we should just be thankful that they were not tasked with dispute resolution in Northern Ireland, the Middle East or say, handling Brexit. But then….

The debate around the issue of merger in the city of Hull was as inflammatory as in any of the centres which were proposed for fusion in the Super League adventure. In an article for *The Independent* on 23 June 1996, David Hadfield interviewed Hull FC's majority shareholder Roy Waudby. Although Waudby expressed his avowed loathing of the Robins, saying that he kept two cats to kill any robin entering his garden, he said he understood the necessity both commercially and for success on the field for two to become one. Perhaps even more controversially, one time Rovers' icon Phil Lowe, who had spent his entire career at Craven Park, barring a very successful stint in club rugby league in Australia, and who was the current Chairman and a legend of the east Hull club, expressed his support for merger. So incensed was the spokesperson for the Robins' Supporters Club that he said that while he had loved Lowe in his playing days, if this was his view he wished the great second rower had stayed in Australia. Thankfully, in the end neither turkey was forced into voting in favour of the traditional yuletide festivities.

In Parliamentary politics, when an MP decides to switch allegiances to the party opposite, they are said to 'cross the floor.' The great poacher turned gamekeeper Churchill did this so frequently, there and back, that his shimmying across the floor would have made him a contender for 'Strictly', like a latter-day Anne Widdicombe or Ed Balls. While politicians may have a change of heart and colours, this option is not really open to sports supporters. In his wonderful insight into what it is to be a fan, Nick Hornby in *Fever Pitch* explains the purgatory of the supporter's lot. It's for life – for better and, usually since winners are in the tiny minority, for worse. Fans carry their clubs like a millstone in their lives. Not for nothing do Hull FC belt out *Old Faithful*, a tribute inspired by an old Gene Autry song of 1933 dedicated to his faithful horse and sung by those in the Threepenny Stand to their deadly goalkicking marksman Joe Oliver, so becoming the club anthem. Faithful unto death is the fan's lot!

But for players it's a different story. They are compelled to adopt a more quasi-mercenary approach in pursuit of their professional careers. Clubs see players as human assets to be acquired and disposed of as circumstances dictate. Players must move on to don the colours of former foes if they are the highest bidders. Even 'The Old Firm' in Glasgow now deal on a non-sectarian basis since Grame Souness took Mo Johnston to Ibrox in 1989, thus breaking the unwritten ban on Catholics joining Rangers.

But in a city as claustrophobic and self-contained as Hull, crossing the great divide must have its consequences personally, socially and for one's family. The potential hostility when visiting your old stamping ground thereafter must set the heart racing! Yet the men who have made this precarious journey are not so rare as might be imagined. Writing in the *Hull Daily Mail* in 2020, James Smailes listed the 132 players who had crossed the city divide. These include some who have gone on to make more than 100 appearances for both clubs including, Len Casey, Shaun Briscoe and Graham Horne. Other famous members of the group have much deeper roots at one club than the other, with perhaps Peter 'Flash' Flanagan being the best example. While the Great Britain hooker had a brief sojourn at the Boulevard, he is much more associated with Craven Park where it is planned that a statue will be erected in his honour.

Doubtless these dual club players will have suffered the slings and arrows, the barbed insults and the derisory chants but there is one exception. When you leave the M62 to drive into Kingston upon Hull you follow the A63 named in honour of one of the city's most loved adopted sons. I cannot imagine even the most one-eyed, partisan Airlie Bird or Robin, making a detour to avoid driving down – Clive Sullivan Way.

'Sully' as he was universally known, was born in the Splott region of Cardiff on 9 April 1943 to parents of Antiguan and Jamaican heritage. When he was a teenager, he experienced injuries which necessitated several operations to his feet, knees and shoulders. Doctors doubted that he would ever be able to walk properly, let alone play sports. Upon leaving school, young Clive became a car mechanic before joining the Army. He was posted to Catterick in north Yorkshire where his CO invited him to play rugby on account of him being Welsh. Sullivan feared that a failure to comply with the request might highlight his physical difficulties and even lead to him being discharged on medical grounds.

He played in the match and realised he had talent. So promising was the winger that a trial was arranged with my hometown club Bradford Northern. Just as Hunslet and Leeds had let the great Brian Bevan slip through their fingers some years before, so Northern's directors wrinkled their noses at the willowy Welshman. Our loss was Hull's gain as he went on to make 352 appearances for the Airlie Birds, scoring 250 tries.

During his years at the Boulevard, Clive won international recognition, gaining the first of his 13 Great Britain caps in 1967 and being selected for the 1968 World Cup. Four years later he was made the captain of the national side and thus he became the first ever black captain of a British team in any major sport. This was six years before association football bestowed its first cap on a black player at full international level when Viv Anderson won that honour. The 1972 team won the World Cup final in Paris with a length of the field solo try from Sully.

There were no wild fanfares or ticker-tape street parades for the returning cup kings. Sullivan was a part-time professional, as were all the players from his era and he supplemented his income by working at the Hawker-Siddeley Aircraft factory near Hull. Instead of being greeted by a smiling Prime Minister, eager to bask in some reflected glory, Clive took the World Cup to the factory to show his mates.

In 1974, Sullivan left Hull FC and joined the team in east Hull for a fee of £3,250. Incredibly, he spent six years in the red and white shirt, playing 213 games and scoring 118 tries. The highlight of his time at Craven Park was winning at Wembley in the 1980 Cup Final involving both Hull clubs which saw the famous invitation on a banner for the last person to leave the city to turn the lights out!

Later that year he was released at his own request and joined Oldham where he played 18 games, before the lure of Humberside became too great and he returned to the coaching staff at Hull FC. Clive had indeed been 'To Hull and Back' – but this was not the end of the story. After drawing with Widnes in only the second ever Wembley final to end all-square in 1981, Clive was called up for the Elland Road replay when Dane O'Hara, the New Zealand winger, was dropped for a breach of club discipline. Hull duly defeated the Chemics providing him with a second winner's medal in a fairy tale ending to a wonderful career,

Tragically he died only three years later at the age of 42 having received a cancer diagnosis only six months before. Clive Sullivan was awarded an MBE in 1974 and his status as a 'national treasure' was ensured when he became one of that very rare breed of sports stars to appear on *This Is Your Life* in recognition of his achievements. Sully is the only player ever to have made over 200 appearances for both clubs scoring more than 100 tries in black and white and red and white. There is a great deal to divide east and west Hull in rugby league, but when the two teams now meet, they compete for the Clive Sullivan trophy in honour of a giant who bestrode this divide with ease and grace.

5. Cec Thompson

Theodore Cecil 'Cec' Thompson's life story is the very epitome of a rags to riches tale of a man who overcame every obstacle which life placed in his path. It is an object lesson of how sheer determination against seemingly insurmountable odds can help someone to elevate their circumstance however difficult a hand life deals them.

Cec was born in 1926 in Birtley in the north east of England to a local miner's daughter and a father from Trinidad who earned his living as a painter and decorator. He worked in Leeds and one job saw him applying gold leaf to the walls of the City Hall there. Sadly, he died shortly before Cec was born so he had been dealt his first major body blow before he was even born.

His mother moved back to the north east of England where poverty prevented her from raising her four young children. In those harsh times almost a century ago there was little or no help from the state and the youngsters were separated. Cec, who was initially fostered, was sent to different orphanages across the country as were his older siblings. Looking through the lens of history, this beginning sounds like the start of a Dickens novel. Although the family was reunited in 1938, their formative years had been blighted and in Leeds they faced the casual racism which was prevalent back then and Cec says, "In those days, there were very few Black people away from the seaports... and I felt like I had walked out of a freak show."

In 1995, Cec Thompson told his own story in a moving autobiography fittingly entitled *Born on the Wrong Side.* He received a woefully inadequate education and left school unable to read or write. He describes the often racially motivated bullying he faced at the various institutions he was passed between in Wiltshire, Cheshire and the north east. He also describes the varying degrees of callous neglect and unkindness meted out to him. He said, "By the time I left school at 14, I was utterly desensitised and virtually unemployable."

Nevertheless, Thompson did seek and find employment, becoming a labourer and in 1944 he joined the Navy, where he served for three years. Perhaps like other youngsters who are deprived of a loving family and who become institutionalised, Cec was looking for a tribe and found it in his life at sea.

Upon leaving the Navy, he returned to Leeds and found work as a driver's mate at the Yorkshire Copper Works. Cec was invited to play for the firm's rugby league team in a works tournament in Bramley. He accepted the offer and played even though he did not know the rules. He credited years of hard physical toil as having been excellent preparation and he showed a natural aptitude for the sport. After only two outings Thompson was spotted by a Hunslet scout. He joined the Parkside outfit for the princely sum of £250 which was more money than he had ever seen and he described how he felt "like a millionaire."

He quickly adapted to the demands of the professional game and very soon he was being touted as a future international. Eddie Waring showed himself to be a man ahead of his time in not being afraid to call out prejudice when he wrote in his column in the *Sunday Pictorial*, "If Cec Thompson is not chosen for the Great Britain squad, the selectors must be racists." England had capped brothers Val and Jimmy Cumberbatch before the war and Wales had included George Bennett and Alex Givvons on international duty. In 1947, Roy Francis was the first Black player to play for Great Britain.

In 1951, Cec Thompson became the second black player to pull on a red, white and blue international jersey when he was selected to play against New Zealand in the first test at Odsal Stadium. His side won 21–15. This was many years ahead of any equivalent selection in association football. However, before we get carried away with self-congratulatory zeal at the game's liberal credentials, we must refer to one piece of offensive language applied to Cec in a *Daily Herald* headline. Decency prevents me from repeating how he was described in the article. Suffice to say the pejorative term applied to him would have earned the writer an appearance in court in modern Britain. This is a sad reflection of the bigotry which Cec faced in some quarters and testimony to his courage in overcoming it. He showed up well in the Odsal test and was selected to play in the second game at Swinton which ended in a narrow 20–19 victory. This game was also the first league international ever to be shown on the BBC.

In 1953, Thompson was transferred from Hunslet to Workington Town. Given an almost total lack of racial diversity in that region in the 1950s, Cec said he felt he stood out "like a Martian". But he was full of praise for the area saying: "I felt immediately that I had made the right decision. Just as welcoming as the hills and the lakes were the people of Cumbria, warm-hearted, hospitable and generous." In fact, he must have felt very much at home at Derwent Park because he referred to his teammates as his "siblings". Perhaps this provides some insight into the sense of dislocation and loss that he bore as a result of his early separation from his real family as a child.

Cec Thompson's most successful season with Town was in 1958. In that year, the club reached both the Challenge Cup Final and the Championship Final. Sadly for them they were runners-up in both competitions. Wigan defeated them at Wembley 13–9. Winger Ike Southwood scored all Workington's points with three goals and a try. In the Championship decider, they went down to Hull FC 20–3 and Cec sustained a serious knee injury in the game which was to blight his last couple of seasons in the sport.

When he finally drew down the curtain on his playing days, he had made 96 appearances for Hunslet and 192 for Workington Town in a career lasting from 1948 to 1960. Thereafter, Thompson joined Barrow as a coach. No doubt he will have received help and advice from the great Gus Risman with whom he had formed a firm friendship during his years at Workington. Their friendship endured throughout their lives and Cec delivered the eulogy at Risman's funeral in 1994. In accepting the Barrow job, Cec Thompson became only the second black coach in the game. Again, the first was the trailblazing Roy Francis. At one point Barrow were depleted by injuries and the coach was pressed into playing for the stricken side in games against Bramley and Blackpool Borough.

Thompson began a very successful window cleaning company and he was determined to better himself. As a young player he dreaded being asked for his autograph as he could only print his name. Rather than cursing the darkness, he lit a candle of self-improvement. On long bus journeys to away matches he taught himself to read and studied books from *Reader's Digest* to extend his vocabulary. When he was cleaning windows at schools, Cec said "...I would see the teachers at work and imagine how pleasant it would be if I could do their job."

Cec developed a passion for opera and art and passed his English 'O' Level after studying at night school before enrolling at Huddersfield Technical College in 1962. His thirst for learning led him to begin studying at Leeds University in 1965 at the age of 39. Cec studied for a degree in Economics and followed this with a postgraduate teaching qualification. While at Leeds University, he set up the first ever student rugby league team and to this day, the player-of-the-season receives a trophy in his name. As well as becoming coach and president of the team, he was co-founder of the Student Rugby League helping the game expand to other universities.

While simultaneously establishing and managing a large cleaning company which employed over 600 workers, Cec embarked on the teaching career he had once envied when cleaning windows. Cec exemplified the saying, "If you want a job doing, ask a busy person!" He secured his first post at Dinnington Comprehensive School in south Yorkshire where he taught for five years. He was then promoted to become Head of Economics at Chesterfield Grammar School where he served with distinction for 17 years.

Cec was not afraid to challenge racism should it arise. He advised *Look North* on matters of diversity and his wife Anne said that after his notorious "Rivers of Blood" speech by the MP Enoch Powell, Cec had said he felt sorry for Mr Powell as he did not understand the issue he was talking about. Such a mild rebuke against such a rant has a certain dignity.

This wonderful self-starter and truly inspirational man died on 19 July 2011 leaving behind his wife and their son Mark. After his passing, a spokesperson from Leeds University, which had awarded him an honorary Master's degree in 1994 said, "Cec Thompson's …. remarkable rise on the rugby field is matched only by his achievements off it, as he pushed himself from illiteracy to graduation." His story of overcoming every adversity encountered in his life is as remarkable as it is humbling.

6. Headingley Heritage

Leeds as a city bristles with civic pride. The magnificent neoclassical Leeds Town Hall is a municipal palace which proudly puffs out its chest as a symbol of Victorian grandeur. It is guarded by two enormous stone lions, which legend has it, should the Town Hall clock ever strike 13, would descend from their plinths and roam the streets. Stuart MacConie refers to the city as one of "brass and bravado" in his book describing his retracing of the Jarrow March. He details the lavish reception which the hunger marchers received in that building reflecting the generosity of the city fathers. Leeds Rhinos as a club have maintained this generosity as I learned when I was given a marvellous reception when I visited their stadium.

Headingley is a state-of-the-art sports ground serving Yorkshire cricket and rugby league. But while it has been developed with futuristic looking stands, a hotel, restaurants and media facilities, it remains on the same site on which it has been situated since 1890. Like the Roman God Janus, it simultaneously manages to look backwards and forwards. As more founder members' grounds disappear to make way for supermarkets and housing estates, we have fewer and fewer physical historical reference points to reflect the proud history of traditional northern clubs and their contributions to the communities they represent.

Parochialism and tribal rivalries can be an obstacle to celebrating the game of rugby league in a wider, collective sense, but we should understand the need to have our own shrine at which we can pay homage – and this from a Bradford lad. Cricket has Lord's, tennis has Wimbledon and Union has its 'Twickers'. Headingley can be our spiritual home and the wonderful work already undertaken is testimony to the commitment of everyone at the club to uphold the finest traditions of our sport. One of the features that impressed me most was the diligence of the volunteers of the Leeds Rhinos Heritage Committee in researching the history of the Loiners.

Gary Hetherington invited me to view the fantastic heritage facility underneath the North Stand at Headingley Stadium. It is a credit to the determination of the Leeds club and its Foundation to commemorate both the club and the game in general. Gary feels very strongly that the ground should be showcased as the home of our sport. The fantastic resource was designed by the club's Head of Media and PR, Phil Daly. Although a native of Luton, he has lived in Leeds for 28 years since arriving in the city as a student. He joined the club on a work placement and has never left. His knowledge of the club's history is truly encyclopaedic and he and Gary beamed with pride as they gave me the tour.

The first part of the display is devoted to the Leeds club itself. The faces of Victorian gentlemen with starched collars and impressive, luxurious moustaches stare unsmiling from the walls. These are the city fathers, aldermen and captains of industry who doubtless upheld the amateur ideals which were the order of the day when football and cricket clubs were founded in Victorian cities. The resource has details about the club in its rugby union days before the 'Great Schism' of 1895 over broken time, as well as into the Northern Union era.

The next part of the exhibition is a set of 13 illuminated boards, each containing the images of the 10 'best' players to represent Leeds in each position. Any popularity contest attributing the status of GOAT to former players is always a subjective affair and the cause of great debate but it is an exercise in which all fans love to engage.

For example, among the full-backs, there is Frank Young, a Welsh recruit prior to the First World War alongside Jim Brough, who gave almost 20 years service to the club, starting in the 1920s, who went on to become a great coach to the national team. There is Brough's predecessor, Syd Walmsley and then the great New Zealander Bert Cook from immediately after the Second World War.

The next representatives are from my boyhood. Ken Thornett, the Australian with the looks of a matinee film idol, was in the first Leeds team I saw when they came to Odsal. There too is the recently deceased Bev Risman. The word on the terraces had been that Bradford were well placed to sign the former England rugby union international from Leigh, but that dad Gus, then in charge at Northern, was reluctant to do the deal fearing that accusations of nepotism could be laid at his door. More modern incumbents in the full-back berth are represented by 'ET' Andrew Ettinghausen, Brent Webb and Iestyn Harris. That's a selection to spark a great debate down at the Mechanics Arms.

Phil Daly explained that he had received some stick from stars of recent times about non-inclusion and even complaints about representing players out of position. For instance, Garry Schofield is to be found among the centres, whereas some might argue his natural home was in the number six shirt. Phil, though, maintains that he was signed as a centre and he is sticking to his guns. It is also not as if there would be any shortage of talent in the stand-off category. Here we find John Holmes, Alan Hardisty, Mick Shoebottom and the like, so fitting everybody in would become something of a tight squeeze.

Inevitably, the sight of so many great past stars evokes many memories and anecdotes about exploits we have witnessed across the years. There is the fearsome Barrie McDermott. Off the pitch he is mild mannered and lovely company though he can lay claim to being the first man in England to be tasered some years ago. I spot Geoff Wrigglesworth who I greatly admired in the 1960s and Gary tells me the former farmer from York is still going strong which I'm pleased to hear. All of the great three-quarters I recall tormenting us visitors are there in the form of John Atkinson, Alan Smith, Les Dyl and Syd Hynes, all pictured in their full pomp and majesty. I spot Roy Powell who was taken from us far too soon. The plasterer from Batley helped to coach a Bradford Boys' team with me on a couple of occasions and I enjoyed a pint with him in the 'Top House' after our exertions.

Among the array of outstanding players to have graced the number seven shirt I spot Keith Hepworth and of course, Rob Burrow. There too is Barry Seabourne. He always put me in mind of George Formby with his banjo and toothy grin and Gary tells me this likeness earned him a nickname connected to the comic genius among his teammates. Les 'Juicy' Adams who was born in the Hyde Park area of Leeds in 1909 is there alongside Joe 'Chimpy' Busch, the Australian star with whom he vied for the number seven shirt in the 1930s. Adams was killed in Burma when serving as a rear gunner with the RAF.

As we continued down the corridor past the palatial dressing rooms with their individual bays and widescreen television, a crucial visual aid to enhance the review process, we pass other details of club victories and photos of players like Lewis Jones, the recently departed and much-lamented club legend, holding the 1961 Championship trophy, hoisted high on teammates' shoulders in time honoured fashion. We see a life-size photo of Rob Burrow in his kit with Jamie Peacock, JJB and company. It brings a bitter-sweet recollection of that beautiful, moving testimonial match in 2020 when Rob managed to take the field for one last time with that wonderful band of brothers with whom he had created such a dynasty. The image puts into sharp relief the dreadful ravaging effects of MND and it serves to highlight the courage and dignity of this inspirational man.

Before we leave this part of the exhibition, we come to the blue boards emblazoned with white lettering containing the names, debut details and heritage numbers of all of the players to have graced this great club. This incredible catalogue of each member of every Leeds team down the ages is testimony to the marvellous efforts of the Heritage Committee.

Detailed scrutiny of this amazing scroll reveals some incredible information. I must own up to being a sucker for a cenotaph. As Albert Schweitzer observed, monuments to those killed in wars are the greatest tool in preaching peace. I find them, as I find this Headingley roll of honour, an act of defiance against the dread threat of obscurity. There is something touchingly inclusive and egalitarian in this honours board. It says that the seemingly merest of these men is as equally meritorious of mention as any leviathan of the game. Furthermore, it is a living, ever changing record as the club advances into its future, as their anthem states, "Marching on Together!" It is great to see the women Rhino players celebrated alongside the men and this resource will doubtless grow as their game goes from strength to strength.

I look for my former pupil Liam Hood and allow myself to momentarily bask in a little reflected glory for my part in encouraging the nine-year-old's early forays in the game. Gary Hetherington sheepishly points to his own details and I quip that I've heard of that guy. Phil draws our attention to a couple of unusual entrants. At number 746 is Joe Dixon who guested for the club in the Second World War, playing against Wigan and is listed as belonging to the Royal Australian Air Force. Guest players were allowed to turn out for clubs and Gary points out another in Dave Cotton who won Championships with both St Helens and Warrington.

When his famous son Fran, of England and Lions union fame, learned that his dad had played for Leeds, it was a surprise to him and Gary plans to present his dad's heritage certificate at the Saints game this season. Another less mainstream player is at number 925. Al Kirkwood was a former Californian American Football quarterback who turned out in a handful of matches.

One name caught my eye and brought back a particularly poignant memory. I recall an after-match autograph hunting session in the Odsal clubhouse back in the 1960s. Dad sent me over to a very elderly gentleman who he had overheard someone saying was called Joe Winterburn. He had been a Northern player back in the Birch Lane days. I admit to being a bit confused, but approached the obviously ancient man and asked if he would sign my book. He smiled and held up what I now understand to be very arthritic hands. "I can't with these lad," he apologised. My dad took the book and wrote Joe Winterburn in his own hand and the old chap held the pen and made a very spidery cross underneath his name. No doubt my father understood that to be remembered would give the veteran of the game a great deal of pleasure. To my amazement I saw that Joe Winterburn had been assigned heritage number 379 as he guested for Leeds against Dewsbury in 1917. I learned later that the old Birch Lane forward, who joined Northern from Keighley in 1911, had been awarded the Military Medal in the First World War. I must admit to a shiver down the spine moment as I recalled our brief encounter those 60 years ago!

We then proceeded through the doors in the corridor to the section of the exhibition which is devoted to the wider game of rugby league and its history. All of the landmark moments are recorded, from the formation of the Northern Union by the 21 original members following the meeting at the George Hotel, to the formation of the Women's Super League in 2018. A great deal of thought has been given to the design of the resource as a parallel timeline runs beneath the events in the game referencing wider global and national landmarks.

One in particular caught my eye. It transpires that two members of the Suffragette movement were in the act of setting fire to the main stand when a policeman coming off his night shift thwarted their protest by arresting the suffragists. Using sport for political protest in pursuit of women's suffrage took its most dramatic turn when Emily Wilding Davison famously died when she threw herself under the King's horse Anmer at the 1913 Derby. I recall that years later, just over the back of this very stand we found ourselves in, that the supporters of a convicted bank robber brought their cause to the attention of the nation when they gouged into the Headingley cricket pitch their declaration that 'George Davies Is Innocent', thus bringing a premature conclusion to the Ashes test of 1975.

Prior to 1895, rugby union was held here with Leeds competing in their first ever game in 1890. The home side wore terra cotta and green jerseys as they beat Manningham, who would later become Bradford City, by a drop-goal and a try to nil. Three years later, the Scottish Rugby Union moved their home Calcutta Cup game against England to Headingley in the hope of attracting a larger crowd. Perhaps it would be an unfair stereotype to claim that the Scots were once again showing a hard nosed attitude in matters of finance but "many a mickle *does* make a muckle" as they say.

Pictorial evidence reminds us that the first ever test was played here between the Northern Union and Henry Baskerville's New Zealand All Golds and that Batley beat St Helens in the first ever Challenge Cup Final at this stadium. A second Challenge Cup Final was staged here in 1906 when Bradford FC, who later split to become Bradford Park Avenue FC and Bradford Northern, beat Salford. We also learn that in 1916, the RFU allowed the first ever league players to play in a union match when Northern Command lined up against the Australian military to raise funds for the war effort.

Rugby league has always been closely associated with social history. We see a photo of Lucius Banks above a door where players are called to give post-match specimens as part of anti-doping procedures. Banks was the first black rugby league player to play in England. Prior to the First World War, a couple of directors from the Hunslet club were on business in America. They took in a game of American football and spotted the New York born player. They approached him after the game and offered him a chance to join Hunslet. Banks accepted but could only join them when they paid for him to be released from his duties with the US Cavalry! Lucius Banks became the first black player to grace Headingley when he took part in the first ever Lazenby Cup fixture between Leeds and Hunslet in 1912.

Pioneers of 'the greatest game' are lionised in the exhibition. Roy Francis is pictured with players from the club in the 1960s. His revolutionary coaching techniques were certainly ahead of their time. Albeit rather late in the day, he is now widely recognised as a trailblazer and a statue of him was unveiled in his native South Wales in 2023. He shares the distinction of being the first black player to represent Great Britain and the first black professional team coach in any sport in this country. Alongside him is the figure of Jean Galia who is often referred to as 'the Founding Father of French Rugby League.' The former professional boxer brought a group of French union players to Headingley to learn the rudiments of the game.

On his return home he established 'rugby a treize' in France in 1934 before the Vichy government collaborated with their Nazi partners in an unsuccessful attempt to kill the game.

It is fitting that as players of the modern game emerge from the changing rooms and line up to take to the stadium's hallowed turf, they stand adjacent to the 30 all-time greatest players who stare down on those who are about to do battle. Gary Hetherington and his colleagues canvassed pundits, historians, former coaches and players both in this country and Australasia, inviting them to nominate their greatest 20 players ever to have played at Headingley. From their responses, they narrowed the results down to a list of 30 whose names and images are now emblazoned on the walls. From Lewis Jones to Wally Lewis, Jamie Peacock to Jonty Parkin and Neil Fox to Jim Sullivan, they stand as a wonderful bond between the present, the future and the past. To paraphrase the cultural icon that was Marcus Garvey, we do well to understand that to jettison our heritage is to become like a tree without roots. Leeds Rhinos have taken this message to heart.

Roy Francis with Jack Nelson, John Atkinson and Alan Smith prior to the 1968 'Watersplash' Challenge Cup Final. (Courtesy Geoff Francis)

7. Vince Karalius

Some years ago, I attended a seminar in Bradford which was delivered by Professor Charles de Forges from the University of Exeter. He shook the large audience with his opening comment: "I hate coming to Bradford." Our interest was well and truly grabbed by this inflammatory barb at our wonderful city.

His lecture covered the link between parenting and a child's educational achievement. His contention was that children do well if they are reared in an environment where adults speak with them regularly. He argued that the subjects which are discussed are not relevant – topics need not be, say ballet, opera or the novels of Charles Dickens. De Forges said that the main topic of conversation in his childhood home had been rugby league and Hull Kingston Rovers. His antipathy to my native city was due to reversals for his team at Odsal.

I consider myself blessed to have had lots of time in discussion with my dad who told me tales about the great players from across the ages and this enhanced my anticipation and enjoyment of matches enormously. On Saturday 19 March 1966 we travelled across the Pennines in a Wallace Arnold bus on a rare excursion into Lancashire. In those far off days we only got inter-county games a couple of times a season. Cup games were a treat as we could draw one of the glamour sides from the red rose county and on this particular day we were headed to Naughton Park, Widnes. They had earned their place in the second round draw of the Challenge Cup by beating amateur side Brookhouse 23–5 in the opening round while we had beaten Doncaster by a similar margin.

I was beside myself with excitement because I was going to see the great man that was Vince Karalius. I had been reared on stories of the exploits of 'the Wild Bull of the Pampas' by my old man. Little did I know that this would be his final appearance in a long and distinguished career. I recall it was a crisp and bright early Spring afternoon and we stood right at the front behind the sticks. Much to my delight, Northern won a nail biting 7–6 victory over the Chemics and 'Vinty' called time on his playing days at the game's conclusion. To my nine-year-old eyes, this man was truly scary. A great chiselled jaw and long skeletal face, sallow complexion and wild dark eyes topped off with a mop of black, slicked back hair, Karalius could have passed for a wild west gun slinging villain or a mafia hitman. I feared for my heroes in red, amber and black that day given his fearsome reputation. In dad's mining parlance, Vince had come through 'more fights than a checkweighman', referencing the need of the man who weighed the amount of coal a miner had dug to determine his pay back in the day. He often angered the miners and justified his judgements with his fists.

Vincent Peter Patrick Karalius was given the name of three saints by his Irish mother and Scottish father. He was one of eight children in a large Roman Catholic clan. His paternal grandparents had emigrated from their native Lithuania. Three of his siblings, Terry, Denis and Tony also became professional rugby league players. Although a Widnesian, Vince went down the road to St Helens when he signed professional forms in 1951. Standing just shy of six feet tall and weighing in at 14 stones, he was a fitness fanatic. Part of his training regime involved him running from his Widnes home to St Helens and back, a 20-mile round trip.

Rarely touching alcohol, his frame was honed and if he floored an opponent, they stayed down. But it was not only the destructive element of his game which was impressive.

Vince Karalius with the Challenge Cup at Wembley in 1961 after St Helens had beaten Wigan 12–6 in front of a 94,672 crowd. (Courtesy Alex Service)

For a big man he had nimble hands and was adept at threading teammates through gaps with precision passes.

Vince spent over 10 years at Knowsley Road and played 252 times for Saints, scoring 42 tries for the club. As well as regularly winning the Lancashire Cup, he also enjoyed Wembley success. In 1956 St Helens beat Halifax and in 1961 he skippered the side to glory in a one-sided victory over the arch enemies from Central Park. By the 1960s, Saints had assembled an all-star outfit with standout players like Alex Murphy. The mercurial scrum-half enjoyed the protection of one of the hardest men in the game. However, Murphy also points out that his pal was not beyond bringing him down a peg or two from time to time. He explained that on one particular occasion, "Vinny shouted not to score between the posts because I'd get my head stuck. It was a great way of bringing me down to earth."

Competition for international honours was fierce when it came to the loose-forward berth back in the 1950s. Hull had 'Gentleman' Johnny Whiteley in their ranks and Derek 'Rocky' Turner, another player with reputation as a hard man, was a star with Oldham prior to moving to Wakefield Trinity. Karalius won 12 caps for his country and helped Great Britain to a World Cup on home soil in 1960. In that competition against France, Vince was given first use of the bathing facilities when he was sent off in a particularly bloody encounter. Alongside

French captain Jean Barthe, Karalius was sent from the Station Road pitch by Bordeaux Police Inspector Edouard Martung after a brawl between them in the home side's 33–7 victory.

At international level, Karalius' peak was in 1958 when he was selected for the tour to Australia. Initially Vince's inclusion was in some doubt but larger than life team manager Tom Mitchell fought the loose-forward's corner and insisted on his inclusion. Mitchell explained, "I needed him to tame the likes of Aussie hard men Norman Provan and Kel O'Shea. Karalius was just the strong man for the job." Saints and Widnes colleague Ray French, for many years the BBC voice of rugby league, highlights what a big impression 'Vinty' made down under. He only half jokingly suggested that Australian parents would frighten their kids into bed by saying, "Karalius is coming." French likened his mate's vice-like tackling technique, in which he enveloped hapless opponents, as like being wrapped up "by an octopus." It was on that tour that the Australian press bestowed the 'Wild Bull of the Pampas' moniker on Vince in reference to the great Argentinian boxer of the 1920s, Luis Angel Firpo.

The tour got off to something of an inauspicious start and the first test saw an easy victory for the home side, 25–8. Tom Mitchell then surprised the pundits by giving the players a week's trip to Surfers' Paradise which many members of the press and the Australian management criticised. But the ploy now looks like something of a masterstroke as the team bounced back to gain one of the most iconic wins in the sport's history.

The second test at Brisbane in 1958 has become part of rugby league folklore. Harking back to the 'Rorke's Drift' test of 1914, it is often referred to as 'Rorke's Drift Revisited'. The hero of the piece was Vince's Saints' teammate Alan Prescott. In the opening minutes of the game, the British captain sustained a broken right arm when tackling Rex Mossop. Refusing to leave the fray, Prescott, arm dangling to his side, continued to lead his side.

However, the subtext to the story involves Vince Karalius who sustained a badly bruised spine during the first half. At half-time, his back had seized to a point where he could barely stand as the players were due to resume the second half. Tom Mitchell managed to haul the stricken player to his feet and he staggered back out to do battle.

Great Britain's problems were compounded early in the second stanza when Wigan stand-off Dave Bolton broke his collarbone and was forced to leave the action. In those pre-substitution days, Karalius switched to stand-off to partner Alex Murphy. Writing in 2009, Dave Hadfield records how Vince contributed to the eventual win. The makeshift number six exhibited a deft touch to seal the game and Hadfield wrote "...Karalius, buried in a gang tackle, somehow managed to scoop the ball up to Murphy, whose dazzling pace saw him score under the posts and effectively decide the match." Vince played in the third test as Great Britain won the Ashes.

In the twilight of their playing careers, some players make sentimental journeys back to former clubs or destinations which have personal relevance to them. Perhaps moving to his hometown club, Widnes was an itch which Vince needed to scratch. But the move saw no relaxation in the great man's efforts and he certainly didn't use it as part of a comfortable retirement plan. He signed up at Naughton Park in 1962 and brought success to a club which had recently endured a long period of mid-table mediocrity.

Widnes had last won the Challenge Cup in 1930 so it is fair to say that their supporters did not have huge expectations as the 1964 campaign on the road to Wembley began. In the first round they defeated near neighbours Leigh before heading west to dispose of

Liverpool City in the next round. Continuing their victorious streak against Lancastrian opponents, Swinton were their third round victims before an epic semi-final struggle with Castleford. Their first encounter ended in a 7–7 draw before the Chemics narrowly won the replay 7–5. Coincidentally, the other semi-final between Hull Kingston Rovers and Oldham was also decided on a replay, with the rematch being abandoned in extra time due to bad light. The Humberside club eventually emerged as victors and met Widnes in the final. In a tight encounter, with only one penalty giving the men in black and white a 2–0 half time lead, captain Karalius led his side to a 13–5 victory to end their 34-year wait and to lift the trophy for the third time in the club's history.

Vince retired after the defeat to Bradford Northern on that March afternoon when I had the privilege of ticking off another of the all-time greats I had seen in the flesh. He then took a six year break from the game to continue his successful scrap metal business. In 1972, he returned to Widnes as coach. This move marked the start of a new era at Naughton Park as Vince began to build a side fashioned in his own image based on fitness and honest graft.

By 1974–75, Widnes had become a top side. That season they won the Lancashire Cup and followed this with a Challenge Cup win at Wembley. Following a stint at Wigan, Karalius returned to Widnes and in his second season again led them to the Challenge Cup in 1984.

Vince moved to the Isle of Man in 1981 where he built houses. He remained a devout believer and helped to renovate St Columba's Church in Port Erin. In 2000 he became the first forward to be inducted into the Rugby League Hall of Fame. In an interview at his home, Vince, still an imposing looking man though in his 70s said, "I loved the gladiator approach. When there's a body or two lying about, it makes the job a bit more interesting!" He certainly left a few bodies lying about in his amazing career.

Vince died at the age of 76 in 2008. In his obituary in *Rugby League Journal,* Harry Edgar summed him up saying that he was "...one of the most revered figures in the history of rugby league...a symbol of toughness, strength, aggression, ferocity and determination." In the entire history of our sport, he was right up there with the best.

8. Rugby league in film, fiction and drama

Various sports have been depicted in fictionalised form in books, on stage, television or the silver screen. Probably the earliest example was in Thomas Hughes's classic, *Tom Brown's Schooldays*. The author described a rugby game as Rugby School prepared its young charges to develop into leaders ready to go out into the colonies, the church or commerce. In more recent times there has been the Oscar winning *Chariots of Fire* or the absolute turkey which was *Escape to Victory*, in which Ipswich Town's John Wark's Glaswegian accent was deemed to be so impenetrable that it was dubbed by an educated Edinburgh brogue. Television served up comedy in cricketing form with the series *Outside Edge* in the 1980s. The mini-series *Bodyline* was an ambitious attempt to tell the story of the 1932 Ashes series which almost led to the severing of diplomatic relations as skipper Douglas Jardine unleashed his attack dog, Harold Larwood, on Don Bradman and his chums.

But what of rugby league? Undoubtedly the best-known representation of the game was in David Storey's *This Sporting Life*. Appearing first as a novel in 1960, Storey adapted the work as a screenplay and the film premiered in 1963. Taking the often proffered advice given to budding authors to 'write about what you know', Storey drew on his own experiences. Born in Wakefield in 1933, he played in the Leeds 'A' team as a half-back before he eventually graduated to make a handful of appearances in the senior side.

The moody black and white classic sometimes tipped over into stereotyping of the 'Eee' it's rough oop north' variety in the portrayal of the life and career of loose-forward Frank Machin, but the film did gain widespread acclaim among film-goers. The fascination for rugby league supporters in watching the film is in trying to spot the players in cameo support roles. Eagle eyed viewers may pick out Neil Fox, Derek Turner, Ken Traill and others in the dressing room scenes. Indeed, diminutive will-o-the-wisp stand-off Harold Poynton developed a firm friendship with Richard Harris who played the hard man hero with a total inability to express his true emotions. Harris often wore a fur lined, leather RAF pilot's jacket on set and at the conclusion of filming, Poynton managed to 'cadge' the coat from his new thespian friend.

Given Harold's slight build and vertically challenged stature, and the fact that Harris was well over six feet tall, the fit must have been quite comical and certainly less than snug. Nevertheless, Poynton could be seen wearing his prized possession for many years after as he ran his tobacconist corner shop in the 'Merrie City'.

Playwright Storey followed up the success of *This Sporting Life* when he penned *The Changing Room* in 1971. The play was first performed in the West End in 1973 and it ran for 192 performances. It is an exploration of what it is to be part of a team, its attraction, frustrations and hugely complex dynamics. The play covers an entire match but only ever within the confines of what the Australians call 'the sheds'. It depicts the pre-match, half-time and post-game changing room and the lives and characters of the players and staff who share that intense and intimate space. It progressed to Broadway later that year where it won a New York Critics Award for its portrayal of male relationships.

The proliferation of male nudity may have caused some controversy 50 years ago. However, when Noel Coward saw the West End version he is reputed to have commented, "Fifteen acorns are hardly worth the price of admission." I would hazard a guess that Sir

Noel's evening at the theatre to watch the play will have been his only encounter with any aspect of the game of rugby league.

Playwright Nick Boocock used the intriguing episode in Wakefield Trinity's history in 1983 when they recruited the services of 'The King', Wally Lewis for a 10-match stint, to inspire his screenplay. Sharing the title with the club's fanzine from that era, *Wally Lewis is Coming*, Boocock sets his work in the tense pre-miners' strike days as his main character weighs the conflicting emotions of taking on the might of the establishment as he watches his beloved club fight the perils of relegation. The work was rewarded with the 'Euroscript Screen Story' development award and although not yet commissioned, on the 40th anniversary of that epic dispute, it would be a valuable addition in recording that bitter page in the north's history. Hopefully producers will be found to bring the work to the big screen at this important period of public reflection.

Former teacher John Godber joined the Hull Truck Theatre Company in 1984. Having only been in post for two weeks, he learned that the organisation was £76 000 in debt. Answering the financial imperative of the moment, Godber jettisoned plans to stage some rather highbrow German plays and set about writing *Up 'n' Under* which he completed in only four days. The play was staged at the Edinburgh Festival that year and won a Fringe First and Laurence Olivier Award for best comedy even though Godber said he had not written it as a comedy piece. In its three-week stint, the play made £42 000 and subsequently went on to the West End thus saving Hull Truck which thrives to this day.

The plot centres on a pub seven-a-side team from the Wheatsheaf Arms which is initially hampered by the fact that it only has four players. Its landlord makes a bet to challenge the boastful jibes of a neighbouring publican whose all-conquering team from the Cloggers Arms have beaten all comers to gain their status as 'the cocks of the walk.' In 1998, the play was adapted for the big screen where former St Helen's star Adam Fogerty – son of Terry who played in the Halifax Championship winning side of the 1960s – starred as the hard man enforcer for the Cloggers Arms outfit.

I would not claim to be a true connoisseur of the theatre or a great romantic, but one memorable evening in 2011 stands out in my mind's eye. I decided to make an impromptu gesture and booked a table for two at an eatery at a venue of world renown and secured two tickets to the theatre for my wife and myself. We dined at the George Hotel, the birthplace of rugby league, on steak and ale pies of the highest quality before attending the Lawrence Batley Theatre in Huddersfield. We watched the play *Broken Time* which dealt with the 'Great Schism' and its subsequent consequences.

The play by Mick Martin was presented with a tiny cast of no more than half a dozen actors and the choreography in the depiction of play on the field was superb and enhanced still further by the beautifully haunting brass band music which accompanied the action. A central figure in the play was the real-life character of the Reverend Marshall. He was an anti-professional evangelist who considered that the very souls of those accepting payment for lost time and wages were in peril. He pursued the players and clubs he deemed culpable to have given in to the lure of Mammon with the hysterical zeal of a latter-day Witchfinder General. The play examined the existential struggle between the forces of amateurism and professionalism and the history of the great divide between the codes. Never let it be said that I don't know how to show a girl a good time!

Rugby league in television drama is a rarer beast. However, it can be found and certainly in the cosy Sunday night series about the lives of a group of district nurses, *Where the Heart Is*, created by Ashley Pharoah and Vicky Featherstone and first screened in 1997, a number of scenes were rugby league related. The series was a huge viewing success and ran for 10 seasons until 2006. Set in the fictional town of Skelthwaite, and shot in the Colne valley mainly in the villages of Marsden and Slaithwaite, the players from the cast, most of whom were employed at the local toilet roll factory, turned out for the Skelthwaite Scorpions. The scenes that include rugby footage were shot at The Cross which is the home of Underbank ARLFC where a young Harold Wagstaff first earned his stripes and where fellow Hall of Famer and all-time points record holder Neil Fox once plied his trade.

In 1978, former journalist Brian Finch created the series *Fallen Hero* for Granada TV. Finch decided that he needed to gain experience and like an embedded war correspondent, he went to join training with the Wigan players. So concerned were the managers at Granada that they insured the writer for £100,000 just in case. Thankfully Finch survived the rigours at Central Park and a second series was commissioned in 1979. The drama charters the on-and-off field life of the central character Gareth Hopkins, played by actor Del Henney. The plot follows the Welsh player's fortunes after he travels north to join Horton Rangers, but is subsequently forced into retirement due to a knee injury. *Fallen Hero* maps the difficulties of Hopkins on his return to the valleys and the resentment and prejudices he faces.

The story-line did remind me of the true story of a young Welsh player from Cymmer in South Wales which is the village my father originally hailed from. John Hardcastle was a big fair-haired prop forward who signed for Bradford Northern in the early 1960s. He decided to end his league career after a brutal encounter with Wakefield's Don Vines left him in need of extensive dental treatment. The old man and myself sat with him in the stand after the game as he awaited an ambulance as dad had given assurances he would keep an eye out for the young forward. "I'm going home, Gordon" he announced. Years later when I was a student in Wales, my uncle told me of the difficulties and barriers he had faced on returning to his native land. As Oscar Wilde said, "Life imitates art far more than art imitates Life."

And so we move onto the written word. In 2010, Philip Howard, a retired teacher from St Helens, who was responsible for students with special educational needs at a Sixth Form College, used his specific knowledge and experience in his first novel *Braver Than all the Rest* published by London League Publications. It tells the story of a young rugby mad boy Karl Burgess who lives in the fictional town Castleton and suffers from muscular dystrophy. Karl's bravery inspires one of Castleton's veteran players, Chris Anderton, into making an important life decision.

In 2014 Roy Chester published his novel *The Glory and the Dream,* also with London League Publications Ltd. It is set in the years of austerity and rationing following the Second World War and tells the story of the central character, young Johnny Gregson, the budding star of the Garton rugby league team. His father, a pre-war league hero in the northern town of Four Locks, has been killed in the conflict and Johnny harbours an ambition to follow in dad's famous footsteps. The novel highlights the social class prejudices at work as Johnny faces snobbery and bullying after winning a scholarship to a local public school and how his prowess as a rugby player helps him overcome the social stigma and emerge victorious despite the prevailing prejudices of the day.

In 2019, former rugby journalist Chris Berry had his first novel published. *Tough Season* is set at Hopton Town, a club in the lower echelons of the game and its lead character is Greg Duggan, their loose-forward. Unusually this rugby league novel borrows from the crime and mystery tradition rather than the gritty social reality genre we might expect. Berry says he was inspired by the work of Dick Francis whose prodigious body of crime fiction is often set in the world of horse racing. Like Brian Finch, Berry used his experiences of following Wigan as his muse and says, "I wasn't particularly thinking of players like Denis Betts or Andy Farrell but I've known the players and seen the games over the years so people will see little reflections in there."

Another literary connection with Wigan can be found in the writing of Peter Aspinall, who is something of a polymath with a degree in Greek and ancient history. He was a journalist who reported on the club's glory years when they won eight consecutive Challenge Cup finals between 1988 and 1995 which was the subject of *Simply the Best* by Frank Malley. Aspinall worked for the local *Evening Post and Chronicle* prior to its closure and he also compiled and edited Wigan's match programme. When he ended his career as a journo, he turned his hand to writing novels. In 2019, he produced *Two Weeks to Live*, about George and Gaynor Longworth and their kids, 16-year-old Larry and his sister, Katie. George is suffering terminal cancer and Larry is convinced that the end of the world is nigh as he believes a giant asteroid is on a collision course with the earth. The family makes a 'bucket list' trip Down Under with their St. Bernard dog, Bernard. There Larry meets a young Aboriginal NRL player, Jamal Jamai, who shares the doomsday theory about the end of the world. Can Bernard the psychic dog save the day?

Finally, we reach a rather niche area of literature in the form of the graphic novel. Keith Mason, the self-confessed bad boy and rabble rouser who starred as a prop with Wakefield Trinity, St Helens, Castleford and Huddersfield has made an interesting literary and artistic contribution in this format. He has produced two graphic novels in his *Rugby Blood* series. Stars of the recent past, including such luminaries as Konrad Hurrell, Zak Hardacre and John Bateman appear in cartoon form and readers can witness their adventures and heroic exploits as they confound their dastardly foes. Discussions have taken place with Netflix regarding the possibility of a television adaptation so watch this space!

9. The tragic death of John Davies

Fatalities on the field of play are thankfully extremely rare events. Sadly, they are not unknown. In 1947, Wakefield centre Frank Townsend was fatally injured in a match at Featherstone. In that same year, Halifax's Hudson Irving died of a heart attack playing at Dewsbury. In 1949 another Thrum Hall player, David Craven died of injuries against Workington. On 24 April 1977, Chris Sanderson collapsed while playing for Leeds against Salford. He was taken to hospital and died later that day. In more recent times, Wakefield Trinity's Leon Walker died in a reserve team game at Bridgend in 2009 and six years later, Keighley stand-off Danny Jones died in a game in London.

As a 12-year-old I remember my dad coming home from a night shift with the sad news that a Dewsbury player had passed away in a match at Crown Flatt. On 15 April 1969, Welsh back-row forward John Davies died of a heart attack playing in the Heavy Woollen derby against Batley.

David John Davies was born in Caroline Street in Blaengwynfi in 1941. He was an athletically built back rower who showed great promise as a schoolboy and was selected to represent Wales Youth in the 1958–59 season. He joined the Neath club and became a regular for the 'All Blacks' at the Gnoll. Ironically the club adopted their black strip after a player called Dick Gordon died of injuries sustained in a game in 1880.

In 1962, Davies was picked to play for Wales in their match against Ireland at Lansdowne Road. Interestingly, that season's international matches saw Kel Coslett at full-back for Wales. He failed to land a single goal against either England in a 0–0 draw or against Scotland in an 8–3 defeat. He scored the only points in a 3–0 victory over France and by the time the Ireland match came round he had left to join St Helens, where he became part of the furniture in his long and distinguished career.

John Davies' international debut is remembered as 'the hangover match'. This had nothing to do with the amount of Guinness consumed, but rather because the original fixture had been postponed due to a smallpox epidemic in the Rhondda which caused the deaths of 19 people and led to a widespread vaccination programme. The game was eventually played on 17 November 1962 and resulted in a 3–3 draw. John was one of four newly capped players to debut that afternoon and one of the others to be called up at prop was John Warlow who became a future Great Britain rugby league star after joining Kel Coslett at Knowsley Road.

Neath is the oldest rugby union club in Wales. Rugby league scouts have long been seen as the scourge of the amateur code and agents representing northern sides would often run an eye over Welsh talent. Indeed, former player Rees Stephens writing in his journal for Saturday 13 October 1945 recorded after a defeat to neighbours Newport, "After bathing a Leeds scout asked G. Hughes and myself if we would like to "GO NORTH". I told him to "GO TO HELL!" Given that Stephens' father was the owner of two coal mines then we may presume that the financial imperative was less crucial for him than his less affluent countrymen for many Neath players did succumb to temptation. Over the decades such stars of our game as Lewis Jones, who Robert Gates describes as "arguably the most devastating full-back Wales ever produced", have hailed from Neath. Billy Boston had turned out for the club on occasions and in the modern era Jonathan Davies, Scott Gibbs, Glyn Shaw and Allan Bateman have been former sons of the Gnoll.

No doubt John Davies' cap had brought the six feet one inch back rower's talents to the notice of Leeds. The newly qualified school teacher was at the start of his working life when he decided to accept an offer to join the Loiners. Coincidentally, at the same point in 1963 they also recruited another former Neath forward, Don Devereux, who had won three caps in 1958 and signed for Huddersfield. During the same season that these players were recruited, the Headingley based club also signed the Welsh and British Lions player Alan Rees from Maesteg and Scottish international winger Ronnie Cowan from Selkirk. These union converts however were to be eclipsed by the capture of a young winger from the Wakefield amateur rugby league. Alan Smith scored four tries in his debut against Dewsbury and became a legend at the club and a future member of their illustrious Hall of Fame.

John Davies joined the staff of Foxwood School in Seacroft in Leeds and remained at the school until his passing in 1969. But while his day job kept him busy, he had to wait many weeks to don the famous blue and amber jersey. Phil Daly of the Leeds Heritage Group explains, "This was the season of the big freeze! Not a single game was played at Headingley between 1 December and 3 April, a period of 17 weeks and Leeds finished their First Division programme with 18 games in 55 days." Daly believes that it was this experience which caused the club to follow Murrayfield's lead and install under soil heating involving 30 miles of cable.

The end of season glut of fixtures obviously gave Davies the chance to become familiar with his new surroundings and the requirements of his new game. I recall seeing him play at Odsal. He partnered the South African, Louis Neumann, in the back row in a side which included Ken Thornett at full-back. John Davies was at Leeds for six years.

Throughout the 1960s Leeds were developing into a star-studded outfit. In the 1968–69 season the club enjoyed the longest unbeaten run in the club's history, a sequence of 23 games without defeat. They went on to win the Championship by beating Castleford 16–14 in the Final. They boasted a galaxy of international backs like Mick Shoebottom, John Atkinson, Barry Seabourne and Syn Hynes to name but four and the strength of their pack is worth considering. In John's chosen berth, the club had players such as Bill Ramsey, Graham Joyce, Ray Batten and two young hopefuls in Phil Cookson and Graham Eccles banging on the first team door. Consequently, John found himself surplus to requirements. With a burgeoning teaching career and a new family to support, a move down the road to Dewsbury, who were a good workmanlike outfit, was an attractive proposition.

In signing a former Welsh international from Leeds, Dewsbury were departing a little from their usual modus operandi of relying on the production line of local talent, often from the Shaw Cross amateur club. John gained a first team place and was settling in well at Crown Flatt. And so we come to the fateful night of the game against Batley. David Hymes of the Dewsbury Website remembers attending the match as an 11-year-old with a group of his friends. He explains, "During the game John Davies made a break but he went to ground in a collapsed state. He was carried off and the tannoy called for the assistance of a doctor. The game ended and I don't think anybody of a Red, Amber and Black persuasion was prepared for what unfolded the following morning."

John Davies was only 28 years old when he died. He left behind a wife and two children, Erica aged four and Richard who was approaching his first birthday. Sometime after the sad event, Leeds played a combined Dewsbury and Batley side as a fundraiser for the family. In February 2023, Richard contacted Mike Stephenson who was a teammate of his father in that match. Stevo was over from Australia and he met Richard and his sister Erica who now lives in Bridgend with her husband David. Erica said, "I think Stevo was unsure of whether we would want him to tell us the details of what happened that day. But I think it was important that we knew. It is a bit dramatic to say it gave us closure but it filled in the gap."

Stevo explained how John broke away down the slope at Crown Flatt before being tackled by the Batley full-back. He raced to acting half and told John to play the ball quickly before his colleague collapsed in his arms.

On 16 April 2023 a ceremony was organised by former director Neil Fahey and took place following the Coventry game at the FLAIR Stadium. It was attended by John's family members as well as former players including Stevo and John and Allan Bates. A plaque was unveiled with a picture of John and it will be a permanent tribute to a man Stevo described as "a lovely fella" and "a great character with a dry sense of humour." He added, "It was tragic but it forced the RFL to do something about it." Following John Davies' death from an undetected heart condition, mandatory health checks were instigated for all players and perhaps that is his greatest legacy.

10. Tommy Smales – just like the Lone Ranger

All students of the 'greatest game' must learn the subtle complexities and intricate patterns and vagaries of rugby league if they are to fully appreciate what modern day administrators erroneously refer to as 'the product'. As a child I learned at my father's knee that all team members had their own specialist roles and specific skill sets.

For example, he referred to forwards as 'three quarters' labourers'. To the old man this was not a pejorative term by any means for, as a miner, the dignity and worth of hard graft was central to his creed. The physical toil of the forwards in providing a good supply of ball for the backs and wearing down opposing defences to make space for the glamour boys in the back line to exploit was, I was taught, an essential prerequisite for success. An effective team needed to operate "as smoothly as a well buttered ice rink" (in his words), in order that they produced outcomes which were greater than the sum of the parts. Nowadays your sharp suited management types refer to this as 'synergy.'

Moreover, I learned that since roles were clearly stratified, they leant themselves to a variety of body types and thus our game was one for folk of all shapes and sizes. Back in the day there were piano shifters and piano players and each relied on the other. In an excellent article in *Rugby League Journal*, Stephen Bowes lamented the homogenisation of the world game whereby styles of play by different nations – French flair, British guile and craft, Australian power and pace etc – has morphed into a global 'sameness.' I feel there is a lack of originality in the domestic game and it mitigates against the different physical demands for varying positions. The game today is undoubtedly faster as a result of full-time contracts, the 10-metre rule, superior playing surfaces and constant interchanges of players or 'spelling'. Consequently, all the players tend to look like 200 metre runners or middleweight boxers.

I was brought up to believe that the most influential players in any side were the nimble, fleet of foot men at half-back. The scrum-half was the lynchpin or the conductor of the orchestra. Often diminutive by comparison to their teammates, the player wearing the number seven shirt was pivotal. My attention was always focused on the man who fed the scrum – down the middle in those far off days! – with the sharpest of interest. He was, in dad's Welsh Methodist parlance, "God's chosen own." Anyone doubting the special significance of the number seven would do well to consider the following evidence about the magical and mystical properties which are prescribed to this uniquely special digit.

There are seven colours in the rainbow, seven days in the week, seven wonders of the world. There are seven continents and the same number of oceans. Snow White was surrounded by Bashful and his six other little mates and Yul Brynner had six comrades to help him set the badlands to rights. The number seven has special significance in the Bible as the youngest Sunday School child knows that God created heaven and earth before enjoying a well-earned break on the seventh day. There are seven deadly sins, seven layers of purgatory and Roman Catholics believe in the seven sacraments and St Thomas Aquinas spoke of the seven gifts of the Holy Spirit.

Other faith systems too reflect the spiritual significance of this number. For example, Surya, the Hindu Sun-God, rode a golden chariot led by seven horses across the skies, while the original Buddha, Siddhartha Gautama, lost his mother just seven days after his birth as he took seven steps to mark his arrival on earth. In musical notation there are seven notes to an octave and Shakespeare loved to bang on about the seven ages of man. Mathematically speaking, the number seven is the only number between two and ten which is neither a multiple nor a factor of the others. I could go on but I think I don't wish to labour the point. But in case I need to make an even clearer claim to the number being magical I would offer only two further words. Tommy and Smales. Nuff said.

While Bradford Northern (1964) Ltd initially fielded a team which had been begged, stolen and borrowed following the reformation, the directors indicated their ambition in naming Gus Risman as their team manager. This legendary figure, who years later would be one of the original inductees into the inaugural Hall of Fame, joined after only nine games of the new regime. It had been rather an inauspicious start for the new club with seven defeats and only two victories, against Salford and Batley. Such rugby royalty as Risman represented would surely attract big names and no name was bigger than that of Tommy Smales.

The mercurial Featherstone born scrum-half had played 302 games for Huddersfield, leading them to the Championship trophy and the Challenge Cup Final only two years previously. It is remarkable how the pit town of Featherstone has produced so many scrum halves over the years with the likes of Don Fox, Carl Dooler, Paul Daley and Steve Nash having all been part of that production line of talent.

In his excellent history of the Bradford club, Phil Hodgson highlights how Tommy's move to Odsal transpired. Smales was due a testimonial for his services at Fartown and when this was denied, he stood on a point of principle and demanded a transfer. Hodgson points out that the first impression of the state of his new club led him to doubt the wisdom of his decision when he confided "I remember going to my first training session and thinking – what have you done? On principle have you signed your life and career away?"

But Tommy's doubts were soon allayed and Northern's fortunes turned a corner. His leadership skills galvanised the fledgling team and Tommy became a favourite on the Odsal terraces. His original and distinctive appearance appealed to this young fan's imagination. His compact five feet six inches frame, socks rolled to his ankles and all topped off with a rockabilly quiff, all suggested a maverick personality. He exuded confidence which spread through the ranks and adjectives such as 'intuitive' or 'inspirational' hardly do him justice. His ball handling skills were mesmeric and his distinctive reverse flick to change the angle of an attack brought collective gasps of wonder and incredulity from the ever-increasing crowds. I always took my rugby ball when I was sent to the shop down the road, working scissors moves with every single lamp-post with my version of the reverse flick as I revelled in the roars of the imaginary crowd!

On one occasion, Tommy executed a move with Cumbrian loose-forward Johnny Rae, who improved enormously under Smales' tutelage, which still lives fresh in the memory these many years later. Sadly, *Anno Domini* has erased the exact details of our opponents that day, but thankfully not the memory of the wonder that I witnessed. A scrum was formed about 30 yards from their line. Northern won the ball and Tommy bolted away down the blind side. In those days there were some really tough customers at loose-forward who took it as a personal affront for a cocky scrum-half to encroach down their short side. That area was akin to the proverbial dark alley at night. Tommy was duly belted for his impudence when he was collared. Nobody in attendance doubted that he was the ball carrier. Then a kind of murmur of amazement and recognition grew to a disbelieving roar. Johnny Rae was strolling unopposed under the crossbar having received a smuggled pass disguised after a fashion which would have shamed Sherlock Holmes as Tommy set off on his decoy dash. What modern commentators, who scream their hyperbolic praises of sometimes routine plays, would have made of this, I shudder to think.

In studying the programme for Johnny Rae's benefit match against Huyton after the loose-forward was forced out of the game by injury, I discovered courtesy of 'Old Jack's programme notes, how Tommy's understudy, Bak Diabira, who was also a veritable box of tricks himself, replicated the very same play against Featherstone in 1968. The pupil had learned well from the master craftsman but we should give credit to Tommy as the originator of this wonderful prestidigitation.

Many years later, I was intrigued to learn, when thumbing through the very amusing set of recollections and anecdotes in the book, *No Sand Dunes in Featherstone,* how the 'Fev' loose-forward Keith Bell had been summoned to the 'Travellers' Rest' by the then club coach Tommy who was mine host at the pub which housed his famous gym. It was Christmas Day Night and he and the incumbent scrum-half had been called up to practise the self-same ruse with the aid of a ball and a pub table in advance of their Boxing Day fixture. They were not given permission to leave until the move was perfected. Apparently, Mrs Bell was not amused.

But back to the 1960s. It was 1965, just three weeks before my ninth birthday, when Tommy gave me the greatest gift of all – the Yorkshire Cup. Plenty of supporters – especially of a more mature vintage, lament the passing of the county cup competitions which gave such a sense of excitement to the early season. For me, it was the first ever experience of glory and silverware. Like your first pair of boots, your first car, your first kiss – that feeling is etched into the soul forever. Little did I know how long it would be between drinks at such an early stage in my sporting odyssey.

We attended every round. Keighley were beaten at Lawkholme Lane in round one. Next, Hull KR, our first opponents after our 1964 comeback were disposed of at Odsal and then we confronted Tommy's former side Huddersfield in the semi-finals. We drew the initial encounter 7–7 at home and faced a replay at Fartown the next day – modern players who lament fixture congestion please note. I recall holding onto the metal railings on the touchline where you could smell the wintergreen on a fine autumn evening. I remember the tension and the noise as we toppled the claret and golds 7–4.

So it was off to Headingley for the final, which always felt slightly regal like visiting your posh auntie's house. Memory is a funny thing. As a young teacher I was told by an old sage, "In 20 years they won't remember much of what you said. They'll only remember how you made them feel." So it is with that golden day almost 60 years ago. The record shows we beat a much-fancied Hunslet side 17–8. Only a few months previously they had lost narrowly to a star-studded Wigan at Wembley in what is still considered to be one of the classic finals. They had a fearsome pack crammed with present and future internationals of the calibre of Geoff Gunney, Bill Ramsey, Ken Eyre and Dennis Hartley.

My recollections are of a new Northern pom pom hat and scarf knitted by my mum in honour of the occasion. Outside the ground I was treated to a silk rosette, the size of a small dustbin lid, or so it seemed to me, which was adorned by a plastic rugby ball stuck in the centre. This wonderfully gaudy favour was thereafter stapled to a shelf in my bedroom for years before moving to Wales where it lived alongside my posters of Olivia Newton John in my student digs.

We wore our change strip of red to allow Hunslet to don their distinctive chocolate and white banded jerseys and navy-blue shorts. The day was sunny and the seasonal milky sun made shielding your eyes necessary with your special souvenir programme. In my mind's eye I still can see our centre Ian Brooke charging downfield to our end with his distinctive head bobbing running style for a spectacular long-range individual try. I remember Australian winger Lionel Williamson grabbing a brace, the second of which was courtesy of a pass near the line from Tommy himself. Most of all I recall the great man lifting the enormous silver cup to us delirious fans!

Tommy Smales played 61 games for the club and in 1965 captained Great Britain in all three tests against New Zealand. We were at the Odsal test in which he was partnered with teammate Johnny Rae. A serious arm injury necessitated surgery and the insertion of a metal pin and Tommy was disappointed not to be selected for the 1966 Ashes tour as the selectors deemed the injury to represent too great a risk.

Then he was gone. It all felt like the end of an episode of another of my boyhood heroes – the Lone Ranger. It was as if Tommy had breezed into our troubled town and sorted out all our problems and kicked out all the bad guys, leaving before anyone had the chance to say thank you to the masked man. The illusion is reinforced by the fact that his particular sunset took him to far off North Sydney.

I can almost hear the William Tell Overture.

Tommy Smales with Johnny Rae training at Bradford. (Courtesy *Rugby League Journal*)

11. The Goldthorpes of Stourton

I have always had a soft spot for Hunslet. As a teenager I had some good mates from the Hunslet Boys' Club which had a fine rugby league tradition. One of my former pupils who I coached at Hanson School in Bradford joined the south Leeds club in 1994 and I always looked out to follow his progress. Prop Steve Pryce was a great lad who went on to serve the club for 10 years and was inducted into the club's Hall of Fame in September 2018 and is described as "A true legend of the club" on their website.

Hunslet's motto "And so we shall again" is taken from the supporters' optimistic anthem, 'We've Swept the seas before, boys', which harkens back to the glory years of the club's past and the halcyon days at their old Parkside ground. In 1907–08 they became the first team to win 'All Four Cups'. The love which supporters have for the club is shown by the wonderful work done in chronicling their history by volunteers who have gathered a truly excellent archive of resources and records of the team's exploits. People like Pat Benatmane, Steve Calline and Stephen McGrail have done a magnificent job of bringing together some invaluable sources of evidence which is a real credit to their passion and diligence.

One remarkable feature of Hunslet's history is the part played by one specific family – the Goldthorpes. There were five Goldthorpe brothers who were brought up on the family farm. Their home was at Haigh Farm in Stourton which is in the Belle Isle area and when not performing chores like milking duties, the boys were given the freedom to develop their sporting skills on the land known locally as Goldthorpe Pastures.

'The Great Schism' which resulted in the creation of the Northern Union occurred in August 1895. The careers of the five sons straddled this date so that they played both codes during their days at the club. William (Heritage number 69), was the eldest of the boys and he made 27 union appearances for Hunslet. Sadly, his story is rather a tragic tale as he took his own life at the age of 48. At the inquest in 1913, his younger brother Albert explained that when William was 20, he had an accident when a number of roofing tiles hit his head leading to "severe concussion of the brain". Subsequently William complained of severe bouts of pain in his head and in a final note to his sibling he stated, "my head has started swimming again." It was found that farmer William had shot himself when "of unsound mind".

James Goldthorpe (Heritage number 64), joined the club in 1885 and played 185 union games for Hunslet. He also made four appearances under Northern Union rules. In all he scored 61 tries and 24 goals. James became a teacher following his rugby career. Probably the least successful player of the five sons was John (Heritage number 68). Nevertheless, he did represent the club sporadically, sometimes standing in as a guest and between 1885 and 1892 he made seven appearances. John, who was a serving police officer at various stations in Yorkshire, emigrated to Australia. During the First World War, his own two sons joined up with the ANZAC forces. Harry served in France and returned home having survived, but sadly 18-year-old Arthur died in the disastrous campaign at Gallipoli.

Without doubt, it was the two younger Goldthorpe brothers who enjoyed the most successful rugby careers. In thinking about this, it is perhaps that when there is something of a tribe of brothers, you have to work harder to keep up. I recall inviting some of the Bradford Bulls players into the school I worked at and Sam Burgess talked to the kids about the sibling rivalry that had stood him in good stead. Jack Fairbank, former Huddersfield and Leeds forward was also, like the Goldthorpe brood, a Yorkshire farmer, as were his sons Karl (not for nothing was he nicknamed 'Concrete'!), John, Dick and Mark. The great John Holmes of Leeds was the youngest of three brothers so I believe my theory may hold true.

Hunslet supporter and historian Stephen McGrail has undertaken extensive research on the youngest brother Walter (Heritage number 119). The fifth son was born on 9 January 1874 and he joined his brothers at the club in 1889, making his debut at full-back as a 16-year-old. This made him the youngest debutant at Hunslet, a record which stood for 60 years. Initially Walter played as the last line of defence, but he eventually moved into the centres later in his career.

His first taste of silverware came in 1892 when he helped the club raise 'T' old tin pot', the Yorkshire County Cup, in triumph by beating near neighbours Leeds in the final. That season, still pre-Northern Union, Walter was selected for Yorkshire at full-back. Following the start of the new era, the Parkside club, which had moved from their Woodhouse Hill ground 10 years previously, won the Yorkshire Championship and momentum was maintained with the Yorkshire Cup victory of 1905. During the previous season, Walter and his brother Albert had been awarded a joint testimonial for their long service and the match was attended by 8,000 of the Hunslet faithful.

But the best was yet to come as the club went from strength to strength. In the north of England, the game was still largely played under old union laws but in 1906, the number of players per side was reduced from 15 to 13. This major change and its resultant opening up of space for players to exploit, must have suited their style and in 1907–08, Hunslet became the first of only three teams ever to win 'All Four Cups'.

The competitions in question were the Championship, the Challenge Cup, the County League and County Cup. Only two clubs ever repeated the feat – Huddersfield in 1914–15, with the much-vaunted 'Team of All the Talents', and Swinton in the 1927–28 season. Given the fact that by 1970 the structure of the game had changed and not all of these competitions survived, then this is an achievement which can never be replicated. During the historic season, Walter made 33 appearances, contributing nine tries and seven goals to the cause.

This landmark season marked Walter's 18th at the club. However, in 1908–09, James Goldthorpe became secretary of the Leeds club and he persuaded his little brother to join him at Headingley. Walter was made vice-captain and went on to make 51 appearances for the Loiners. In 1910, he was in the team which beat Hull in the Northern Union Cup – fully 18 years since his first win in the competition. This was Walter's fourth win having repeated this success in 1899 and 1908. He retired after the Final in 1910 to bring down the curtain on a career which had spanned 21 years.

When a player is referred to by the fans as 'Our' it denotes a true sense of affection. It is as if the throngs on the terraces are conferring an almost familial claim to their hero. It was so in the case of Harold Wagstaff who the Fartown faithful nicknamed 'Ahr Waggy'. So it was with the final member of the Goldthorpe clan – the penultimate son Albert (Heritage number 112). Known to Parksiders simply as 'Ahr Albert', he was without doubt the pre-eminent member of the footballing dynasty.

A fellow legend of the Hunslet club, full-back 'Gentleman' Jack Walkington, who made 572 career appearances between 1927 and 1948 and who died in 1997, wrote the following in *Sporting Yorkshire* in 1988: "Four of the Goldthorpe brothers played in a cup match for Hunslet in 1892. But Albert was the best. His record for dropping goals will never be beaten." In 659 games for Hunslet, Albert scored over 1,500 points.

In the all-conquering 1907–08 season he captained the side even though he was by then, a 36-year-old veteran, making 42 appearances and racking up his 800th goal during the campaign. The picture of him standing proudly by the haul of silverware which he had won alongside 'the terrible six', a pack feared and revered in equal measure, is an iconic image of our sport.

After retiring, this tireless servant of the club joined the committee and fitted in his work for Hunslet alongside his business as a dairyman. Albert also found time to captain the Hunslet Cricket Club over a 20-year period. 'Ahr' Albert died exactly a year to the day after his brother James, on 9 January 1943. Prior to his death he had volunteered as a full-time Civil Defence worker to support the war effort.

His place in the pantheon of the greats was ensured when he was inducted into the Rugby League Hall of Fame in 2015, alongside Shaun Edwards OBE. Another lasting tribute to this legend of the game, is the annual award of the Albert Goldthorpe medal, introduced by *The Rugby League Express* in 2008 to mark the centenary of the 'All 4 Cups'. The solid gold medal which is worth several thousand pounds is awarded to the player who gains the most accumulated points over a season as voted by journalists and it mirrors the Australian equivalent 'Dally M' award, which is given to the top NRL player in honour of the legend Dally Messenger. It is an important feature of the award that it is for the best and fairest player and modern recipients have included Sam Tomkins, Danny Brough, Luke Gale and Jonny Lomax. A stipulated criteria is that no player who has been suspended during the season can win the prestigious medal. The medal provides a fitting tribute to a player, who was not only a great footballer, but also a man acknowledged as a true gentleman. As the American sports writer Grantland Rice put it, "When the one great scorer comes to count against your name, he counts not on whether you won or lost, but how you played the game."

12. South Africans in English rugby league

In *What Sport Tells Us About Life*, the former England cricket selector Ed Smith asks whether some sports have a natural home and are fitted to a perceived national temperament. He argues that, "Sports were not only invented in unexpected countries and flourished where you least expect; they have also taken on counter-intuitive national interpretations." This I feel is the case with South Africa and rugby union. Why is it that a game conceived and fashioned on the muddy fields of England's Public Schools should flourish in the land where startled impalas pronk along the sun-baked high veldt?

It is important to say at this point that, using apartheid era terminology, that rugby union was the major winter sport for the white (English and Afrikaner) and 'coloured' communities. It had a small following in the African (black) population, but association football was the main winter sport for the African community, who were and are the majority of the population.

In 2023, the Springboks became the first team to lift the rugby union World Cup for a record fourth time. This is because the game which favours forward power is suited to the Afrikaner character which emphasises strength and machismo as virtues to be desired. Rugby union, with its need to achieve dominance in the scrum, appeals to the collective South African mindset. This is, I believe, why rugby league never took root in 'the rainbow nation' despite a number of abortive attempts to establish it there.

Interestingly, union players from South Africa are not averse to travelling abroad to ply their trade in faraway lands. Writing in *The Rugby Paper* in 2020, former Springbok Andre Snyman points out that of all the players registered by rugby union's Premiership clubs in that year, 10 per cent were of South African origin and Bath had 10 players from the country on its books. Snyman attributed this diaspora of talent to the quota system in operation in his native land, which is an attempt to mitigate the consequences of the decades of abhorrent apartheid laws but which limits the opportunities by squeezing out some players. He also cites the violence and unrest which beset the country in this transitional period of its development as a contributory factor to this exodus.

While English rugby league clubs have traditionally relied on Australasians to bolster their squads, there have been recruits from South Africa and some of them have been a fantastic success! Jamie Bloem, whose career is mapped in Andrew Hardcastle's biography, *In Full Bloem* (2013), is a more recent recruit to the English game. An often-controversial figure who was handed a two-year ban for taking performance enhancing drugs, Bloem served several clubs including Castleford, Oldham, Doncaster and Halifax between 1992 and 2005. Also in the modern era, Mark Johnson had a successful career in British rugby league.

Wigan were one of the first clubs into the market. In 1923 they signed the star winger Adriaan 'Attie' Jacobus van Heerden. Prior to his arrival at the Lancashire club, Attie had represented South Africa in the 1920 Olympics in Antwerp in the 400 metres. A year later he was selected for the Springboks twice against the All Blacks. With the Springboks he toured Australia scoring a then record five tries in their opening match against New South Wales.

The six feet one inch, 13 stone four pounds wingman had pace, power and a magnificent body swerve. He made 127 appearances for the club between 1923 and 1927, scoring 107 tries, making him 10th in Wigan's top try scoring list. Attie scored a try in the 1924 Challenge Cup 21–4 victory over Oldham at Rochdale's Athletic Grounds. He had to dive over the line under the legs of a police horse as it attempted to hold back spectators in the 41,831 crowd.

The following year van Heerden registered another try as Wigan defeated Warrington in the Championship Final at Knowsley Road. On the club's website he is described as, "a flamboyant personality, dancing at times on the tables of hostelries in Wigan, a snappy dresser and popular with the ladies." He twice represented Other Nationalities before he joined Leigh in 1927, playing in 14 games before returning home to the Western Cape.

A contemporary of van Herden was David Booysen who played scrum-half or centre at Central Park between 1924 and 1929. He made 156 appearances and scored 52 tries and two goals. Booysen played scrum-half in the 1925–26 Championship win. He also gained international honours for Other Nationalities against England. Wigan again invested wisely when they signed Rhodesian born goal kicking full-back Fred 'Punchy' Griffiths in 1957. During a five-season stint at the club he contributed 1,455 points in his 161 games.

Continuing to mine this rich seam of player talent, in 1973 the club secured the services of a unique character who it was hoped might become the next Billy Boston. Green Vigo, a black South African fisherman was signed and although the initial expectations may have been rather too ambitious, the free-spirited winger did have an impact at Central Park. He spent seven years at the club with the highlight being a seven try haul in a Lancashire Cup victory against their bitterest rivals, St Helens, in 1976.

In 1984, Maurice Lindsay signed Nick du Toit who had won 18 Springbok caps. He played in 59 matches until his departure for Barrow in 1987. He appeared as a substitute in the 1985 Challenge Cup Final before joining the Cumbrian club where he spent three seasons. After a brief sojourn with Chorley, du Toit rounded off his career at Wakefield where he played in 22 games at a club which, as we shall see, also has a tradition of South African involvement. He returned to Wigan when his playing days were over as a publican. He cycled from Blackpool to Paris to raise funds for the Cystic Fibrosis Charity.

'The Pie Eaters' again raided South Africa the season after du Toit's capture, to sign the Springbok pair Rob Louw and Ray Mordt who had both been frustrated by the lack of opportunities to play international rugby due to the boycotts by other nations against the apartheid policies of their government. When the 1985 tour to New Zealand was called off, they decided to cash in their chips to join the cherry and whites.

Dr Danie Craven the South African rugby supremo condemned their action and referred to the pair as "traitors". Louw had won 19 Springbok caps and for his province had won the Currie Cup on five occasions with Western Province. Before revising his view on the second rower Craven had described him as "fast enough to play among the backs". Louw had to bide his time in the 'A' team but did eventually make enough first team appearances to be awarded a medal when Wigan won the league in the 1986–87 season. Ray Mordt was a winger who, though born in Cape Town, spent most of his childhood in Zimbabwe. He made 25 appearances for the club and scored 16 tries in that league winning campaign.

Wakefield Trinity, as noted previously, has an interesting history of involvement in South Africa. In an excellent article on the club website, *I'm Wakefield 'til I die...* it is explained how the relationship began. In 1962 Trinity responded to a request to tour the country in an attempt to help the game put down roots in the republic. Some star South African guests were co-opted into the squad in the shape of Fred Griffiths (Wigan), Tom van Vollenhoven (St Helens), Wilf Rosenberg (Hull) and Ted Brophy (Leigh). Wakefield made their South African centre Alan Skene captain of the tour in the absence of Derek Turner who was with the Great Britain tour to Australia. Sadly, a power struggle between the two organisations who were vying to run the game, the National Rugby League and Rugby League South Africa contributed to preventing the project becoming a success. It always strikes me that like the Labour Party, rugby league fights harder internally than against any of its natural enemies!

By 1962, Wakefield had already dipped its toe into the South African talent pool. In 1958 they signed five players from Western Province. Jan Lotriet was a six feet three inches centre or winger, but he only made three appearances before returning home. Ivor Dorrington made 12 appearances in the 1958–59 season and it was he who recommended the aforementioned Alan Skene to the club. Skene formed a lethal centre partnership with the legendary Neil Fox and scored 69 tries in 139 appearances for the Belle Vue outfit. He played in Challenge Cup victories in 1960 and 1962 and twice contributed to winning the Yorkshire Cup as Wakefield enjoyed their most successful period in the club's history.

Jan Prinsloo was a twice capped Springbok when he joined St Helens in 1958. He played on the opposite wing to his fellow countryman Tom van Vollenhoven at Knowsley Road before being signed by Trinity for a club record fee of £9,000 in 1961. In June of that year Wakefield's chairman Stuart Hadfield embarked on a scouting mission to the country where he signed Colin Greenwood on a three-year contract for £4,000. In 75 games at the club, Greenwood crossed for 32 tries before moving to play and coach in Australia.

On Trinity's 1962 tour they played against Bloemfontein Aquilia who had in their ranks the union convert Gert Coetze who had represented the Orange Free State on 44 occasions. On that day 'Oupa' (which means 'grandad' in Afrikaans) gave a good account of himself on the wing playing opposite Tom van Vollenhoven. The following season Coetze travelled to England without a club, asked Trinity for a trial and was duly snapped up. He went on to make 191 appearances scoring an impressive 122 tries. He was a try scorer in the victory over Wigan at Wembley in 1963 and he was on the winning side in two Championship campaigns. 'Oupa' was selected for the groundbreaking 1963 South African tour to Australia but a shoulder injury forced his early withdrawal.

Rudolph 'Rudi' Hasse initially joined Bradford Northern prior to their demise in 1963. The second rower was part of a squad which included two non-white South Africans in Goolam Abed and Enslin Diambulo who, had he been in apartheid South Africa, Hasse would have been banned from playing alongside. When Northern went under, he joined Wakefield and played six times for the club before his homesick wife convinced him to take her and their two daughters home.

Ivor Dorrington, who had recommended Alan Skene to Wakefield, again played matchmaker as Trinity signed the black South African winger David Barends for a bargain fee of £1,000. Fast and powerful, the crowd favourite enjoyed three fruitful years at Belle Vue, scoring 22 tries before moving on to enjoy his most successful period under Peter Fox at Odsal. Barends played for Bradford Northern between 1977 and 1983 gaining Championship honours in the process. He played 202 games for the club scoring 70 tries before ending his career with Featherstone Rovers. He settled in West Yorkshire and still lives there today.

Left: David Barends wearing his 'Honorary Springbok' blazer, awarded to players who could not play for the Springboks in the apartheid era. Right: Mark Johnson, who had a successful career in English rugby league before returning home. (Both photos Peter Lush)

Tom van Vollenhoven, Jan Prinsloo and Duggie Greenall training. (Courtesy Alex Service)

During the late 1950s and early 1960s, Leeds delved into the South African market to sign two South Africans to bolster their team. Louis Neumann was a second row forward who played for the club 123 times between 1961 and 1966 before moving to Australia to play with Eastern Suburbs. In 1959 they had acquired the services of a young South African student. Wilf Rosenberg had been capped five times by the Springboks and formed a partnership with Tom van Vollenhoven as his centre against the 1955 touring British Lions. Rosenberg was born in South Africa but moved to Australia as a child where he first played rugby at school. Returning to his homeland as a teenager, Wilf graduated to play for his provincial team, Transvaal, before being selected for international duties. He joined Leeds where he made 81 appearances, scoring 73 tries. His trademark swallow dive finish, which was captured in one of the most iconic rugby league photos ever, earned him the title, 'the flying dentist'. Rosenberg had been studying medicine in South Africa, but was unable to transfer to a course in Leeds, so studied dentistry at Leeds University. Rosenberg was in the 1961 Championship winning side but following a broken jaw he moved to Hull where he played for two seasons bagging a further 42 touchdowns.

Wilf Rosenberg returned to South Africa in 1963 and set up his own dental practice. Sadly, this ended when he suffered a stroke in 1970. Thereafter, he dabbled in various projects including an involvement in boxing promotion. In 1994, he was inducted into the 'International Jewish Hall of Fame'. In 2011, I had the great pleasure of meeting Wilf Rosenberg at a dinner at Headingley to commemorate the fiftieth anniversary of that 1961 Championship team. Alongside teammates like Lewis Jones and Derek Hallas, Wilf was feted and old stories were regaled by the former wingman who had been flown over from Israel where he was then living. I met and shook the hand of a very elderly, stooping gentleman who told me with a twinkle in his eye that he was the only male resident in an old people's home which hosted 20 people! Wilf died in 2019 in Herzliya in Israel.

St Helens were the club who got the most bang for their rand in the signing of two remarkable wingers. Leonard Michael Anthony Killeen joined Saints in 1962 and was that rather rare breed, a goal-kicking winger. He clocked up 187 appearances in his five seasons at Knowsley Road, amassing a points haul of 1,161 in the form of 115 tries and 408 goals.

I remember sitting at home watching our tiny black and white television in 1966 as St Helens demolished near neighbours Wigan 21–2 at Wembley. In the first half they were awarded a penalty near the touchline inside their own half by referee Harry Hunt. Along with the 98,000 plus people at the stadium, I was dumbfounded to see Killeen place the ball for a shot at goal. His playing colleague that day, Ray French estimated that, with the angle, the distance was fully 65 yards. In his toe ended, straight on style, he sent the ball sailing high and handsome through the sticks. Later in the game he went very near to repeating the feat from five yards further out in the swirling winds of the old ground. On that day the man from Port Elizabeth became the only South African to be awarded the Lance Todd Trophy.

Remarkably, the following week he almost surpassed these heroics in the Championship final at Swinton's Station Road against Halifax. 'Leo the lion', as his teammates nicknamed him, grabbed a hat-trick of tries and kicked six goals as Halifax were put to the sword in Saints' 35–12 victory. In 1968 the points machine, left for Balmain in Australia.

And so, in the spirit of saving the best 'til last, we need to talk about 'The Voll'. I feel that it is rather surprising that the man from Bethlehem – albeit the Orange Free State version – was not one of the original inductees to the Rugby League Hall of Fame, only joining the immortals in 2000. Nor was he one of the heroes to be ennobled by inclusion on the Wembley Statue. I find this somewhat perplexing for when we consider the pantheon of the greats, Tom van Vollenhoven is surely right up there.

The story of how St Helen's signed the former police officer by beating rivals Wigan in his pursuit is the stuff of legend. The story goes that the two clubs were involved in a race to present their case to sign to the former Springbok, but that the telegram from the Central Park club was delayed when their dispatch rider suffered a flat tyre and Vollenhoven acting on a 'first come first served' principle opted for Saints. Fate intervened in the form of that puncture and how St Helens benefited from their neighbour's misfortune.

Karel Thomas van Vollenhoven's statistics alone cannot begin to tell his story or demonstrate his greatness. Impressive though his numbers are, 392 tries in 409 games spanning 10 years at the club, it is the style and quality of his play we must consider. Two tries in particular are highlighted by those who were fortunate to witness them.

The first was in the 44–22 1959 Championship Final victory over Hunslet at Odsal. Receiving the ball near his own line, van Vollenhoven set off on a 75-yard mazy run beating six defenders with side steps and swerves before rounding the solo effort off under the posts and all this with a dodgy, tight hamstring.

The second masterpiece was enacted at Wembley in 1961 when his would-be employers Wigan were the cup final opponents. 'The Voll' and his centre partner Ken Large passed inside and out to bamboozle the Wigan left side defence as they progressed 75 yards up field in one of the greatest tries ever to be scored and this can be witnessed by the grainy footage on YouTube accompanied by Eddie Waring's commentary which conveys the breathtaking astonishment at the brilliance of the play.

My wife tells how she bought her dad a 'Jackdaw' folder of documents all about the great man in the 1960s, when she was a child. I asked if it was about St Helens in general but she assured me it was dedicated to Tom van Vollenhoven. My memories of him are that I saw him score a try against Bradford Northern, when Saints beat us in the Championship in April 1967 at Knowsley Road on my first visit there. The try was not spectacular, but came when Brian Lord made a mess of a kick through and Tom merely dotted it down.

My next visit was not until 1995 when I took my son Owain to the ground to watch the clash between New Zealand and PNG in a World Cup pool game. At half-time Tom van Vollenhoven was guest of honour and received rapturous applause from the crowd, so the flying policeman was present on both occasions I visited the ground!

Vollenhoven was 82 when he passed away in 2017. In his obituary in the *Guardian*, Charles Nevin wrote: "At five feet 10 inches, with blond crew-cut hair and all the aloofness of the superior sportsman as he waited on the wing, he had pace and grace ready to explode at an instant, with elusive footwork, deceptive strength and a smooth but sudden surge to an even greater speed that left the finest opponents floundering."

While South Africans may not have been as numerous as some of their overseas counterparts, those who arrived on these shores have left an indelible mark on the history of our game.

13. Modern scrums

Now, I grant you that modern, full time rugby league players are super-fit athletes who benefit from dieticians, sports psychologists and all the army of backroom staff who are there to meet their every need so that they can optimise their performances. But at the risk of sounding like one of those RFU committee members referred to by Will Carling, I do believe that the modern game could learn from the past which is, as L P Hartley opined, a foreign country where things are done differently. Nowhere is this more the case than in one feature of our game: the scrum.

An absolute prerequisite for a sporting encounter to engage and excite the spectator is the need for an element of unpredictability. The possibility of the unexpected excites optimism in the underdog's heart and makes the favourite guard against complacency. The server in tennis is likely to win the game, but does not hold all the aces (pun intended!) as the receiver could break serve. The penalty taker in football should score more often than not, but perhaps the keeper will save one or two in ten kicks from the spot. Dramatic tension relies on this lack of certainty and this is the glorious allure of sporting theatre.

There is an old saying that "Possession is nine tenths of the law", for to state the bleeding obvious, as many an old sage on the terraces would point out, "you can't score without the ball." However, in rugby league today the scrum has given up all pretence of being a contest. Now it is merely a device for handing over possession to the non-offending side following an error by their opponents. The ball is rolled between the last man down's legs – probably not the loose-forward – as the players loll against each other in a manner which looks vaguely ridiculous. By design, there is not a hope in hell of there being a scrum going 'against the head'. In removing any real *raison d' etre* for the scrum, the powers that be have created some unlooked for consequences for the game in general and thus contributed to the predictability which I believe the more traditional spectator finds alienating and which contributes to a more formulaic brand of rugby.

Positional demarcation was always a feature which meant that the game had something for people of all shapes, sizes and physical attributes. Brawn and bulk had their place to play alongside speed, guile and athleticism but at the heart of the game was the fact that you needed ball getters and ball users.

As a kid back in the 1960s I recall a Challenge Cup first round tie in which my beloved Bradford Northern visited Dewsbury. We were favourites to win and had become renowned for our expansive back play having signed stars such as Ian Brooke, Berwyn Jones – the former Olympic sprinter – classy centre Geoff Wrigglesworth and the Australian powerhouse, George Ambrum. On that afternoon at Crown Flatt, I learned that glamour and panache were of little value if you were starved of possession. The formidable Dewsbury pack with forwards of the calibre of Tank Walker, Brian Taylor, 'Dick' Lowe and Harry Beverley did not allow us the ball and lowered our colours 12–2.

The following week having been chastened by proceedings at Crown Flatt, the directors got out the cheque book to sign Peter Mullins the Dewsbury and Great Britain Under-24 hooker in the previous week's match, to solve our ball winning problems. Sadly, he did not enjoy much success at Odsal.

A modern scrum: Bradford versus Leeds in Super League in 2004 at a packed Odsal.
(Photo: Peter Lush)

What made matters even worse in my eyes was that our Australian stand-off Garth Budge, who was my favourite player, was thrown into the bargain and left for Crown Flatt. It transpired that Dewsbury had been willing to release Mullins as waiting patiently for his chance in their 'A' team was Mike Stevenson, who some years later would don the number nine shirt for Great Britain when we won the World Cup in 1972!

My point is that hookers who could win the ball were an invaluable asset to any side. Look back to the 1960s and 1970s and think of those redoubtable ball getters – Bill Sawyers, Don Close, 'Flash' Flanagan, Tony Fisher and later to others like Keith Elwell – the list is endless. Furthermore, they relied on their pack colleagues to aid and abet them in the dark arts, expending their energy for 80 minutes in toiling in scrums and other duties and not merely being used in short spells as athletic battering rams – or 'middles'.

Mick Morgan was a larger-than-life figure, wit and raconteur who served several clubs including Wakefield, Featherstone and Oldham in a career spanning more than 20 years. In *No Sand Dunes in Featherstone*, he explained how Keith Bridges, who he described as the "best ball getter ever", earned Great Britain a 10–10 draw with Australia in a World Cup encounter at the Sydney Cricket Ground. In the dying moments of the match, Bridges used his snake hipped skills to scoop back a ball from the Australian second row on the home side's feed. Steve Nash worked a clever scissors move with Ken Gill near the line so that the spoils were shared and it was the half-backs who were given all the plaudits. Morgan and Mike Coulman were Bridges's two props and they knew that the result was due to that great piece of hooking.

Keith Bridges, in the same book, explained that his duel with his opposite number was a game within a game. He had many epic battles with David Ward of Leeds as each tried to out-do the other. He said: "You played two games. You played a game of rugby and, even if you lost the match, if you beat the hooker, it was a big thing for you." Bridges cites other contemporaries with whom he had terrific scraps in Colin Clarke, Kevin Ashcroft, Graham Liptrot, Tony Karalius and Clive Dickinson.

Modern hookers are often excellent at what they do, but what they do is not hooking. Nowadays, they generally just go into dummy half and throw in the odd 'scoot' for good measure. Their role in the scrum has become entirely redundant. I recall going to a lunch at the invitation of Tony Crosby whose granddaughter, Emma, was a teacher at the school I worked at. Tony, who was originally from York, was the Leeds hooker in the 1960s and played in the 'Watersplash' final in 1968. He regaled our table with some of the tricks of his trade and reminisced about some of the great exponents of his particular craft.

A further advantage of the reintroduction of competitive scrummaging would be that in the physically demanding job of winning possession, the big lads in the pack would be expending energy and this provides more space for the backs. Forwards used to be hefty men and not guys who resemble muscular bodybuilders as they do now. Think of the Chisnalls, Steve Pitchford of Leeds or our own Peter Goddard at Odsal – hardly Adonises, but essential to their teams in pursuit of their share of the ball.

Now I hope that I am not falling into the trap of lauding all things ancient as superior in a kind of "four legs good, two legs bad" Orwellian tirade. Nor am I calling for our game to adopt the rugby union approach of making the scrum a sacred cow with a life of its own which is allowed to dominate proceedings and consume huge tracts of time within a match. Ironically after the referee has chanted the latest entreaty to "crouch, bind, engage" or "take your partner by the hand" or some such nonsense, they now seem to follow our lead and allow the crooked feed as standard having spent an age in creating an even keel in the formation of the scrum. But a return to some form of contest with the ball going down the middle of the tunnel and a requirement to bind the forwards together in some form of cohesive unit would be an interesting experiment and a way to bring back some element of challenge and unpredictability to mitigate against increasingly unoriginal patterns of play!

When I get into one of these rants my wife usually appears at about this point, takes my elbow and leads me quietly away.

14. Alex Murphy OBE

I am fascinated by the subject of leadership. The death of Terry Venables in 2023 prompted much media debate on the subject of what makes a great leader. The former Barcelona and England football supremo was lauded as a great mentor and manager by many of the players who he had worked with during his long career, as they queued up to pay homage following his passing in November.

As fans and journalists contributed to the debate, I found my hackles rising as the terms 'leadership' and 'management' were used interchangeably, as though they were synonyms describing the same concept. In their inspection of schools, OFSTED often fall into this same trap as a section of each report deals with, 'Leadership and Management'. While these are overlapping areas, we need to understand that there are some subtle, but important, differences between these two skills.

Managers are vital in every organisation. They focus on the nuts and bolts of getting the job done on a day-to-day basis. They deal with the practicalities such as budgets, resource allocation and logistics. Leaders are much more focused on the big picture. They are all about people. They inspire others to contribute to a collective goal. Leaders have a vision which they articulate clearly and which they can get team members to buy into so that their organisation or team succeeds as a collective. It has been said that leaders see the whole forest, whereas managers deal with the individual trees. Alex Murphy could manage but more importantly he was a great leader.

Born in the Thatto Heath area of St Helens on 22 April 1939, 'the lad from Donkey Common' attended St Austin's school where he first played rugby league. So talented was the boy prodigy that he was playing with the senior side when he was aged only 10. At 15 years old he was attending a summer school at Knowsley Road when the first team coach, and giant of the game, Jim Sullivan, spotted his precocious talent. He immediately invited Murphy to train with the first team, even though he was not old enough yet to sign professional forms. Sullivan was a huge influence on the scrum-half's development as he moulded his raw talent in the vital early phase of Murph's career.

While other would-be suitors lined up to try to sign him, the St Helens board spirited him away to chairman Joe Harrison's home on the eve of his 16th birthday. The group ate sandwiches and played snooker until he signed at midnight, for the bargain price of £80.

After a short period in the 'A' team, the young Murphy grew rather impatient and even at this early stage, he put in a transfer request which was promptly refused. Before the 1956 Challenge Cup final, Saints had a fixture backlog which required them to play three games in a five-day period. On 11 April, Jim Sullivan selected almost the whole 'A' team to play against Whitehaven at home and so Murphy was handed his first team debut in a 21–7 win.

This was the start of a meteoric rise to stardom for the teenage half-back. In his first full season, 1957–58, he scored 27 tries and helped St Helens to second place in the league behind Oldham. The Great Britain selectors were undeterred by his relative inexperience and decided that his exceptional speed would be a great asset on the hard grounds in Australia.

Saints had six players in the squad which headed to Australia and New Zealand and Alex was selected to play in all three tests. What a baptism of fire that series must have been for an 18-year-old, but then it is said that 'the finest folk are fashioned in the fiercest flames.' Murphy played second fiddle to his Australian counterpart Keith Holden in the first test 25–8 defeat. But then the callow starlet bounced back to play a vital role in the second test in 'the Second Battle of Brisbane' as the game has gone down in rugby league folklore. The epic match has been likened to 'the Rorke's Drift test' of 1914 when Harold Wagstaff led his 10-man team to heroic victory. The 1958 version saw fellow Saint Alan Prescott lead his team to a 25–18 series equalling win. Prescott played virtually the entire game with a shattered forearm in a team which lost stand-off Dave Bolton to a broken collarbone and left five members needing hospital attention following the final whistle.

Miraculously, the comeback was complete when Britain beat the Australians 40–17 at the Sydney Cricket Ground in the final test. The incensed home crowd threw oranges and beer glasses onto the pitch to express their displeasure and as Mick Sullivan refreshed himself by peeling and eating an unexpected citrus treat, Murph picked up a beer glass and ceremoniously toasted all four points of the crowd in a moment of comedic genius. The teenage scrum-half later paid tribute to his Saints' 'minder', Vince Karalius, for looking after him in those formative days. Years later he told Dave Hadfield, "It was like having one of the Kray twins as your best mate." This auspicious beginning was the prelude to a 13-year international career in which he wore the Great Britain jersey on 27 occasions.

On returning home, silverware came thick and fast with a Championship in 1958–59 and a 1961 Cup Final win over Wigan, in which Murphy bagged the opening try. 1962 saw him selected for a second tour to Australasia which sadly ended in a shoulder injury which led to him missing the first three months of the following season. Alex returned with renewed vigour and by 1964 he had been rewarded with the captaincy at Knowsley Road.

Murphy's team-mate Ray French tells an amusing anecdote which sheds light on Murphy's self-confidence which often bordered on arrogance, but which also reveals a sharp sense of humour. French explained that only a couple of minutes before the side were to take to the pitch, Murphy was standing in front of the mirror applying Brylcreem and slicking his hair back into its immaculately groomed style. When French asked him what he was doing Alex replied, "Ray, your mum and dad have come to see you, but 22 000 have come to see me!"

In 1966, Saints won a one-sided Cup Final against the old enemy from Central Park. Under the old rules, any penalty which was kicked into touch was followed by a scrum. Wigan were without their first-choice hooker Colin (father of Sky pundit Phil) Clarke and Saints had the arch ball-getter Bill Sawyer in their ranks. Such was their scrum dominance that Murphy realised that persistent infringing would subsequently lead to his side winning back possession in a tactic which many believe led to the legislators bringing in the tap following a penalty to touch rule shortly afterwards. St Helens completed 'the Double' with a 35–12 win over Halifax in the Championship Final, but this turned out to be 'Mr Magic's' last appearance for his hometown club.

It is at this point that we first glimpse the fractious and volatile aspects of Murphy's nature which make him such a complex and intriguing character. He had declined taking part in what would have been his third Ashes tour in 1966. He gave 'business commitments' as the reason for his unavailability but many believe he was 'spitting the dummy' because the selectors favoured Harry Poole as captain rather than him.

Left: Alex Murphy scoring against Widnes for St Helens in the 1960s.
(Courtesy Alex Service)

Ironically, Tommy Bishop, who Saints had signed from Blackpool Borough, was the favoured scrum-half in the squad. It was Bishop who was central to Alex's eventual departure from Knowsley Road when the management asked him to move into the centre berth to make way for the new arrival. The club captain refused to comply and was banned from training at the club. Murphy trained alone at the Pilkington Recs ground and put in a transfer request. The club granted this and placed the huge fee of £12,000 on their prize asset (well over £200,000 in today's prices). The club probably felt that the huge fee would be prohibitive and that Murphy would become frustrated and return to the fold.

If the St Helens board thought that he would wait out his time before returning with his tail between his legs, then they were sadly mistaken. Near neighbours Leigh contacted Alex and chairman Jack Harding offered him £30 per week to join them as a coach. This masterstroke meant that no fee was payable because Murphy would not be registered as a player. Following this unprecedented move, the RFL outlawed signing a player registered with another club in any capacity. The ensuing impasse would eventually be resolved 12 months later when the Hilton Park club paid £6,000 to employ Murphy as their player-coach. I believe that this phase of his career really highlights Alex Murphy's true leadership genius.

At St Helens, he had been surrounded by a whole galaxy of superstars of the calibre of Tom van Vollenhoven, Len Killeen, John Mantle, Kel Coslett and hosts more. It is true that Murphy stood out even in such exalted company, but now he was faced with the task of reaching the heights with colleagues who were journeymen footballers who had little to offer but the proverbial 'blood, sweat and tears.' In 1971, he did reach the top of the rugby league mountain with a club that had not won the Challenge Cup for 50 years.

One aspect of Murphy's genius was his understanding of which players he could get to do a job for him. He recruited men who he knew would follow him into hell should the need arise. One of his most important lieutenants was the hooker Kevin Ashcroft who became his right-hand man. Ashcroft told the *Manchester Evening News* how he joined Murphy's men and said "I was playing for Rochdale...A message was sent to me that Alex Murphy wanted to see me outside the ground after I'd broken his nose during a game. I thought he wanted to settle this once and for all – I then found out he wanted to sign me."

Murphy and Ashcroft led their colleagues through the 1971 Cup rounds with a relatively easy first round 19–2 victory over Bradford Northern. A much tighter second round away victory over Widnes 14–11 followed. Thereafter in the quarter and semi-finals, Leigh managed to progress without scoring a try as they beat Hull and Huddersfield to reach the final. Jack Bentley, who was the voice of rugby league in the *Daily Express*, described the 10–4 semi-final as, "The bore to beat all bores." Murphy responded that the team would reserve playing their rugby until the final at Wembley.

A crowd of 85,514 turned up to witness the finale of the competition which very few outside Murphy's inner-sanctum thought the Lancashire side could win. Recently I rewatched the game on YouTube and it was really an illuminating experience. I was extremely impressed by Murphy's on-field leadership. The ace American Football coach Vince Lombardi commented on the difficult judgement required for a leader to be of and yet detached from the group and the judgement required to get this call correct. This dichotomy is all the more acute for a player-coach. "The leader can never close the gap between himself and the group," explained Lombardi, "If he does, he is no longer what he must be. He must walk a tightrope between the consent he must win and the control he must exert."

In studying Murphy's body language in that final, we can see how he cajoles and guides his team, leading by his actions and example. We also see how his influential co-leaders like Pete Smethurst, Geoff Clarkson and David Eckersley play their key parts in the overall performance. This is another remarkable feature of Murphy's leadership for as the American political activist of the 1960s, Ralph Nader points out "The function of leadership is to produce more leaders, not more followers."

The game itself was a fierce affair with fireworks like El Alamein only with less Health and Safety. Former Wakefield full-back Les Sheard, writing in the *Rugby League Journal,* explained how Murphy, "luxuriated in the tumult and sense of anarchy that he created around himself." Some 15 minutes from time, the Leeds captain Syd Hynes gained the dubious distinction of becoming the first player to be sent off in a Wembley final when he head-butted Murphy, who was left prostrate on the turf and stretchered off. Controversy still reigns as Hynes always maintained his innocence and some claimed Murphy winked to spectators as he was on the stretcher. For his part, Alex said, "A lot of people said I winked... but the only thing I did was close my eyes." Conspiracy theories abound but as with claims of gun shots from the grassy knoll, we will never really know. Suffice to say, Leigh won 24–7 and Murphy was rightly awarded the Lance Todd Trophy.

Their remarkable giant killing act was Alex's finest hour and the club would not repeat the feat until 2023 under the flamboyant patronage of Derek Beaumont, who was ironically born in 1971, in their new guise of the Leigh Leopards. Yet within days of this historic victory, the hearts of the faithful at Hilton Park were broken as Murphy moved on to pastures new with Warrington. Leigh secretary John Stringer and the board had known of their talisman's departure for almost five weeks and had kept it secret so as to not affect team morale.

Murphy again scaled the heights as he assembled a formidable team at Wilderspool with recruits like his old pal Ashcroft along with Welsh rugby union international winger John Bevan, half-back Ken Kelly and tough as teak forwards like Dave Chisnall and union signing Mike Nicholas from Aberavon. I recall a steamy encounter at Odsal in the early 1970s when Murphy sparked a brawl which erupted to involve all but three members on the field – the two wingers furthest from the fray and Murphy himself who repaired to the centre spot until the fighting ended. Murph's script writers were again working overtime in 1973–74. Warrington won the treble of the Captain Morgan Cup and John Player Final and the Challenge Cup, in a 24–9 victory over the cup holders Featherstone.

When he eventually retired he touted his leadership skills coaching Salford. Les Sheard tells one amusing story about Murph's time at the Willows. Les was caretaker manager at Trinity when they encountered the Red Devils. Murphy was getting increasingly frustrated and shouted at the official, "Gerr 'em on side ref!" Sheard wound him up, saying, "That's what they all shout Murphy when they know nowt about t' game." Alex gave the Trinity coach a look of derision adding, "Who the f*****g hell are you?" Les explained he had played one game for England and the man who had selected him was Alex Murphy. He concluded that he must not have made much of an impression on the great man.

Later in his managerial career he joined St Helens (again) and Huddersfield. In a turbulent term of office at Wigan, Murphy apparently punched Maurice Lindsay in a less than polite pay negotiation following a pre-season sevens tournament. Always good copy, and perennially controversial, Alex was an original inductee into the Hall of Fame and was awarded the OBE in 1998. A friend of mine used to joke that OBE should stand for 'Other Buggers' Efforts' but I can't apply this to Murph's award as he was one of the greatest leaders our game has ever seen.

15. Shaw Cross

As a teenager in the 1970s I was fortunate to have grown up in an era when youth services were thriving. In 1960, the Albermarle Report was published, championing the cause of providing informal educational and social development opportunities for young people. It captured the zeitgeist that nurturing the adults of tomorrow was the best bulwark against future conflict in a post war world.

I spent the majority of my post-school hours at Sedbergh Youth Club in Bradford. I hung out with mates and we played rugby, football and table tennis as well as having a go at drama and art. We went on visits and residentials which included jaunts to the Lake District, Snowdonia and even Germany, all at minimal cost. Trevor Foster coached us as we represented YABC – Yorkshire Association of Boys' Clubs – against a touring French rugby league team who stayed at our homes. This gave us a chance to practise our very rudimentary French language skills. Indeed, my first job prior to becoming a teacher was as a youth worker in the east end of London where I saw the incredible work of boxing clubs, like Repton and Arbour Youth, helping generations of kids to develop self-discipline and respect for the virtues of dedication and hard work.

Sadly, because the provision of youth services was never a statutory requirement placed on local authorities, austerity measures from the 1980s to the present day led to the erosion of these opportunities. Any available resources were diverted to 'outreach' work on drug awareness and the like. As modern politicians grapple with the challenge to address anti-social behaviour and the modern scourge of knife crime, perhaps they would do well to reflect on the demise of opportunities for young people. They should learn from the hope and optimism of the post-Albemarle era rather than cursing some perceived inherent moral turpitude among today's adolescents.

Thankfully, while councils may have cut back on providing positive chances to develop citizenship skills, volunteers have stepped into the breach to plug the gaps for some lucky boys and girls in community sports clubs. One incredible organisation which has done so is the Shaw Cross club in Dewsbury. Founded in 1947, the club celebrated its 75th anniversary in 2022 and in that time, it has provided over 250 players for the professional game.

The club erected its first premises in 1949 in the form of an old Army Nissen Hut. The Shaw Cross motto is "Reaching Forward" and it has certainly lived up to its creed over the decades. In 1977, it became the first BARLA club to tour Australia and New Zealand and in 2003 the club made its third trip to South Africa where the team members visited black townships to coach youngsters in the skills of rugby league. In 1988 the club were rewarded with a National Lottery grant to build a new clubhouse and in the same year they were named as 'Sports Club of the Year' by Sport England. Their website is a colourful and professionally managed source of information and the Shaw Cross Sharks, as they are now branded, continue to thrive. In 2017 Graham Williams provided an invaluable record of the history of the club and its achievements in his 70 *Years of Reaching Forward: Shaw Cross Rugby League Club* (London League Publications Ltd).

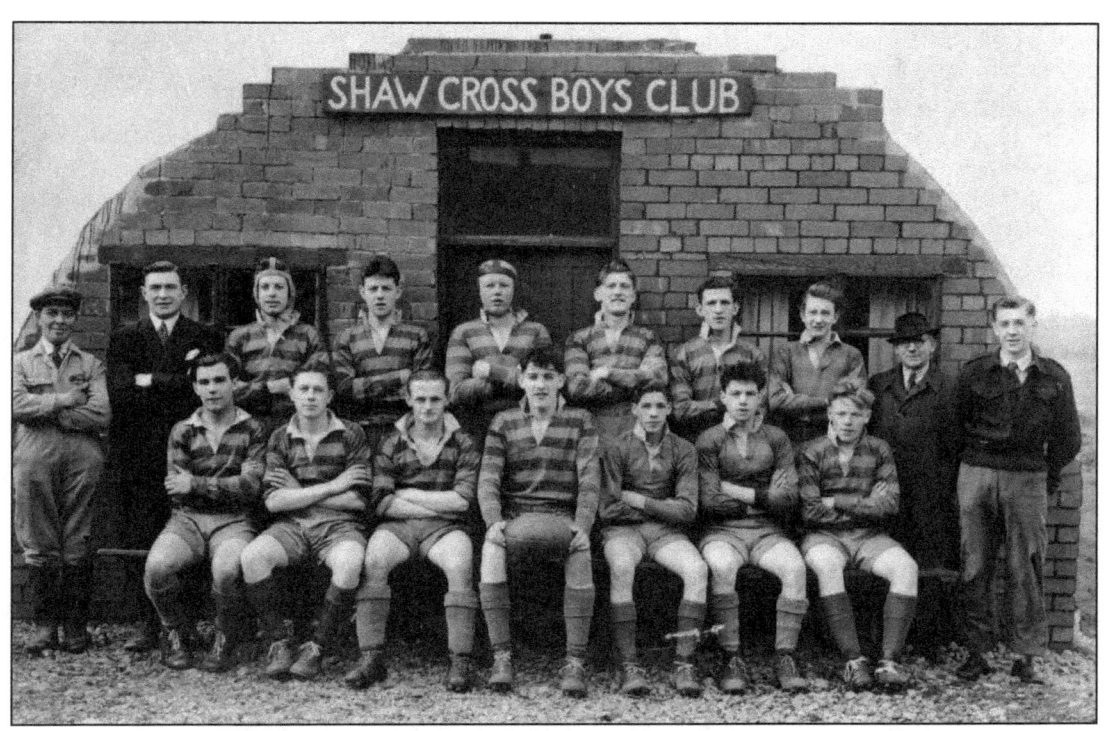

The 1949–50 Shaw Cross team, in front of their Nissen hut headquarters.
(Courtesy Shaw Cross ARLFC)

Williams highlights how Brearley Bailey, the Dewsbury president in the 1960s, fostered strong links with Shaw Cross. The cash strapped professional club made a virtue of necessity and recruited players in a more frugal fashion than some of their more affluent neighbours. As a result, in one match in the 1964–65 season, Dewsbury fielded a team consisting of 11 Shaw Cross lads. Nor did this penny-wise approach hamper the club as they reached the Challenge Cup semi-finals in two consecutive years. In 1966 they lost narrowly to a star-studded St Helens side led by Alex Murphy with six of their 15 players from Shaw Cross. The following season they went down 14–9 to Barrow with another half dozen recruits from the amateur club in their ranks at Station Road, Swinton on that afternoon.

Studying the club's own Hall of Fame*, which is housed at their clubhouse, we become aware of the huge debt of gratitude the game owes to Shaw Cross. One criterion for inclusion to this auspicious band is to have gained international honours in the professional game. There is incredible rugby pedigree among those who have been honoured. Two legends of the game who are included are renowned throughout the world of rugby league. They are Derek Turner and Mick Sullivan. As a young fan in the mid-1960s, I had the privilege of seeing the two play, albeit in the twilight of their long careers.

Derek Turner's nickname 'Rocky' tells us all we need to know about this granite hard man of the game. Former Saint's second rower and latter-day BBC commentator Ray French included him in his list of the six hardest ever players along with Vince Karalius, Barrie McDermott, Ray Price, Gordon Tallis and Cliff Watson. But Turner was much more than a hit man in an era of tough guys. He was also a gifted footballer who could create space for others although as John Lindley in his history of Wakefield Trinity *100 Years of Rugby* said, "He did not create openings ... he forced them!"

In 1950, his hometown club, Wakefield, missed signing him from Shaw Cross having deemed him "too small". This judgement would appear about as wise as telling the Beatles they lacked the musical wow factor or that George Best was a bit on the slow side and lacked ball skills. Turner joined Hull KR and later Oldham before finally returning to the Belle Vue outfit where he spent his glory years. Rocky became the first man to lead a club to three Wembley Challenge Cup victories as Trinity triumphed in 1960, 1962 and 1963.

He won 24 caps for Great Britain. This statistic is all the more remarkable when we consider that he played in an era when the country was spoilt for choice in the loose-forward position. During that period the equally fearsome Vince Karalius won 12 caps and the legend that was 'Gentleman' Johnny Whiteley gained 15. Turner won a World Cup winners medal in 1960 and in 1962 he captained Great Britain on the New Zealand leg of their tour when skipper Eric Ashton was forced to return home through injury. He was inducted into the Rugby League Hall of Fame in 2018 appropriately in the same cohort as his former rival for the 13 shirt, Johnny Whiteley. After retiring, Derek Turner enjoyed a successful career in coaching at Castleford, Leeds and Wakefield and he was at the helm there in 1983–84 when the whisper that "Wally Lewis is coming" turned out to be more than a rumour. Alongside his coaching duties, he also ran a successful removals business with his son David.

Mick Sullivan was one of Rocky Turner's contemporaries. Pudsey born 'Sully' joined Shaw Cross when studying to become a plumber at technical college in Dewsbury. The two had much in common as pugnacious, combative and feisty characters. Perhaps it's something in the water in the heavy woollen district.

In 1952, Mick joined Huddersfield where he honed his professional skills prior to a record-breaking signing on fee of £9,500 being paid by Wigan for his services. While at Central Park he won two Challenge Cup winners' medals in 1958 and 1959 and he helped the club to gain the Championship in 1960. Neighbours St Helens then swooped to beat the Cup deadline and signed Sullivan for a new record price of £11,000. Following a three-year stint at Knowsley Road, he again moved on to pastures new joining York. He eventually returned to his roots with Dewsbury where he led the club to their near miraculous Challenge Cup feats of the mid-1960s.

The hard running, tough tackling wingman became the holder of the record number of Great Britain caps with 46 and while Garry Schofield equalled this many years later, it is a record which will never be beaten. Again, it is appropriate that Sullivan and Schofield were simultaneously welcomed into the Rugby League Hall of Fame in 2016. Mick Sullivan scored 120 tries in 102 appearances in the Great Britain shirt and won two World Cup winners medals in 1954 and 1960 as well as Ashes victories in four series between 1956 and 1962.

The Australians loved Sullivan's character and he had a couple of spells in club rugby there. In 1958, he was part of the Great Britain team to win the fabled second test in Brisbane when captain Alan Prescott played for 77 minutes with a broken arm. But what I recall most was the story my dad told me about the final test in that series in Sydney. The partisan crowd was growing increasingly hostile and ugly scenes threatened to halt proceedings as the Aussies pelted the British players with oranges. In a spontaneous comedic gesture

Sullivan picked up an orange and peeled it before eating the fruit and the atmosphere of anger evaporated and turned to mirth.

Mick passed away in 2016, shortly after he had attended his induction into the Hall of Fame with fellow legends Billy Boston and Neil Fox. Paying tribute to him, a fellow Shaw Cross Hall of Famer, Mike 'Stevo' Stephenson said, "Mick lived for rugby league and never forgot his grass roots, endlessly and eagerly giving enormous support to his junior club, Shaw Cross, the club that put him on the road to stardom." At a commemorative event in Mick's honour, a friend recounted how, when asked what the best club he had ever played for, bearing in mind the calibre of professional clubs he had represented over the years, he answered without a second's hesitation – "Shaw Cross."

There is an old African proverb which says, "Those who would drink the water should thank those who built the well." In the spirit of this sentiment there are generations of fans who have had their spectating experiences enhanced by players who graduated from this breeding ground of rugby league excellence. But those who came through on this conveyor belt of rugby talent from this most auspicious nursery owe a further debt of gratitude to Shaw Cross' founders for as Stevo explained: "It didn't only teach kids to be better rugby players but it also showed them how to be better human beings."

*The full list of ex-players in the Shaw Cross Hall of Fame is:
John Dalgreen, Nick Fozzard, Brian Gabbitas, Carl Gibson, Lee Gilmour, Tony Halmshaw, Alan Redfearn, David Redfearn, David Smith, Michael Stephenson MBE, Nigel Stephenson, Michael Sullivan, Derek Turner, Norman Wainwright and David Ward.

16. Statues and memorials

In recent years there has been much discussion about the place of statues of historic Britons. The toppling of the slave trader Edward Colston's statue and his subsequent unceremonious dumping in Bristol Dock caused an avalanche of comment in the media. It kick started a greater debate about how we memorialise the figures from the past. According to the Public Monuments and Sculpture Association (PMSA), there are over 800 public statues in the UK with Queen Victoria being the most frequently represented figure.

Thankfully, given that sports people tend to be less controversial figures than say politicians, monarchs or champions of industry, the erection of statues to working class heroes from the sporting world tends to bring with it less criticism from the public in general.

Sheffield University set out to catalogue the more than one hundred sporting statues in Britain in a project called, 'From Pitch to Plinth'. Doctor Chris Stride explains that the commemoration of sports people in the form of statues is a relatively new phenomenon. He points out, "There were just a handful, maybe four or five that had been erected before 1980, then maybe another 10 before 1995." Stride attributes this recent surge to the cult of celebrity in modern times and to the decline in mass religious observation. He believes that sport is, in many ways, the new religion and that these statues provide a focal point for communities to pay homage to past glories and to mourn fallen icons. We saw this outpouring of emotions recently at Old Trafford where the faithful made a shrine at the statue to the 'Holy Trinity' of Charlton, Best and Law on the occasion of Bobby Charlton's passing away.

Perhaps the best-known rugby league statue is the one which was unveiled at Wembley Stadium in 2015. Sculptor Steve Winterburn's impressive work features Eric Ashton MBE, Billy Boston MBE, Martin Offiah MBE, Alex Murphy OBE and Gus Risman. A panel of fans, journalists, coaches, players, MPs and newspaper editors contributed to the debate about who should be included. Perhaps controversy was inevitable and many fans bemoaned the exclusion of some greats of the game who performed heroic deeds on that hallowed turf including, for instance, Neil Fox MBE, Shaun Edwards OBE or the South African Tom van Vollenhoven. However, perhaps an even more glaring omission occurred as Wembley celebrated its 100th Anniversary this year by naming 100 icons to be involved with the famous venue. While some like the Spice Girls and Elton John made the cut, not one single rugby league player was included in the list – not even one of those legends on the Wembley statue itself!

Winterburn's other ensemble piece is to be found in Cardiff Bay. 'The Rugby Codebreakers Statue' is a monument to those Welsh union players Billy Boston, Clive Sullivan and Gus Risman who 'went north' and became stars in the professional code. Reviled for decades as turncoats, these men are now afforded the respect which is so richly deserved. 14,000 votes were cast for a list of 13 candidates of players who crossed the great divide from the south Cardiff areas of Tiger Bay, Butetown, Grangetown, Adamsdown and Splott. The three top nominees are depicted on the plinth and the sole survivor of the three Billy Boston described the unveiling in July 2023 as a "highlight in my life." This colossus of the game is also the subject of an individual statue by the same sculptor which stands in Believe Square in his beloved adopted hometown in Wigan.

Above: The Roy Francis statue in Brynmawr, his home town in South Wales.

Left: The rugby league statue at Wembley Stadium.

(Both photos: Peter Lush)

The 'Codebreakers Statue' is unique in that it is the first in Wales to depict non-fictionalised, named black men. Indeed, Sullivan was the first black athlete in Britain to captain his national team as he did when leading Great Britain to World Cup glory in 1972. Gus Risman, father to the recently deceased Bev Risman, was the son of Russian immigrants who played in five successful Ashes victories in his long and illustrious career.

On 23 October 2023 during Black History Month, a statue of Roy Francis was unveiled in his hometown of Brynmawr in Blaenau Gwent. The project was the idea of Ian Haywood and the twice life-size statue was unveiled by Welsh great, Jonathan Davies. It is a fitting tribute to a man Davies referred to as "a trailblazer", having been the first black man to play for Great Britain and the first black professional coach. Francis joined Wigan as a 17-year-old in 1936 and was capped in 1947 before embarking on an incredible coaching career. He won honours with Hull and Leeds before moving to Australia where entrenched attitudes on matters of ethnicity hampered success. Roy's final coaching job was with Bradford Northern before his death in Leeds in 1989. His methods were far ahead of his time and he revolutionised coaching. Thankfully recent research into his career means he may now be regarded as a prophet in his own land. A blue plaque about Roy is on display at Brynmawr rugby (union) club where he started his career. A biography of him was published in 2022 by London League Publications Ltd.

It is interesting that former converts to rugby league are being recognised in their native land which is to be welcomed as for many years their achievements went unrecognised. Recently I spoke to Dai Davies, clerk to the Llanedi Council who explained that in Hendy, funds have been raised to commemorate Terry Price. The Welsh international joined Bradford Northern when I was a young fan and he went on the 1968 Great Britain tour to Australia. He was a prodigious marksman and eventually plied his trade as a kicker for the Buffalo Bills in American football playing in the same side as a certain OJ Simpson.

Sadly, Terry died in 1993 when he was struck by a car when he stopped to aid a motorist who had broken down on the motorway. His brother Geraint Price serves as a councillor in Hendy and he told me that there will be some form of memorial at a new community centre which is due to open later this year. Every year the council awards the 'Terry Price Prize' to a young person who has demonstrated sporting or academic excellence.

Most of the statues of former players are to be found in the vicinity of the club grounds at which they played or at their new grounds if the club has changed homes. In 2011, St Helens moved to Langtree Park and a statue of Kieron Cunningham was unveiled to mark the occasion. The veteran of 500 appearances for the club beat greats such as Tom van Vollenhoven and Alex Murphy in a poll of fans. The statue is unusual in two regards. First, it is the only one which was produced by a female sculptor in Vanessa Marston. Second, the majority of subjects who have been immortalised in metal have been backs whereas Cunningham was a hooker. It is perhaps unsurprising that it is the glamour players among what my old man referred to as 'the Brylcreem boys' who run in the tries and thus capture the public's adoration who are the subjects of statues.

Just a short drive down the East Lancs Road stands the impressive Leigh Sports Village where the resurgent Challenge Cup winners thrilled fans in 2023. It is there we find the statue simply entitled 'Woody' dedicated to John Woods who was the darling of the Hilton Park faithful. John and his family witnessed the unveiling of the nine-foot bronze figure by local artist Stephen Charnock on 17 September 2016 before the club's match against Batley Bulldogs. Fans, local businesses and Wigan Council helped to raise £30,000 to pay for it.

Another stand-off who has been similarly honoured by his hometown club is Barrow's Willie Horne. His statue stands in Duke Street, just a drop kick away from the club's Craven Park home. As a 33-year-old veteran, Horne captained the club to a rare Challenge Cup victory in 1955. Three years before this famous day, Willie skippered Great Britain to Ashes glory. The plaque on the sculpture by Chris Kelly which was unveiled in 2004 describes him as, "A quiet hero...revered throughout the global rugby league community but most of all here, in his own backyard, where he was idolised as a sporting genius, and respected as a decent man... with magic in his fingers and humility in his heart."

Visitors to the Warrington Wolves' Halliwell Jones Stadium will see the impressive statue of Brian Beven elevated from the ground as if on the crossbar of rugby posts. The figure is the work of Philip Bews and was originally situated on the Causeway Roundabout near the club's Wilderspool ground before being moved in 2012. The sculptor captures beautifully the unlikely looking star's frail frame, bald head and knee strappings which were the probable cause of his rejection by Leeds when the Australian sailor pitched up at Headingley in the hope of a trial. The Loiners' loss was the Wire's gain as Bevan went on to score 796 tries in 688 games between 1946 and 1964.

On Sunday 11 July 2021, I was honoured to be the guest of Gary Hetherington at Headingley as David Ward unveiled the statue of his friend and teammate John Holmes. The work by Steve Winterburn is dedicated to 'The Reluctant Hero' and stands in front of the South Stand as a tribute to the Kirkstall lad who made a record 625 appearances for the club having made a fantastic debut as a 16-year-old. The versatile stand-off or full-back retired in 1990 and was taken from us far too early at the age of 57. At a splendid lunch to announce the most recent inductees to the Hall of Fame, friends and colleagues told stories of John's prowess and Kevin Dick amused us all with a tale of how some Americans had thought the great man was the adult film actor of the same name. Phil Caplan, the chair of the Rhinos' Heritage group said, "To have the ultimate, reluctant local hero, looking out over Kirkstall, where he came from, could not be more appropriate, fitting or poignant."

Douglas 'Duggy' Clark was a loose-forward and member of the immortal Huddersfield 'Team of All the Talents' and was in the famous team led by Harold Wagstaff in 'the Rorke's Drift Test' of 1914. Awarded the Military Medal for bravery in the First World War, Douglas was severely wounded by shrapnel and invalided home where medics said that he should never play again. Defying advice, he returned to the front before returning home at the end of the War to continue playing domestically and internationally until 1927.

Thereafter he became a superstar and world champion as a wrestler. His remarkable story is told in Steven Bell's excellent biography published in 2020, *The Man of All Talents*. A bronze bust of Douglas had been on display at the Wave Museum in Maryport where he was born. In 2010 his then 81-year-old niece Joyce Dempsey finally won her campaign to have the bust returned to Huddersfield where she unveiled it alongside former Fartown stalwart Ken Senior and it is now on display in the club's media centre.

Both Hull clubs have plans in the offing to commemorate two sons of the city. Hull Kingston Rovers have council approval to erect a statue by Steve Winterburn of Peter 'Flash' Flanagan in the Colin Hutton Stand at the Lightstream Stadium. The stylish hooker played

415 games for Rovers and 14 for Great Britain. The Airlie Birds have already placed a beautiful tribute to Jack Harrison outside the KCOM Stadium and it was unveiled in 2014. Harrison is the only rugby league player to have been awarded the Victoria Cross and the citation from the *Times* which highlights how he died at Oppy Wood in 1917 is on display on a commemorative bronze plaque at the Hull Guildhall. Local playwright Ian Judson is spearheading a campaign to raise funds to commission a life-size statue of Harrison and in 2019 he wrote a play entitled *An Ordinary Hero.* The play was performed by the Pony Express Theatre Company and all the proceeds went to the fundraising project. Judson hopes to raise £100,000 by 2025 and feels that the site for the statue should be outside Hull Minster or in Queens Gardens.

I have a particularly soft spot for statue of a rugby player in Dewsbury which is not to commemorate a famous former star of the game. There are in fact two figures in the composition. Alongside the man in his rugby kit is the second figure of a Victorian mill girl in a shawl and clogs. The two are positioned as though they have just walked past one another and are glancing over their shoulder to admire the other. The beautiful, rather whimsical piece is entitled 'Flirting with the Past' and was produced by sculptor Jason Thomson. It stands by railway arches in Northgate near the town centre and was unveiled by Mike Stephenson in 2005 as a tribute to the part played by textiles and rugby league in Dewsbury's history and the statues were partially financed by Kirklees Council.

The Blue Plaques scheme dates back to 1866 and is currently administered by English Heritage. Rugby league grounds or sites of significance have been awarded plaques but so too have some individual players including Albert Goldthorpe, Harold Wagstaff, Billy Ivison, Gus Risman, Neil Fox and Roy Francis.

It was Pericles, the Greek politician and general, writing in the fifth century BCE, who said, "What you leave behind is not what is engraved in stone monuments, but what is woven in the lives of others." The stars of the past who have bedazzled the fans and have illuminated our lives will live long in the hearts and minds of those who witnessed their heroic deeds.

17. Harry Pinner's socks

In November 2022, during the football World Cup in Qatar, an episode occurred which challenged my assumptions about the prima donna-like antics and egos of England's association football stars.

Upon scoring England's sixth goal against Iran, Jack Grealish celebrated by gyrating his body into what we now know to be 'the worm'. It transpired that the inspiration for this had been 11-year-old Finlay back in Manchester who Jack met prior to leaving for the competition in the Arabian Peninsula. The youngster suffers from cerebral palsy, as does Grealish's little sister. After the game it was revealed that the star had promised Finlay to do 'the worm' in the event of him scoring. True to his word, Grealish delivered, even in such a moment of personal euphoria in which he had fulfilled his own lifetime ambition of scoring in a World Cup finals match.

As a retired teacher I know that heroes are important for young sports fans as they provide inspiration and motivation to reach for the stars and to have ambitions for the future. Whether athletes like it or not, they are role models. As a child, my twin passion alongside rugby league was cricket and it remains so to this day, even though it brought me one stinging disappointment which I have never forgotten.

I had my very own 'Say it ain't so Joe' episode which stayed with me long after and was a real moment of innocence turning to bitter experience. I felt like the kid in 1919 who implored his hero 'Shoeless' Joe Jackson to deny taking a bribe to throw the World Series. The incident involved the Chicago White Sox player inspired the haunting rock lament by Murray Head.

I witnessed my first live county game in the mid-1960s when I went with a school pal to watch Yorkshire play Somerset at Bradford Park Avenue. At close of play I ventured towards the pavilion in the hope of adding to my extensive collection of rugby league autographs. My particular cricketing hero approached so with great excitement I trotted out my well-rehearsed, super polite entreaty, "Excuse me, please may I have your autograph Mr....," only to be invited by the world-famous fast bowler to "bugger off!" It always rather stuck in my throat that, for many years after, this man dined out on a public image of being 'a down-to-earth northerner' and 'a man of the people'. On this occasion he certainly proved to be a 'plain speaking Yorkshireman!'

Just like the youngster on the steps of the Grand Jury hearing in 1919, my hero too revealed himself to have feet of clay and my loss of innocence was palpable. These contrasting examples exemplify how the responses of sports stars to their fans can cause either jubilation or despondency.

The beauty of rugby league back then was that those who performed Herculean acts on Saturday afternoons at the likes of Odsal, Thrum Hall or Crown Flatt, were for the rest of the week mere mortals who lived among us as teachers, miners or pub landlords. They adopted no airs and graces as they were part of our communities. They lived alongside those who cheered their exploits and achievements on the pitch and, as such, they were accessible heroes.

As suggested earlier, I was an avid autograph hunter in my early years. My dad would take me into the clubhouse at Odsal after home games. He would have a pint and smoke his pipe. I would have a lemonade into which the old man would pour a tiny amount of his ale which made me feel very grown up as I consumed my very weak shandy. He would point me in the direction of the players as they mingled among us following their afternoon's exertions. Not a single autograph was ever refused and the signatories would often share a little banter with us kids. I remember when 16-year-old Keith Toohey made his debut in the mid-1960s and I asked the player, who was barely out of school, for his autograph. how the more experienced players teased him about his new found stardom.

One specific episode lives on in my memory to this day and exemplifies the calibre of these humble heroes. On 20 April 1968, Wigan were the visitors to Odsal in the end of season play-offs. In the days of the Yorkshire and Lancashire Leagues, we were rather starved of access to the stars from the west of the Pennines as only a handful of cross border fixtures were allocated to each club at the start of the season. Prior to this occasion I had only seen the mighty Wigan 'live' in a home third round evening Challenge Cup game in 1966. Robert Gate's excellent biography of Billy Boston records that the crowd that night was 27,453 and that Bradford Northern lost 15–6.

In 1968, Billy Boston had announced that he would end his career when Wigan's Championship campaign concluded. Billy was a particular hero of mine almost by proxy as I was reared on tales of the exploits of this giant of the game. I learned from my Welsh father how he escaped the racist colour-bar which operated in rugby union at international level when he had burst onto the scene in the 1950s. Denied any hope of a cap in his native land, Boston opted to 'go north' and joined Wigan. Within weeks he had been included as a member of the Great Britain squad to tour Australia.

His uniquely powerful build for a winger and his ram-rod hand-off and man-and-ball crash tackle were legendary trademark features of his game. On that afternoon in 1968 Robert Gates records: "The nearest Billy came to a try was soon after half time, when he was energetically bundled into touch a foot or so from the Bradford goal-line. He had been given a standing ovation at half-time and he was called up amid thunderous applause to convert the last two Wigan tries, which he duly did. A police escort was required to clear his way back up the slope at the final whistle." Wigan won the game 28–8.

The density of the massed ranks of Billy's admirers prevented me from getting anywhere near the great man for his autograph, but I had a clear strategy and aimed to play the long game. Dad allowed me to carry out my plan as I camped outside the players' bar and resolved to wait for as long as it took. Slowly, but surely, the crowd eventually dispersed and my 11-year-old self became an almost solitary presence. Across the rutted car park, I spotted our robust second-rower Terry Clawson approaching. He was a no-nonsense forward from Featherstone who years later wrote my favourite sporting biography of all time cataloguing his nomadic rugby odyssey, *All the Wrong Moves.* He asked me what I was doing and I explained I was waiting for Billy Boston. He took my autograph book and went inside. About ten minutes later he emerged with the book adorned with all the player's autographs with Billy's in pride of place on a separate page. He ruffled my hair and said, "Right lad, now go and get your tea."

Left: Terry Clawson
(Courtesy *Rugby League Journal*)

Below: Billy Boston with a young fan at Waterstones in Wigan where Billy was doing a book signing for his biography by Robert Gate.
(Photo: Peter Lush)

Left: Harry Pinner scoring for St Helens. (Courtesy Alex Service)

When I learned of Terry's passing in the *Rugby League Journal* in 2013, I wrote to his son Martin, who was Bradford Bulls strength and conditioning coach at the time, to tell him of his father's random act of kindness and how much it had meant to me. I told the children the story in my next school assembly and quoted the Dalai Lama who advised his followers, "Be kind whenever possible and remember, it is *always* possible."

Finally, another example of the generosity of spirit within the rugby league fraternity takes me to St Helens. My wife hails from the town and we sometimes joke that ours is a mixed marriage. She qualified as a Grade One coach and started a team at Gregory Middle School in Bradford where she worked. I managed to beg a kit for them from my old amateur club and she repaid the kindness by bringing her boys to beat my current school team. We met as students in Wales and eventually it was decided that I should meet her parents. As I drove rather nervously down the street where they lived in Denton's Green, I noticed a tall man tending his garden. "That's Kel Coslett!" I exclaimed. My future spouse confirmed the fact and added nonchalantly, pointing at other nearby abodes, saying, "John Mantle lives there and Frank Wilson lives round the back. Geoff Pimblett works at the school over there and my mum teaches with his wife." She told me that she had been at Knowsley Road School with Harry Pinner and even been 'a bit sweet' on the future international loose-forward.

In the mid-2000s, I was invited to a British Lions dinner by Chris Rostron from the RFL. Chris is a Rochdalian with the build and demeanour of a cheeky, feisty scrum-half who was instrumental in forming the charity Rugby League Cares which supports the welfare of former players. It was a brilliant event and I was in awe as I met several of my childhood heroes. As my wife was driving me there, she warned me not to return home with any old items of sporting kit like a former international's jock-strap, costing a small fortune should an auction take place. I quipped that I suppose this warning would not hold good should the items in question be Harry Pinner's socks.

When the dinner was concluded and one or two shandies had been taken, I spotted my wife's former classmate and told him the story. Without a moment's hesitation the socks were off and when she came to pick me up Harry came out to the car park to present them in person. They say you should never meet your heroes but I'm not sure this is so in the case of those who have played 'the greatest game.' The finest exponents of our sport have always had a great rapport with supporters and genuinely are men of the people.

18. The Arkwrights of St Helens

"There's allus been an Arkwright at Arkwright's Mill 'n there allus will be!" is a line often trawled out by comics to typify the kind of no-nonsense, hard-nosed spirit of dour northernness, which says it like it is in the spirit of calling a spade a bloody shovel. The quote gives the nod to the 18th century textile entrepreneur Richard Arkwright whose invention of the water frame began the industrialisation of the textile industry and shaped the Pennine landscape we know today. But at St Helens, a dynasty of Arkwrights were perennial as those at t' mill as three generations of the same family served the Knowsley Road club.

It was some 45 years back when I was first introduced to my future father-in-law, Alf King, who I came to love and respect. A native of St Helens, he was a keen student of the game having first donned the colours of the Cowley Boys' First Team as a teenager. The school, where years later, Ray French introduced hundreds of lads to the game during his lengthy spell of service as a teacher, was a veritable production line of future talent. Alf could talk with eye witness knowledge about such legends of the Saints as Alf Ellaby from the 1930s. In an early conversation, I casually tossed in the name Jack Arkwright into our discussion and I recall the look of incredulity on his face given that I had not long since celebrated my 21st birthday. Thereafter Alf and I were destined to be kindred spirits.

The first member of the Arkwright clan to represent Saints was Jack Arkwright who joined the club from Sutton Commercial amateurs for £50 in 1928. Born in Sutton in 1902, he was a huge man by the standards of the day. Initially he was a prop but eventually found his niche as a second row forward who enjoyed a fruitful partnership alongside Ben Halfpenny in the engine room of the scrum. In 1930, 'Big Jack' was unhappy to be overlooked for the St Helens team which made the final of the Challenge Cup to face Widnes. Setting aside his own disappointment, Jack hopped onto his motorcycle to travel to London where he witnessed his teammates go down to the Chemics 10–3.

In all, Jack Arkwright Senior served Saints from 1928 to 1934. He made 174 appearances for his hometown club, scoring 39 tries and kicking 21 goals. During his time at Knowsley Road, he won honours for Lancashire and England. However, Saints struggled in the harsh economic climate of 'the hungry 1930s' and the financially challenged club decided to cash in one of their most valuable assets and Jack was transferred to Warrington. St Helens received £800 for Arkwright who enjoyed a nine-year stint with the Wire. In 1936, Jack was selected to go on the Ashes tour Down Under with Great Britain.

On that tour, Arkwright earned the unique distinction of becoming the only player ever to have been sent off twice in the same match! The tourists were involved in a feisty affair against the Northern Districts when he was ordered from the field for rough play by the referee. However, following protestations from the home side's skipper, Kingston, for a stay of execution to spare him the ignominy of dismissal, the official broke with the usual protocol and reversed his initial decision. Sadly for Jack, a later violent misdemeanour tried the ref's patience once too often and he was granted first use of the bathing facilities. Doubtless the referee would later cite illness and fatigue as factors in his decision – he had obviously been sick and tired of the Warrington man's antics.

Jack Arkwright eventually made 164 appearances in the primrose and blue of the Wilderspool club. He enjoys the distinction of inclusion in both the St Helens and Warrington Halls of Fame. He died aged 87 in January 1990.

Emerging from the giant shadow – in Jack Senior's case, both literally and metaphorically – of a parent who has starred in the game must be a daunting prospect. Jack Arkwright Junior's time in the rugby league spotlight was relatively short lived and somewhat turbulent. Initially he exploited his huge frame and athletic prowess as a goalkeeper with Liverpool and Wigan Athletic before turning his attention to the oval ball. St Helens were in a state of flux in the early 1960s as they parted company with some star forwards like Vince Karalius and Abe Terry. Jack Junior was recruited from Warrington, the club where his dad had served with distinction. He had played for them in the 1959 Lancashire Cup final against Saints and now joined his former adversaries in August 1962.

He made his debut that month in a 16–9 away victory over Liverpool City. In his first six matches for the Knowsley Road outfit, Arkwright contributed to six successive victories. After this positive start, Jack found himself facing Swinton, a powerhouse of the game at that time, in the final of the Lancashire Cup at Central Park on 27 October. Saints eventually won 7–4 in vile weather as the wind and rain created the conditions for a dogfight in the mud. Swinton's Welsh second row Ron Morgan and Jack locked horns and both were dismissed as a fierce fight ensued. The protagonists left the field side by side and by the time the two reached the centre spot, the baying crowd witnessed the two men resume hostilities before they were eventually separated and escorted to the changing rooms. Since the Disciplinary Committee had not convened during the next week, Arkwright was selected to play against Leeds at Headingley the following Saturday. Sadly for him, he was sent off for a second week in succession. The powers that be took a dim view of his repeat offending and handed Jack a lengthy ban from the game. The severity of the sanction meted out seemingly led to Jack drifting out of the game having only made 14 appearances in the famous red and white jersey. Jack died on 13 June 2003 at the age of 70.

The third dynastic cab off the Arkwright rank was Jack Junior's son, Chris. Unlike his dad and grandad, the six- foot, fair haired footballer rather broke the family mould as he emerged through the ranks of the St Helens Colts as a classy, tough tackling centre. Born on 8 February 1959, he was signed by the club in 1978 and eventually went on to make 273 appearances, scoring 90 tries. He proved equally adept in the stand-off berth and won two Great Britain caps, both as a substitute in the home series against New Zealand in 1985.

The late 1970s and early eighties had been somewhat of a lean period for a club so used to league and cup success. In 1984, Chris Arkwright was a member of the team to end the club's seven-year drought in winning any silverware as the team lifted the Lancashire Cup and the Premiership Trophy. Although plagued by injuries which denied him further international honours, Chris battled back and adapted as his set-backs caused some loss of speed, but he made up for this with tenacious tackling and ball distribution. When Harry Pinner departed for Widnes in 1987, Chris assumed the club captaincy and the number 13 shirt.

In his new loose-forward role, Arkwright led his side to the Challenge Cup final at Wembley following victories over Swinton, Dewsbury, Oldham, Whitehaven and Leigh. Under the Twin Towers they confronted a Halifax team including the Aussie stars Chris Anderson and Lance Todd winner Graham Eadie, as the Yorkshire side emerged victorious by 19-18 in a classic nailbiter. That season under Arkwright's leadership, the club finished second on the league ladder behind arch rivals Wigan.

Arkwright's struggle with knee injuries did not prevent him from enjoying one final swansong when he joined Runcorn Highfield in 1990. The club played their fixtures in St Helens at Sutton's Houghton Road ground and Chris eventually called time on his career in 1992. When the final member of this remarkable dynasty hung up his boots, the family's connection with the club could be traced back over a period stretching some eight decades.

19. Roger Millward MBE

It is an oft heard axiom in sport that 'a good big 'un will always beat a good little 'un". As ever though, it is the exception that proves the rule and such an exception was Roger Millward. Nicknamed 'Roger the Dodger' by Eddie Waring, he enjoyed a stellar career and was a unique player.

He first came to the attention of the wider league watching public in the early 1960s. Every Sunday, Keith Macklin covered a game for ABC television showing an inter-town schoolboy match. Castleford were one of the standout teams in the competition and their star asset was a tiny lad who looked years younger than his peers. On the grainy black and white footage, this tiny kid ran rings around his opponents like a little street urchin cheeking off the bigger boys in the school playground. Schoolboy rugby typically favours those who develop early and some people feel there is a case for organising the game in weight bands rather like boxing. Those who hit puberty first usually scatter their less developed counterparts like so many swatted flies. Indeed, the early developers in schoolboy rugby don't always fulfil their potential as the need to hone their skills to the same degree as their smaller colleagues is less imperative when they can rely on brute strength.

Roger Millward certainly worked on his skills. He was the full package. He had a mesmerising sidestep, fantastic hands and was a dead eyed Dick in the goalkicking department. His tackling was exemplary and he had pace to burn. Castleford snapped up the hometown prodigy on his 16th birthday. The Weldon Lane outfit had an abundance of resources in the half-back department with their iconic pairing of Hepworth and Hardisty earning the club the title, 'Classy Cas'. Consequently, Millward enjoyed only limited opportunities at stand-off and often found himself turning out on the wing.

Notwithstanding all of this, he was selected for Great Britain by the age of 18. This is when I first clapped eyes on the little wizard in the flesh. On 23 October 1965, two weeks before my ninth birthday, my dad and I were in attendance with almost 16,000 other spectators at Odsal Stadium for the second test against the touring Kiwis. The home side won with tries from Bill Burgess, Geoff Shelton and Johnny Stopford and three goals from the big Cumbrian prop Bill Holliday. We stood on the banking by the long path leading to the dressing rooms at the conclusion of the game and the old man pointed out the diminutive figure in a claret-coloured tracksuit and explained he was the non-playing back substitute, Roger Millward. He barely looked much older or bigger than me and I remember thinking that he looked out of place among these great man mountains. How wrong could I be? In March 1966, Roger was picked in the starting lineup against France who were renowned for their ferocious tactics back in the day. He partnered Alex Murphy in an 8–4 defeat at Wigan's Central Park.

In 1965, very few people had BBC2. We were in that majority which did not enjoy access to the new third channel. Those who did had a special aerial marking them out as televisual high rollers. My dad used to go for a pint in the Coll Hotel, just a stone's throw from Odsal Stadium where mine host was Harry Womersley, Bradford Northern chairman and Great Britain tour manager. An elderly couple also made the pub their local as it stood in close proximity to their home in Halifax Road.

Left: Roger Millward (Courtesy Peter Lush)

Mona and Charlie had no kids of their own, but lavished loving care on their two Yorkshire terriers. They had BBC2! To my absolute delight they invited my dad and me to their home at 8pm every Tuesday. Being without children they spoiled me rotten and gave me juice and crisps as they each had a bottle of light ale. We watched the BBC2 Floodlit Trophy – second half only – in black and white and barring Saturdays at live games, this was the highlight of my week!

The Floodlit Trophy was won by Castleford in the first three years of its existence and given that my beloved Northern didn't have any skin in that particular game, to adopt modern parlance, I favoured Cas and still retain a soft spot for the club. The RFL used the competition to experiment with rule changes and in its second year it was the testing ground for the Four-Tackle rule. In the 1965 Final, Roger played at scrum-half as Castleford beat St Helens 4–0 at Knowsley Road. Sitting on Mona and Charlie's settee stroking a Yorkshire terrier I basked in a little reflected glory. Given my team's lack of silverware, the 1965 Yorkshire Cup apart, I deemed it okay to take my delights vicariously.

To digress for a moment, during the Covid 19 lockdown I was helping some former players on 'Zoom', to put together presentations to use in a Rugby League Cares programme. 'Ahead of the Game', was a brilliant project designed to get men to open up about their mental health and I have nothing but admiration for the players who got involved. What struck me was that of several former-pros who had been on Castleford's books at different times, a good proportion described it as the happiest time in their careers. When pressed on why this was, they said they were respected around the town, but also not idolised or intruded upon. There are almost unique circumstances which make Cas such a fertile breeding ground for rugby league stock and such a thriving and happy environment to be in as a player and supporter. I think it is what the French refer to as the 'terroir'.

Back to the mid-1960s then, and Hull Kingston Rovers were keeping a watchful eye on the Millward situation. Wilf Spaven, the club chairman, approached Cas and brokered an agreement that should the west Yorkshire club sell the mercurial stand-off, that they would have first refusal. A benefactor was found to donate £6,000 and the Robins made a bid which was accepted. Roger joined Rovers in August 1966. The club reaped an early return on their investment when he scored 38 tries in his first full season at Craven Park. In the early days he was fortunate to have Cumbrian hard man Frank Foster as his minder. Some years ago, I attended a coaching course and met Les Sellars who played with Foster during his time at Odsal. Les said he was more scared of his colleague than any opponent because incurring his displeasure could easily lead to an invitation to "meet him at the back of the stand."

In all, Millward played 406 matches for the red and whites, scoring 207 tries and kicking 607 goals. In the final couple of years in his playing career, Roger was joined at Rovers by his cousin, Brian Lockwood, a fine ball playing forward who had been a teammate at Weldon Road. He had enjoyed great success in club rugby league in Australia. In 1976, Millward tried his hand in Australia, turning out for the Cronulla Sharks. The following year, after the death of coach Harry Poole, Millward combined playing duties with the role of first team coach.

Without doubt his finest hour in club rugby came at Wembley in 1980 in what turned out to be his final game as a player. The match was an all-Hull affair as Rovers took on the Airlie Birds from across the river. Earlier that season Roger had missed several matches having suffered a broken jaw. After 13 minutes in the final he received a recurrence of the injury. He later explained that he knew immediately how serious the break was as the jaw had been knocked out of place. Nowadays he would have been compelled to leave the field, but back then they were made of sterner stuff. He stayed on the field and shortly after he tackled Hull's Steve 'Knocker' Norton and as his jaw hit the rampaging forwards knee it knocked (appropriately!) his jaw back into place. With typical humility he credits fellow half Allan Agar with getting him through the period immediately after the injury when he described himself as "being in cuckoo land".

This single act exemplifies the courage and leadership of the man. Spurred on by his brave example, Hull KR went on to win 10–5, with Millward contributing a drop-goal. However, it was his cousin Brian Lockwood who was awarded the Lance Todd on that day, but perhaps the full extent of the little man's heroics was not realised when the journalists cast their votes shortly before the conclusion of the match.

When Millward hung up his playing boots, he continued as club coach to the Robins. He remained at the helm for 11 years in what would be the club's most successful era. Millward's men brought six trophies to Craven Park during his tenure. When he finally called time with Rovers, Roger spent 17 months as coach of Halifax.

On the world stage he played 29 times for Great Britain and 17 times for England. Roger played in the 1967 Ashes series against Australia and in the 1968 World Cup. While both of these campaigns ended unsuccessfully, his finest achievement at international level lay ahead. Exactly a decade before his remarkable Wembley triumph, Millward became a member of the last touring Lions team to lower the Australians' colours on their home soil.

The 1970 series did not get off to an auspicious start. In the first test at Brisbane, the selectors opted for Roger's boyhood hero Alan Hardisty at stand-off. The tourists were hammered 37–15. The axe was wielded with several changes being made for the second test. Millward replaced the man who had barred his way for so long at Castleford as he was handed the number six jersey. He rewarded the management's faith in him with an almost perfect performance. He grabbed a brace of tries and kicked seven goals from seven attempts in Great Britain's 28–7 win. I recall reading the match report in our local paper, *The Telegraph and Argus* and sticking the picture of one of Roger's tries in my scrapbook.

The final, deciding test was a close-run affair. Fittingly, it was Roger who was the difference as he dashed fully 40 yards to round off a move and to score the winning try in a 21–17 triumph. It is now 54 years of hurt since that historic series. Roger's international longevity is quite remarkable given the way he was often targeted by opponents. Peter Fox turned to the little magician in 1978 when he masterminded a shock victory over the Australians.

In the second test at Odsal, which has gone down in history as the 'Dad's Army' test due to the number of Britain's team who were entering the veteran stage of their careers, Roger played a pivotal part. Against the odds, the ageing home side gained victory against Bobby

Fulton's men and true to form, Roger was so badly knocked about by the Australians that he was forced to leave the fray in the second half and was replaced by John Holmes.

Shortly before his death on 2 May 2016 at the age of 68, I had the honour of meeting the great man at a dinner at Headingley. It was widely known that Roger had not been well for some time and his ill health was apparent as I shook his hand and chatted to him. The cause of his illness was certainly in part, a result of his courage and bravery shown in his illustrious career. The repeated injuries to his jaw had left a gap in the bone. Sadly, a cancer formed there and he had a number of operations which he bore with all the resilience and fortitude he demonstrated on the playing field. His colleague and fellow Craven Park legend, the late Phil Lowe, described him as "the best player I've seen in my life".

Roger was inducted into the Hall of Fame in 2000, having been awarded an MBE for his services to the game in 1983. Following his death, the club retired his number six shirt as a mark of respect and a stand at Craven Park is named in his honour. Like that fellow hero of the city of Kingston Upon Hull, Clive Sullivan, Roger Millward has a road named in his honour. Roger Millward Way is named as a permanent reminder of the high esteem in which he was held. A small man in stature, he was a giant of our game.

20. The Rorke's Drift test

Lovers of sport can be guilty of taking it too seriously. We often speak of sporting contests as though they were military conflicts. The great Australian cricketer Keith Miller flew fighter planes in the Second World War. In an interview following one particular test match he was asked about how he dealt with pressure. He brought some perspective to the question when he responded, "Pressure is having a Messerschmidt up your arse mate!" The iconic commentator Richie Benaud made much the same point about getting things out of proportion in our consideration of sport when he said, "The Titanic was a tragedy, the Ethiopian Drought a disaster and neither bears any resemblance to a dropped catch." We might all do well to remember this in our reactions to sports ups and downs for it is, as the great broadcaster Cliff Morgan stated, "A glorious irrelevance".

Nevertheless, our game does borrow from the common lexicon of military conflict in the vocabulary we use to discuss it. 'Up-and-unders' are now 'bombs', teams 'battle' for supremacy in games and in test matches against the Kangaroos we talk about the 'old enemy'. Although it was played back in 1914, the year in which the first truly industrial war began, the 'Rorke's Drift Test' is probably the best recorded and thus most famous in test history. The game has gone down as being the greatest 'rearguard action' in the history of the sport.

We need to remember that in the year when the First World War began, the actual Battle of Rorke's Drift had occurred well within living memory, only 34 years earlier. To set this in context, looking back in 2024, we are harking back only to 1990 in equivalent terms. Consequently, we become aware that the narrative relating to the Zulu Wars was still relatively fresh in the national psyche. History can be seen as the way a nation tells stories about itself and these tales shape the way that a country comes to feel about its identity. Often viewing heroic deeds from the past confers on those studying the events a kind of delusion of national exceptionalism.

The subtext of the Battle of Rorke's Drift is that a garrison of gallant British soldiers numbering barely 150, repulsed some 3,000 fierce Zulu warriors at a mission hospital in 1879. It is a *Boys' Own* story of victory against overwhelming odds gained by devotion to duty and British pluck. In winning the day 11 VCs were earned and this is the highest number ever given in a single action. But this is not the whole picture. It is true that history is recorded by the victors. It is also the case that the first casualty of war is the truth.

To gain a better understanding of the story we need to set the battle in context. On 22 January 1879, a Zulu army numbering about 20,000 warriors wiped out a British force of about 1,300 soldiers and native allies at Isandlwana. The defeat was largely the result of the hubris of Lord Chelmsford who had led the invasion into Zululand less than a fortnight earlier. Believing implicitly in his troops superiority and thus failing to set up sufficient defences around the camp at Isandlwana, his column suffered the greatest ever reversal against any indigenous force which had ever been suffered. Later that day, a section of that larger Zulu contingent headed to the mission station at Rorke's Drift.

The government and British press were desperate to alleviate the collective national shock at the news of the humiliation. The defence of Rorke's Drift against supposedly insurmountable odds acted as a means to salve the nation's anxiety and to restore faith that 'the Empire on which the sun never sets' was not in peril. While the bravery of those who fought at Rorke's Drift cannot be denied, there are many details about the battle which did not come to light until many years later.

In 1964, Stanley Baker co-produced and starred in the epic film *Zulu* which dealt with the battle. As a child aged eight, I vividly recall going to see the blockbuster with my mum and dad at the Odeon in Bradford. It is through this film that most people became familiar with the history of that action. However, it omits a good deal which is of relevance and also perpetuated and sometimes created myths about the actual events.

The greatest omission is the account of what happened after the battle. Chelmsford decreed that there would be no prisoners. On the day after the fighting, some 500 wounded Zulu warriors were killed, bayoneted (to save on bullets), or stabbed by their own assegies or hanged from cattle carts to die by slow strangulation. This atrocity would obviously constitute a war crime by today's standards. Justifying the butchery, Commandant Hamilton-Browne who oversaw the slaughter said "It was beastly but there was nothing else to do. War is war and savage war is the worst of the lot." A war against native 'savage' soldiers was not deemed to be fought to the same standards of conduct as that against 'civilised' European foes.

The film laid great emphasis on the Welsh influence of those soldiers of the South Wales Borderers during the battle. However, in 1879, the 24th Regiment was in fact the 2nd Warwickshires. They did not become the South Wales Borderers until 1881, so Ivor Emmanuel would not have been leading them in a defiant rendition of 'Men of Harlech'. Scrutiny of the roll call from the battle suggests that only about 15 percent of the soldiers hailed from the Principality.

Notwithstanding these historical anomalies, the Battle of Rorke's Drift did live on in public consciousness and when news of the third test between Harold Wagstaff's Northern Union and Australia broke, it seemed to provide sufficient parallels to be applied to the epic sporting encounter. Just as with the actual battle, an appreciation of the back story of the causes of the conflict shed greater light on our understanding of the subsequent significance of the event.

So convoluted and intractable are the root causes leading up to the match that it provided historian Tom Mather – father of the dual league and union international Barrie-Jon Mather – with sufficient material for an entire book on the preamble to the game. In his book *The Rorke's Drift Rugby League Test Fiasco,* published in 2021, he examines the roots of the dispute between the Northern Union (NU) and the New South Wales Rugby League (NSWRL) which subsequently led to the fixture congestion which ensued.

In his book *Backs to the Wall,* published in 2020, about Harold Wagstaff's contribution to the third test at Sydney, author Bryn Woodworth lays out the role played by the NU's inspirational captain on that day. Bryn kindly contacted me to clarify the background to the dispute. He explained that on the original tour itinerary, the first test had been scheduled for 20 June 1914. However, the New South Wales RL players did not relish the 550-mile journey north to take part in the fixture and so it was downgraded to a match against Queensland. The first test was rescheduled for 27 June meaning that the tourists would now face playing four games in eight days, three of which would be test matches. Given that matches coming so thick and fast had already contributed to a lengthy injury list, the co-managers, Joe Houghton of St Helens and Huddersfield's John Clifford objected to this level of fixture congestion. Initially they received a sympathetic hearing from the NSW Management Committee and a recommendation was made that the final test should take place in Melbourne six weeks later on 15 August when the tourists had completed the New Zealand leg of the tour.

Labouring under the misapprehension that they had additional time which would have bolstered their ranks with the return of some of the walking wounded, the team went on an arduous midweek journey to Bathurst where they defeated Western District 42–3. But as they were completing their victory, the NSWRL was over-ruling the recommendation of their Management Committee and insisting that the tests must all be completed within the narrow window as originally outlined. The British management were adamant that they would not comply with this hectic schedule and the NSWRL responded, "If the NU do not play, they should pack their bags and go home."

Secretary Ted Larkin dispatched a telegram to his opposite number, Joe Platt, in England explaining that there would be no postponement and that a refusal to play would have serious ramifications for the finances of the tour and even possible legal implications. In mitigation of the NSWRL position, they were reluctant to create a clash with the New Zealand All Blacks Rugby Union tour which would be underway in August and there would be an Australian Rules tournament taking place in Melbourne, also competing for the spectators' attention.

We must bear in mind that the XIII-a-side code was in its infancy and fighting to gain a foothold in an already crowded sporting landscape. It was left to Platt to send the message which was, to paraphrase, 'get on with it and play.' He told the tour management, "We hope that you will expend every atom of energy and skill you possess to secure victory; failing which, we hope you will lose like sportsmen."

By the time the third test at the Sydney Cricket Ground came round, the series stood at 1–1. The NU had won the first test 23–5, while the Kangaroos took the second 12–7. Between these dates, in far off Europe, an event took place, the seismic significance of which could hardly have been grasped at the time, as Austrian Archduke Franz Ferdinand and his wife were shot dead by Bosnian Serb student Gavrilo Princip.

On 4 July, the third test was to be played at the SCG. Four members of the second test team, Gwyn Thomas, Johnny Rogers, Bert Jenkins and Fred Longstaff had been added to an already extensive list of the battered combatants of an arduous tour who were unavailable due to injury. Replacement full-back Alf Wood had to play with a badly broken nose and one can only imagine that the selection meeting must have resembled a hospital exercise of triaging the injured rather than picking a test team!

It was left to manager John Clifford to rally the troops with some impassioned oratory in which he invoked the spirit of Nelson at the Battle of Trafalgar. He stirred his beleaguered troops saying, "You are playing a game of football this afternoon but more than that you are playing for England, and more than that, you are playing for right versus wrong. You will win because you have to win. Don't forget that message from home. England expects every one of you to do his duty." Many years later, skipper Wagstaff told a reporter that his fellow Huddersfield colleague Clifford's words galvanised his team to great effect and said, "I was impressed and thrilled as never before or since by a speech."

Early in the match, the NU winger Frank Williams picked up a serious knee injury. Although he limped on for some time, he was eventually forced to leave the field. In those days long before substitutions were permitted, Albert 'Chick' Johnson was pressed into service as a makeshift winger, leaving the forwards one member light. The Huddersfield back-rower Douglas Clark then sustained a broken thumb, but insisted on staying on the field. In the second half he then broke his shoulder and eventually left the pitch with tears of frustration rolling down his cheeks. Later in the game the British team was down to 10 men as Billy Hall suffered concussion.

To some extent, the depletion of numbers for the tourists was a self-inflicted wound. On the first tour to the Antipodes in 1910, there had been a disagreement between the NU and Australian officials regarding replacements. The home side allowed for a replacement to be used should a player be forced to leave the field due to injury before half-time. However, officials in England felt that allowing substitutions to be made was contrary to the spirit of the game. They believed that allowing replacements was open to skulduggery and tactical jiggery-pokery. In 1914, the NU stubbornly stuck to this position meaning that in effect, the two sides were operating under two different sets of rules. John Clifford's entreaties to the NU back home fell upon deaf ears so the consequent difficulties were of their own making.

Be that as it may, the depleted tourists managed to build a half time lead of 9–0 courtesy of a Willie Davies try and three goals from Oldham's Alf Wood. They extended their lead in the second half when Wagstaff, 'The Prince of Centres' lived up to his nickname and broke through the Australian lines before sending out a pass to 'Chick' Johnson. The forward confounded the full-back Howard Hallett by dropping the ball on his foot to round him and dribble over the line to touch down and extend the lead to 14–0. Although the home side hit back with two tries, both went unconverted by Wally Messenger, less famous brother of Dally, the tourists won the day 14–6.

Harold Wagstaff was hailed as the inspiration of the victory and he was feted by the *Sydney Morning Herald* for tackling "with the tenacity of a grizzly bear." His opposing captain Sid Deane complimented his opposite number for being, "brilliant in attack and wonderful in defence" adding that "his leadership was a most important factor in the team's success." Ironically it was the Australian journalist who wrote under the name 'Arawa' who first alluded to the 1879 battle in South Africa, dubbing the game 'The Rorke's Drift Test'.

Little could any of the participants on that fateful day have known that they were living in those last days of innocence when young men only spilt blood on fields pursuing their chosen sporting passions. By the time the tourists set off for home, war had been declared and their ship had to be escorted home for part of the journey by the Royal Navy.

The ensuing hostilities would eventually claim the lives of three of the NU's squad in Fred Longstaff, Billy Jarman and Walter Roman as well as the Australian centre on that July afternoon, Bob Tidyman. Ted Larkin, who had been a central figure in the pre-match wranglings as Secretary of the NSWRL and who was elected as Labour MP for Willoughby on Sydney's north shore, was killed along with many of his ANZAC colleagues on Churchill's disastrous Dardanelles Campaign. It was as if that metaphorical 'Rorke's Drift Test', epitomising the values of courage, comradery and resilience in the best 'backs to the wall' tradition, was little more than a preparation for the real horrors to come.

21. Wally Lewis is coming!

Wakefield, which was granted city status in 1888, is recorded in the Domesday book of 1086 as both Wachefield and Wachfield, deriving its name from either an ancient soul called Waca, who had a field, or from an open space where a wake or fete took place. You take your choice. It was a royalist stronghold in the Civil War and the site of a famous battle in 1460 in the Wars of the Roses. The Wakefield district comprises the five towns of Featherstone, Knottingley, Normanton, Castleford and Pontefract – the latter two known affectionately by locals as 'Cas Vegas' and 'Ponte Carlo'.

It is famously the centre of the hallowed 'Rhubarb Triangle', a nine square mile area taking in Morley and Rothwell, which is to 'forced' rhubarb what Melton Mowbray is to the pork pie or Kendal is to mint cake. The beautiful pinky, green fruit sticks serve not only to make mouth-watering desserts, but were famously used by Geoff Boycott's mum. This son of 'the Merrie City' and former *Test Match Special* co-commentator, would often refer to how she would enjoy greater success in warding off hostile fast bowling with her "stick of rhubarb" than the batters of the modern era with their excessive, protective padding and helmets.

It's a surprising place and it is believed the city provided the inspiration for the nursery rhyme, *Here We Go Round the Mulberry Bush*. The little ditty refers to a particulary large version of that plant variety which became established at Wakefield Prison, around which women inmates took their exercise during nightly moonlight walks. Nocturnal jaunts of an entirely different kind are made on the famous (or infamous, according to your viewpoint) city centre, 'Westgate Run'. This involves sampling beverages in the plethora of bars and pubs in that neck of the woods, where the odd bout of fisticuffs is apparently not uncommon!

Also in the centre of the city, along the route from the Bull Ring to the Waterfront, in Thorne's Lane, visitors will find *The Wakefield Walk of Fame*. The Hollywood-style homage to the famous sons and daughters of the city is a charming exercise in expressing collective pride in those who have left their mark in the wider world. Blue stars are set in the pavements recording the names and achievements of Wakefield's most famous residents. As well as those for Trinity's own Neil Fox and Dave Topliss, there are nods to the Indie band, *The Cribs* and singer and television presenter, Jane McDonald.

As well as these icons of more modern, popular culture, there are a couple which reference figures from more traditional historical fields. John Harrison was a famous carpenter and clockmaker who is credited with solving an age-old problem of calculating longitude at sea, thus greatly enhancing the safety and accuracy of navigation for generations of maritime voyagers. His fictional Lesser H6 watch's discovery also gave us a wonderful *Only Fools and Horses* episode in 1996, when Del and Rodney found it and sold it at Sotheby's for £6.2million, thus fulfilling Del's prophecy that "this time next year we'll be millionaires." Charles Waterton, who was born at Walton Hall in Wakefield, is referred to as 'an explorer'. However, a deeper delve into his past shows that as well as his work in conservation, he also ran his uncle's slave plantation in Georgetown. In the light of recent developments regarding the memorialisation of the past, the council might consider a re-think. Just a thought.

The Wakefield Trinity club owes its name to being founded by Christians from the nearby Holy Trinity Church. It could be said then that the club could claim, "Wakefield's first export was not rugby league, but Christianity." This spiritual theme can be extended as Wakefield curate, the Reverend Sabine Baring-Gould is to be thanked for giving the hymn, *Onward Christian Soldiers* to the world. Although it has rather fallen out of favour given its undertones of militarism, which many now baulk at, the hymn was written for the children of the city to march to as they carried banners between Horbury Bridge and Horbury St Peter's Church on Whit Mondays. In the modern age, many argue that sport has become the new secular religion. Given their passion for the new faith and their more formal religious roots, Trinity are perennially on the lookout for a new saviour to arrive and deliver them from doom and despair. Hope springs eternal that there will be a second coming in the form of a new Messiah. It was in this spirit of eternal hope that the first rumours began to dare whisper themselves on the Belle Vue terraces that, "Wally Lewis is coming!"

During the 1980s, the cult of the fanzine emerged. These locally generated, low budget, supporter written periodicals were an expression of fans' desire to give voice to their feelings about their teams. They were often an irritant to the clubs they referenced and could not be sold in their home ground's immediate environs. They had strong editorial lines, caustic, often irreverent humour and were critical of authority and the pious pomposity of directors, administrators and officials. They had that whiff of gunpowder about them like dissenting pamphlets on city streets in the 17th century, Civil War England. Eventually these homespun publications were rendered obsolete by the internet and social media, but like the mullet and acid-wash jeans, they were fun while they lasted.

Bradford had *The Steam Pig*, referencing the pack from the old Birch Lane days which was produced by an old West Bowling teammate of mine, 'Syd' Fielding. In Leeds, supporters circulated copies of *Another Bloody Sunday*, while on the Fylde coast, Blackpool Borough fans rejoiced in the *Tangerine Dream*. There was *The Roughyed* in Oldham and *The House of Pain* in Warrington. But I always thought that the most evocative title was that of Trinity's fanzine, *Wally Lewis is Coming!* which was the brainchild of coal miner Richard Clarkson and his wife Tracy, capturing the joy and disbelief of that moment in time when the great man graced Trinity with his presence.

The 1960s represented the most glorious period in the old club's history. These were the days of Neil Fox, the greatest points machine our game has ever witnessed. Along with the fearsome figure of Derek 'Rocky' Turner, it was as if these twin Gods had descended Mount Olympus to delight the humble citizens and provide a glimpse of the eternal realm beyond. With a dazzling cast including the likes of Gerry Round, Harold Poynton, Berwyn Jones and South Africans like Gert Coetzer, Alan Skene and Jan Prinsloo, they provided an abundance of silverware for the Belle Vue faithful. From a personal point of view, I loved it when they came to Odsal as my dad's workmates from Hartley Bank Pit in Netherton would come and I'd drop for a few bob as Jock O'Donnell and company who worked with the old man would bestow their generosity on me!

Following something of a hiatus in the early 1970s, the club rallied in the middle part of the decade under the guidance of Dave Topliss with his silken grace and the powerful presence of forwards of the calibre of Trevor Skerrett and Bill Ashurst in the pack. 'The

Dreadnoughts', again earned the right to visit the Twin Towers, only to sink back into mediocrity thereafter following the inevitable cycle of boom and bust.

In the 1970s, the Australian authorities had placed an embargo on players travelling abroad to sell their services so clubs in England could only look on and salivate at the quality of the players in the 1982 'Invincibles' team which toured these isles. In 1982, Wally Lewis had also visited when the State of Queensland undertook a European tour. At this point the restrictions on playing abroad were lifted and eventually clubs could access these antipodean colossi to bolster their squads with the likes of Peter Sterling joining Hull and a season later, Mal Meninga and Phil Veivers joining Saints.

During the 1983 season, a palpable sense of foreboding could be felt in the air at Trinity, but behind the scenes, unknown to the fans, a consortium of local businessmen was hatching a daring plan. The season was well advanced and with four of the 16 teams in the top flight to be relegated, things looked ominous and Wakefield seemed highly likely to become one of the four to fall through the trap door. But could the man hailed as 'The King' and 'The Emperor of Lang Park' be enticed to join the Yorkshire outfit and effect the 'Great Escape'?

Walter James Lewis is still considered by many Australian pundits, including the late Arthur Beetson and Andrew Johns, to be the GOAT. He is one of that very rare breed to be included as an 'Immortal', a group of legendary players from across history which was founded in 1981 and still only consists of 13 members. He is also one of the six original inductees into the Australian Hall of Fame. Lewis played in 31 'State of Origin' matches, captaining Queensland in 30 of them and winning the award for player-of-the-match on eight occasions. In a decade-long international career, the maestro whose statue now graces the Suncorp Stadium, represented his country in 34 matches.

Overtures to the great man began in 1983, but having spent a large amount of time on tour the preceding year, Lewis was reluctant to be away from home for another protracted period of time. Years later he revealed to a journalist at the *Yorkshire Post* how negotiations developed. Trinity came in with an initial offer of £150 per match, but the player was not interested. Incremental increases were then muted and Wally professed, "I needed to piss this bloke off and get rid of him, so I came up with ... £1,000. He nearly had a heart attack to start with, but then said 'yes'." Lewis still expressed reluctance but the club representative said he had named his price and the acceptance amounted to a verbal contract.

We can only imagine with what excitement Trinity fans greeted the news of the deal. It must have been like anticipating receiving a Timex as a birthday present only to remove the gift wrapping to discover a Rolex. Yet the response of everyone at the club was not unbridled delight. Wally revealed that some members of the squad were openly resentful of him and his huge price tag. Captain Nigel Stephenson explained why some of his teammates were jealous. Grumbles and murmurings in the dressing room were barely concealed and matters came to a head when Wally issued something of an ultimatum to 'put up or shut up.' He told them he had come to help them avoid the drop and if they didn't like that then they had no need to play. They played.

Many years later, I got to know Colin Maskill who was a young hooker in that Trinity team. The goalkicking forward, who went on to play for Leeds with distinction and who became England manager before moving on to a role with Rugby League Cares, told me they became firm friends. The two remain in touch these 40 years on and Colin could not speak highly enough of Lewis, describing the Australian stand-off as a "top bloke."

The set up at Belle Vue must have come as something of a culture shock to the mega-star. Most of the players then were part-time professionals. Lewis described how those who worked underground would arrive at training with coal blackened faces, covered "... in dirt and s..t after getting out of the mines. I used to think, they're busting their arses all day long working, then coming here, half as they like their football and half as they needed the money." Lewis sympathised with them and understood why, in his estimation our domestic players did about five to 10 percent of the fitness work which Australian players undertook.

In his months at the club, Wally was billeted at the British Oak Hotel in Stanley, which was run by former Wakefield player Brian Briggs. He explained that one of the main sponsors of the deal came to the pub almost every night and he felt duty bound to join him. The pleasures of endless socialising obviously began to wear thin. Lewis said, "Everyday I remember thinking, I just want to go to the movies tonight, or go anywhere just to get away from the grog." Talk about First World problems!

A fact which is often overlooked is that as part of the hard bargain that Wally struck, Trinity had to agree to also take his younger brother Scott as part of the deal. The versatile threequarter, who was then with the Fortitude Valley club, played in six matches with his brother and averaged a try a game. Scott made five appearances in the centre and one on the wing. Both played their first game against Hull in a 32–16 defeat.

Wally Lewis played 10 games for Trinity. Of those games, the team won five and he contributed six tries. However, in the fixture against Leeds at Headingley, he was dismissed for verbally abusing the referee. He later claimed that the official had misunderstood his comments due to his Australian twang but the ref would have none of it. As Brian's mum in *The Life of Brian* claimed, "He wasn't the Messiah – just a very naughty boy!"

Wally's finest hour in the red, white and blue came in the home game against St Helens. In 2019, *The St Helens Star* took a nostalgic dive into their archives to record the exploits of the great man in that particular game. In the forthcoming seasons, the Lancashire side would enter the Australian market themselves to great effect, but back in that match in 1983 they fielded 11 local lads. Billy Benyon's men were on a poor run having lost six of their last seven games, but probably felt they would have enough ammunition to dispose of lowly Trinity.

Early indications were that this would be the case as Saints took an early lead with tries from their tough, durable centre, Roy Haggerty, Shaun Allen, Andy Platt and twinkle toed winger Barrie Ledger. But Wakefield hung on to their coat-tails and with 'the King' crossing for two tries, Trinity only trailed 22–16 at the interval. Wakefield shut up shop in the second stanza and Lewis continued to be their tormentor-in-chief, completing his hat trick and almost single-handedly orchestrating a 31–22 victory for the home side. Nigel Bell, then a lithe and nimble scrum-half grabbed two tries himself that night. In later years Bell beefed up quite significantly and became a fully paid-up member of the front row union.

While the man who bears the Heritage Number 928 did have a galvanising effect in his short tenure at Belle Vue, sadly the effect was only transitory. When Wally and Scott returned from whence they came, 'the Dreadnoughts' failed to win a further game in the whole season. Ultimately then, the project must be filed under the section 'gallant failures'. I am willing to bet though, that those who witnessed those days would do it all again in a heartbeat!

22. Lance Todd

Lancelot Beaumont Todd was a true pioneer in rugby league. His name has become almost synonymous with the annual Challenge Cup final at Wembley where the player-of-the-match receives the award which is dedicated to his memory.

He was born in New Zealand in 1883 and was a tailor by trade. Initially he played rugby union for the Otahuhu club before graduating to play for Auckland in 1905. He then moved to the Parnell club the following year. In the 1907–08 season an event occurred that changed the course of Todd's life forever.

In 1907, a young postal clerk from Wellington, called Albert Henry Baskerville (the spelling of whose name has been the subject of some conjecture, often incorrectly spelt Baskiville) had written a book on rugby tactics. 'Bert' Baskerville's *Modern Rugby Football: New Zealand Methods: Points for the Beginner, the Player, the Spectator,* showed him to be a clear and original thinker about the sport. That same year he contacted the infant Northern Union authorities in the north of England with the germ of an idea about the possibility of a professional tour to 'the Mother Country'. Following an encouraging response, he began a cloak and dagger exercise in recruiting possible players for the proposed tour. Discovery by the home union authorities of any professional involvement meant an automatic life ban from the game, so the stakes were incredibly high. Those who agreed to sign up for the adventure knew they were cutting themselves adrift from union forever. For Baskerville himself, it was to end in tragedy. He died of influenza on the return trip, but not before the endeavour succeeded in spreading the gospel of the new sport of Northern Union, now rugby league.

The tour was to breathe some much-needed life into the game in England. Only 12 years into its existence, the code was isolated, mainly played in the north of England. Giving the game an international profile could only improve its image on the national stage and demonstrate the potential for expansion.

There were some very high-profile players on that first tour. Dally Messenger was recruited from Australia and another superstar who had toured with the 1905 All Blacks was George Smith. He was an amazing athlete who won many athletics championships in his native land. He travelled to England in 1902 to compete in the AAA Championships in the 100 yards and 440 yards hurdles. During his visit to these shores, the Manningham club approached Smith with an offer to join them for £100, but he declined. After the All Golds tour of 1907–08, he became one of five players to stay on and join an English club by signing for Oldham. In the Great Britain versus New Zealand series in the modern era, the player of the series is awarded the George Smith medal in his memory.

Another of the players who agreed to join Baskerville was Lance Todd. Having signed up, Todd helped to organise the tour and to recruit others. He demonstrated an early flair for leadership by serving on the Management Committee. The dashing centre enjoyed a very successful tour, played in all four tests and scored eight tries in all matches. In doing so, Todd caught the attention of the Wigan directors. He accepted an offer of £400 to join the Central Park team and become club captain.

Left: Lance Todd
(Courtesy *Rugby League Journal*)

He did not return home with the team, but did receive his £300 share of the tour profits to add to his signing on fee. His tourist teammate Massa Johnston did make the journey back home, but later returned to play alongside Todd with the Lancashire side.

When Lance Todd joined Wigan, they had not yet emerged to be the powerhouse of the game which they would become. He made 185 appearances in cherry and white and led the team to four Lancashire League titles, three Lancashire Cup wins and their only Championship victory in the first 25 years of their existence. He led Wigan to the 1911 Challenge Cup Final where they lost to Broughton Rangers 4–0. It came as something of a shock when he made a cross Pennine move to Dewsbury for a £450 fee. His chance to shine at Crown Flatt was cut short with the outbreak of the First World War. Lance Todd answered his country's call to arms, joining the ANZAC forces for the duration of the conflict.

Returning to England when hostilities ceased, Todd became a pub manager for a spell before joining struggling club Salford in 1928. This phase of his career was to be even more remarkable than his playing days. Salford were languishing in rugby league's basement and were barely making ends meet. In his first season in charge, Todd improved their league position from 26th to fourth. He transformed the club so it became a force in the game in 'the hungry 1930s'. The decade was to be their heyday as their New Zealand manager assembled a star-studded outfit under the inspirational captaincy of Gus Risman. Both Risman and Lance Todd, along with the star of the 1960s, Dai Watkins, have roads named in their honour in Salford.

The great ambassador of Hunslet and Leeds rugby league, Harry Jepson OBE, explained how far ahead of his time Lance Todd was. In *No Sand Dunes in Featherstone* he explained, "We now have in rugby league, a scholarship scheme. Well Lance Todd who was manager of Salford in the 1930s, he virtually had a scholarship scheme. He used to sign players on – young players from South Wales ... and found them somewhere to live, often together, well-chosen lodgings where the lady of the house would look after them and sometimes get them a job on the ground staff ... he got a great side together."

The club's roll of honour during Lance Todd's time at the club is quite outstanding. They won the Lancashire League Championship five times, the Lancashire Cup on four occasions and the League Championship three times. He led them to two Wembley Challenge Cup finals, winning the competition for the only time in their history with a 7–4 victory over Barrow in 1938. As well as sweeping all before them domestically, Todd proved his pioneering prowess again in 1934. The game across the Channel was in its first year and the authorities were seeking means of promoting the new sport. Salford agreed to make a two-month tour to the south of France to help the establishment of the game there. So impressed were the French journalists that they nicknamed them 'Les Diables Rouge' – 'The Red Devils', a sobriquet which persists to this day. The enduring nature of this French connection is evidenced by the fact that the club invited the Catalans Dragons to be the last visitors to 'The Willows' when the ground was finally closed in 2011.

Lance Todd's contract at Salford ended with the advent of the Second World War. Too old for military service, he became a Commandant in the Salford branch of the LDV (Local Defence Volunteers). It was while returning from a Home Guard parade in 1942, that he lost his life. On a foggy night on 14 November 1942, Todd was driving three other members of the group back to their homes. His car swerved to miss a tram but hit a lamp-post killing Lance Todd and Colonel Frank Sewell who was a front seat passenger. Thousands of rugby league fans turned up to pay their respects at his funeral. His grave can be seen in the Lower Ince Cemetery in Wigan.

Following Todd's death at the age of 59, Harry Sunderland, who later gave his name to the award for the stand out player in the Championship, later to be the Grand Final, mooted the idea of a commemorative award in Lance Todd's honour. It was decided that the Lance Todd Trophy would be awarded to the man of the match in the annual Challenge Cup final. When the competition was resumed in 1946, the first recipient of the award was Wakefield Trinity's Billy Stott. The accolade is highly prized as it allows winners to be part of a very elite group of players from down the ages. Every year members of the Rugby League Writers Association in attendance cast their vote for their choice just a few minutes before the end of the final.

Neil Ormiston of the Rugby League Record Keepers Club was quite horrified to learn that Jeff Lima, who won the award in 2011, did not even know who Lance Todd was. This is, I believe, a reflection of how we are in danger of denying our heritage and history in the age of Super League. Lima is ironically a fellow Kiwi who became the fifth player from New Zealand to gain the honour when he scored two tries for Wigan in their 28–18 victory over Leeds in that year.

Ormiston points out some interesting facts relating to the Lance Todd trophy. Up until 1956, the winner received a cash prize to invest in a fitting memento of their own choosing. Then the Red Devils Association of former players paid for a trophy for the award and a replica is presented to the winner to keep in perpetuity. This is done at an annual dinner which many former winners attend to mark the prestigious occasion.

Sean Long is the only player to have received the Lance Todd trophy three times. The first player to win a second award was Warrington's Gerry Helme. He is also unique in that he won the 1954 prize after the draw at Wembley against Halifax before a world record crowd attended the replay at Odsal Stadium in Bradford. The trophy has been shared on two occasions. The first was in 1965 in a final seen as one of the greatest in the game's history between Wigan and Hunslet, when Ray Ashby and Brian Gabbitas shared the award. In 2007, two St Helens players, Paul Wellens and Leon Pryce, were jointly awarded it .

In the vast majority of finals, the award has gone to a member of the winning team. However, there are a small group of players who have won the trophy despite being on the losing side. The first to do so was Bradford Northern's Cardiff born prop Frank Witcombe whose grandson Martin wrote an entertaining biography of the life of this larger-than-life character. He was given the award in the 1948 defeat by Wigan. In 1960, fellow Welshman Tommy 'Bomber' Harris was the next man to repeat the feat with Hull. The hooker, who hailed originally from Crumlin, played most of the match against Wakefield with concussion as his side went down to a record 38–5 defeat. My father attended the match and I recall him telling me that Harris tackled like a demon despite showing obvious signs of the head injury on a sweltering afternoon.

In the 1960s, Brian Gabbitas was the joint winner from the vanquished Hunslet team in 1965. Probably the most famous losing winner was Don Fox. In the notorious 'Watersplash' final against Leeds he famously missed the conversion of Ken Hirst's last minute try and the black and white footage still makes for agonising watching. In the current century, Gary Connelly, Kevin Sinfield, Niall Evans and Chris McQueen have joined this exclusive group of players to win a Lance Todd trophy in a beaten side.

My now grown-up son and daughter still laugh about a speech I delivered after my Bradford team had lost the final we had attended in 1996. Robbie Paul won the Lance Todd trophy having become the first man to score a Wembley hat-trick in a losing cause against my wife's hometown team of St Helens. In what amounted to an intention to divorce the team I had followed since 1964, I uttered the line they still quote back to me, "They've broken my bloody heart one time too many now!" We four attended the final and our divided loyalties lent an incendiary potential to the proceedings. Our full-back Nathan Graham was hit with an aerial assault of 'bombs', or 'up-and-unders' in old money, which he failed to diffuse by catching them cleanly, resulting in what felt like several Saints tries as a half time lead slipped through his and our fingers. Following that fateful day I had never seen Nathan Graham again. Then in 2021 he was interviewed as I watched Scotland in the World Cup on television and I was surprised to see he was their manager. I swear I had a flashback.

Lance Todd was a man of vision and courage who was in many ways ahead of his time. As a member of Baskerville's band of brothers who braved the condemnation and banishment of the union authorities on that groundbreaking first tour he is truly a founding father of international rugby league. His name lives on in a much-coveted award to ensure he will remain one of the immortals of our game.

23. Phil and John Holmes – Brothers in Arms

I recently went for lunch and a pint with Phil Holmes. He is secretary of the Leeds Players Association. He was kind enough to bring me a copy of his brother John's biography, *Reluctant Hero,* which his son, Phil Junior, had written in honour of his uncle. Following the Leeds legend's untimely death, Phil described how he had managed to hold himself together as well as one can, while making funeral plans and all the attendant arrangements following a family bereavement. On the morning of the funeral, the hearse drove slowly past the Headingley Stadium at which he played for some 22 years, as John made his final journey. Phil described how the outpouring of public grief and the palpable sense of collective loss left him in awe. He visibly filled up when he recalled the sheer wave of emotion he witnessed on that day, as adoring fans lined the streets to say farewell to a man they claimed as one of their own.

In recent times, we seem to have got better at expressing our emotions and have thankfully shunned 'the stiff upper lip', buttoned up approach in the grieving process. Phil delivered the eulogy for a much-loved brother, which was relayed on loudspeakers to the crowd who had gathered outside St. Michael's Church as well as the 700 plus who managed to fit inside the building. To puncture the mood of solemnity he explained that his brother seldom lost his temper, but did so on one particular occasion. The object of his anger was surprisingly his dear old mum. "Where's my *Beano* and *Dandy* delivery?" John demanded to know. "I've cancelled it," said his mother. "But why?" exclaimed the distraught lad. "Because you're 26 and have been away for six months in Australia," said his mum. This certainly chimed with me as I always receive a *Beano* annual every Christmas having complained to my wife that, "Christmas became crap when I got too old to get one every year!" John and I must have been kindred spirits with similar tastes in reading matter.

Phil explained that the Holmes family consisted of four children who arrived at four-year intervals. Brian was the eldest, then Phil, John and little sister Barbera, who sadly died at the tender age of 27. I asked if their father had been the gatekeeper to the game for them, but Phil said that as an Ulsterman who moved to Leeds, he had no interest in the sport. The rugby gene came from the maternal side of the family. Mum's brother Johnnie Feather played professionally for Leeds, Leigh and Oldham and took the boys to Headingley where they rubbed shoulders with the likes of the great Australian Arthur Clues. Tragically, uncle John died in a car crash as he drove back from training across the Pennines when he was just 28 years of age.

Many scholarly research articles have been written on the effect of family birth order and how it affects individuals in matters such as personality and attitude. What seems obvious to me, is that boys who have big brothers can often look after themselves as they have to fight hard to keep up with their elder siblings. This is particularly the case in matters pertaining to sport. Phil told me that he and John would take a ball – when they eventually got one – with them wherever they went. Prior to owning their own ball, scrunched up papers or, better still, a rolled-up woodwork apron, would have to suffice. The family home was situated alongside a school so the boys would climb over the wall to avail themselves of the wide-open spaces of the playground for their endless games of kick and catch.

Right: The statue of John Holmes at Headingley. The wording on the plinth is:

The Reluctant Hero
John S. Holmes
(21 March 1952 – 26 September 2009)
Born in Kirkstall
Leeds debut – 19 August 1968, last match – 10 September 1989
Club record appearance holder, 625 games
19 major finals, 14 winners' medals
Points scored 1,555 – 153 tries, 525 goals, 29 drop goals
World Cup winner 1972
Record Great Britain points in a match – 26
Great Britain appearances 20, England caps 7
"The greatest player to have worn the blue and amber" – Harry Jepson OBE

(Photo: Dave Jones)

Both lads were fans of the great Leeds stand-off, Lewis Jones and Phil explained how they both mastered the technique of kicking the ball across the panel to effect torpedo spin which causes the ball to fade in its descent by copying the Welsh maestro. The finest exponent of this skill who I attempted to emulate as a youngster was Terry Price.

Practice, they say, makes perfect. In a famous piece of psychological research in the 1970s published in *American Scientific,* Herbert Simon and William Chase came up with 'the ten thousand hours rule.' The two expounded the view that to fully perfect a skill takes that amount of time for an individual to truly master a particular technique. Doubtless the Holmes lads more than spent hours honing their rugby crafts in the streets around Kirkstall.

However, the world nearly missed seeing John playing the game. In my experience, the youngest children are often daredevils. Whether they are more confident because they have older 'minders' in attendance or they just like to show that they are capable beyond their years, we cannot know. Whatever the case, when John was four or five his intrepid spirit brought him to grief. Phil was with him as he clambered up a high wall in a cobbled snicket. The tiny, would-be Blondin walked, high wire style, along the coping stones before dismounting with a gymnastic flourish at the end. Unfortunately, a rusty metal spike was protruding out of the stonework and our young hero ripped open the back of his thigh. Fearing the reaction of his parents, Phil carried him home as the claret flowed,. John was rushed to hospital where he was sewn up both internally and externally. Thankfully, and more by luck than management, he had not torn tendons or his hamstring as this would have led to permanent incapacitation. Feeling responsible for his little brother, Phil went out and managed to procure a battered old pram from somewhere and for the many weeks when John could not get about under his own steam, Phil lovingly transported him around their boyhood haunts on this improvised mode of transportation.

Phil and John both attended Burley National School. The school was a hotbed of rugby league and both boys excelled, dominating neighbouring schools and collecting silverware in the Watson Trophy. Both lads played for the Leeds City Schools sides at a time when places in those teams were hotly contested by the large number of youngsters playing the game.

On leaving school, Phil and John both joined the newly established Kirkstall Boys Club. Phil says that it was great to finally be able to put on shoulder pads and get stuck in against older players. As the elder brother, it was Phil who first attracted the attention of the Leeds club. Although it was strictly against the rules, it appears to have been common practice for clubs to sign lads at 15 to ward off poachers from other clubs and to announce the signing on their 16th birthday. First team coach Joe Wareham and director Sir Noel Stockdale visited their home and Phil still has the building society book in which they deposited £500 to secure his services when he 'came of age'. John would join him at the club some years later.

Phil spent most of his time at Headingley learning his trade in the second team. Leeds had a plethora of talent in the centres with Les Dyl, Syd Hynes and even stand-off specialist Mick Shoebottom who could turn his hand to play centre. He did get one opportunity to play alongside John in the first team when he deputised for an injured John Atkinson on the wing. Phil admits to having had a thorough dislike of Syd Hynes who he "wanted to belt" for keeping him out of the first team. Syd now lives in Australia and Phil and the Leeds Players Association were instrumental in bringing a man, with whom he now shares a close friendship, over for a Hall of Fame event recently. Phil grew increasingly frustrated at his lack of opportunities at Leeds and expressed this to one of his neighbours who happened to be first team coach at Batley. He was persuaded to join the Mount Pleasant outfit and says that Batley was a "fantastic club."

During his years with the 'Gallant Youths', Phil played against some of the greats. The side included the classy Stan Gittens at full-back, and the pack contained the mighty 'Tank' Walker and Brian Taylor, who had both enjoyed great success with Dewsbury. For several seasons, the club volunteered to play in the Lancashire competition because extra money was given to the side agreeing to do this by the RFL.

Phil told me about playing against the colossus that was Billy Boston in his brief career at Blackpool Borough. Phil played centre to a slightly built speed merchant called Geoff Marsh, who lined up opposite the man-mountain. Holmes feared for his diminutive wingman so early in the piece he switched to the outside position and when Billy received the ball, Phil hit him with all he had in a tackle which by today's strict guidelines would have earned him a stretch in Armley. He knew that Boston would leap in off the wing to seek retribution at the earliest available opportunity. Phil told the acting half to miss him out on the next move down Boston's side knowing that Billy would employ his murderous smother tackle which was a famous feature of his repertoire. The instruction to miss him out was followed to the letter but Boston hit on suspicion and as he pinned Phil Holmes to the ground he growled a warning to him in his Welsh accent. The Batley centre was not cowed and gave Billy plenty more treatment during the match. When the referee blew for time Boston approached and Phil wondered if hostilities were to be continued. "Well played," grinned the Bomber.

Blackpool featured in Phil Holmes' career again sometime later. He was playing against the 'Seasiders' when someone stood on his heel and he was forced to leave the field. In a most unusual gesture, Borough's manager Albert Fearnley, who had enjoyed great success with Halifax in the 1960s, went onto the pitch to help the injured Batley man off. As he put his arm around the player to support his weight, he quietly mouthed the words, "Call me next week, we want to sign you." This was certainly a novel approach to conducting a transfer negotiation. Phil still has the programme on which Fearnley wrote his phone number.

It transpired that the damage was more serious than Phil thought and was in fact a torn Achilles tendon, a career threatening injury. Their family had moved to Liverpool where he had opened a new DIY business, but they decided to relocate to Blackpool where his sister Barbera and her husband Chris had a hotel. A Borough director pulled some strings to get his Achilles operated on, but the period of inactivity had led to him gaining weight. In the summer he asked if he could train with the team, simply to get back into shape. They invited him to play in some pre-season friendlies and noticing a loss of some of his former pace a mutual decision was made for him to move to the second row.

One of Phil's most treasured memories is of a visit to Headingley with his Blackpool teammates. They travelled across the Pennines, but were delayed on their journey. The players were forced to change on the bus due to pressure of time. That week the club had sacked coach Graham Rees after a string of poor results so circumstances did not augur well. Leeds took the opportunity to rest some players given their opponents lowly status and John Holmes and David Ward were on the bench. By half-time the men in tangerine were still in with a shout and Phil said he warned the Borough players at half-time that Leeds would probably send on their two international substitutes which they duly did. Phil took an early opportunity to collar his little brother in the second half and taunt him that they were about to lose. His prediction came to pass and Phil said that John was pretty livid given that he was a "sore loser." It was the legendary Green Bay Packers' coach Vince Lombardi who said, "Show me a good loser and I'll show you a loser." Phil certainly dined out on that victory and told me, "I never let him forget it!"

I read somewhere that the renowned horticulturist and landscaping genius Capability Brown had a younger brother who only did window boxes, called Inability Brown. This may or may not be true. I spoke with Phil about how it felt to have more famous kin or to be constantly introduced as "John Holmes's brother." He laughed and gave a shrug and I could tell that he genuinely did not feel he lived in the shadows. Wally Messenger may have been less famous than brother Dally, or Brian Sullivan may not have enjoyed the same star billing as brother Clive, but in both cases the less famous sibling *did* make it into the professional ranks. So it is with Phil who enjoyed many years in the game. Indeed, he and his own son Phil Junior, who wrote his uncle's biography, both received their heritage numbered certificates in the same ceremony at Batley, as the son followed in his father's footsteps.

John Holmes' burst onto the scene in a record breaking Lazenby Cup game against Hunslet as a 16-year-old as Bev Risman finally succumbed to a persistent knee injury. The youngster contributed 10 goals and a try to announce his arrival. His statistics are phenomenal. But it is not about the maths, it is about the man. Suffice to say he played in

625 games for the club in a career which began in 1968 and spanned 22 years. He appeared in 19 cup finals in various competitions, winning 14. In that time, he played for Great Britain in an era where players of the calibre of Alan Hardisty, Roger Millward, Frank Myler, Dennis O'Neill and David Watkins were all vying for the number six shirt.

I asked Phil what he believed was John's rugby superpower. Without a moment's hesitation he replied, "awareness." He told me that Alan Smith had described how in a mud bath at Oldham, the maestro told him to stand out wide as he was going to put him over in the corner and he did exactly that. Gary Mercer said to Phil that when he joined the club, John said to him, "You find a gap and I'll find you."

Phil Hogan from Hull Kingston Rovers was chatting to Phil at the recent England versus Tonga game at Headingley as they reminisced at a Rugby League Cares reception. He described his international debut in a fiery contest with France. When he was waiting with trepidation to take his first drive, John provided him with a pass to fire him through a hole in the French line and over for a try. Hogan said he was a master of communication on the field and that might only involve a look or a nod as he explained, "If he said it, we did it."

John was the youngest member of the World Cup winning team in France in 1972. Phil told me that he was not due to play in the final because Dennis O'Neill from Widnes had been given the nod. Back in those less abstemious times when the odd drink was taken in the team bonding process, O'Neill was performing a balancing trick involving some stacked bar stools. His resulting injury from the fall ruled him out of the final and John benefitted from his colleague's bad luck.

Leeds were regular visitors to Wembley during John's time at the club. Phil explained that supporters sometimes forget that he did not see John play as much as they did. In those pre-video days, live television or attendance in the flesh were the only options and he was playing at the same time as his brother. He did sometimes get to see his cup exploits though because he said that the clubs he represented tended to exit competitions before Leeds. John played in four Wembley cup finals, winning two. He received his first winner's medal in 1977 in a win over Widnes. Many believe that his defining performance came a year later.

In 1978, Leeds played St Helens beneath the Twin Towers. As the match entered the final quarter, the Loiners found themselves 10 points in arrears. The clock was against them as John took control of affairs. He served up three passes to create three tries and then topped off a virtuoso performance with a piece of magic to grace the great occasion. Leeds were pinned back in their own half and needed to advance down the field to get in range to score. Phil described how his brother made a 50-yard break down field before being brought to ground by the desperate Saints defence. He then slid into position to slot over a left footed drop-goal as he was felled by an opponent who was unable to prevent the *coup de grace*.

As Phil Cookson lifted him to his feet, John allowed himself to jubilantly punch the air. So late in the day were John Holmes' heroics that the members of the press who voted for the Lance Todd trophy had already awarded it to 'Gorgeous' George Nicolls of St Helens. In the dressing room afterwards some of the journalists apologised to John, who with typical good grace said he was not disappointed as the team's victory was all that mattered.

When John Holmes retired from first team rugby, he gladly turned out in the 'A' Team. This, I believe, speaks volumes about a man who loved our game for its own sake. The enormous benefit this gave to youngsters destined for future stardom, such as David

Creasser, cannot be underestimated. The skills passed on from master tradesman to apprentice proved invaluable. It is credit to John that he was willing to serve the club in this capacity and he later went on to coach the second team.

One particular anecdote which Phil Holmes shared is indicative of the 'reluctant hero's' modest character. John was on a bus when a group of youths spotted him. They did not behave inappropriately but were obviously excited to spot the star player and were loudly pointing out, "that's John Holmes, that is!" John quietly got off the bus and waited for the next one. Phil was less awkward about dining out on local celebrity status. He told me that in their younger days the two of them bore a close resemblance to one another. Back in the days when they were footloose and fancy free, on nights out, if approached by young ladies and asked if he was John Holmes, Phil would respond, "Indeed I am!"

John was only 57 when he died from cancer and his passing saddened the whole of the rugby league fraternity. Shortly after his death, former colleagues and opponents stood shoulder to shoulder at the Super League qualifying semi-final against Catalans. They stretched the full width of the Headingley pitch and many a tear was shed by these old warriors as they mourned one of their own. When Leeds won the Grand Final the next week, captain Kevin Sinfield dedicated the win to the memory of the lad from Kirkstall whose statue now graces the car park adjoining the South Stand. In praising John's ability to use his spatial awareness to put others in the clear with his precision passing, Phil may be somewhat biassed. But this more objective assessment in *The Independent* paying tribute to him seems to back up his brother's claims entirely as it says, "It is as a creator of tries for others ... that John Holmes was peerless, with a rare gift for getting exactly the right weight on a pass to put a teammate through a gap that others had not even seen." One spectator entered the following accolade on a website of condolences which neatly sums up John Holmes unique gifts. "Rugby League has lost its Leonardo di Vinci - a true artist among the artisans."

24. Billy Thompson MBE

All sports need officials to rule on the laws of the game and to oversee the principles and practices of fair play. Without referees, there simply would be no game. However, when I consider why someone might take on the role, I find myself being puzzled. Why would you put yourself through it? They must be very special men and women who can develop skin so thick they could put a rhino's backside to shame. Thankfully these brave – or foolhardy – individuals are ready to take up the thankless task of adjudication and I say, "God bless 'em!"

Odsal Stadium, Bradford was the shrine at which I worshipped throughout my boyhood years. One feature of the ground which gave it a unique feel was the location of the dressing rooms. Unlike other venues where the players emerged at ground level from the side of the pitch, Odsal's facilities at that time were situated at the top of the huge bowl. Players and officials had to walk down a slope about 100 metres long before descending the steep, railway sleeper steps, to reach the field of play. This lent a certain intimacy to proceedings as the combatants had to walk through the crowds which lined the path. The proximity this afforded the spectators, meant we could smell the liniment and wintergreen and see the glistening Vaseline on the ears and eyebrows of our heroes as we gave them a hearty pat on the back to wish them well, as we eagerly anticipated what we were about to receive.

However, following the game, the mood music could be quite different. I recall one bespectacled old chap who could have only been about five foot tall, who wore a blue gabardine overcoat, who was an ever-present post-match critic. In a megaphone voice, he would provide a full and frank appraisal of players' performances if their efforts had fallen below his expectations, always in the most Anglo-Saxon expletives. But the crowd's ire was generally reserved for one man in particular.

Referees must have felt a high degree of trepidation when they were told they were to officiate at a Bradford Northern home game. At the conclusion of the match, they ran the gauntlet of returning to the safe haven of the changing rooms, through a crowd of angry spectators. They would be surrounded by a phalanx of police officers and the experience must have felt like being an aristocrat in revolutionary France being carted off to the guillotine on a tumbrel, to the hysterical screams of the baying mob!

One incident springs to mind following a particularly controversial afternoon involving a referee in the 1970s called Mr Campbell. As he ascended the pathway of pain, I noticed an angry looking lady walking a few steps behind the official. As the abuse reached a crescendo, the brave woman shouted to one man who was reverting to dreadful personal insults, "Oy! You! – That's my husband so shut yer face!" We would all do well to remember that even referees have loved ones.

One man who would have suffered these frightening experiences on many occasions was Billy Thompson. There were some high-profile whistlers in the 1960s and 1970s, like 'Sergeant Major' Eric Clay, as Eddie Waring dubbed him, or the youthful Fred Lindop, but probably the foremost exponent of the refereeing craft was William Henry Thompson from Huddersfield. Stern of countenance, with slicked black Brylcreemed hair, he carried himself with all the assurance of one who was not to be messed with.

Although his father and uncle had played rugby league professionally, Billy's first passion was for the round ball game. A promising junior, he had been on the books at Gillingham, but failed to make the grade. Returning north, Billy decided to try his hand at refereeing and officiated in his first game in an Under-17s encounter between Rastrick and Queens Road. By 1966, he had progressed to the senior referees list.

The world of sports adjudication was very different back when Billy began his career. Nowadays, referees and umpires have all manner of technical and video evidence to assist in decision making. A small army of backup staff, hidden in underground bunkers like espionage agents acting on behalf of international intelligence agencies, await their call to action. In rugby league games, where the television cameras are present – in recent times that means every Super League game – the referee seldom rejects the opportunity to send his decision 'upstairs' for a second opinion.

Football was one of the last sports to embrace technological intervention in the form of VAR. Many supporters now repeat the mantra, "Be careful what you wish for." Spectators and pundits increasingly despair as the unseen judges back at a business estate called Stockley Park suck the spontaneous joy from every premiership goal as they draw lines on a screen to see if someone's little finger had strayed offside. In cricket, players have a certain number of chances to overturn an umpire's on field call with the DRS system. In tennis, it is unlikely we will see the antics of a young John McEnroe ever again berating the umpire, "You cannot be serious!" as line judges are increasingly replaced by beeps and buzzers.

In rugby union, they have not so much embraced technology as venerated the video in a process of deification to the new futuristic world of virtual wonder. Miked up officials gather beneath the big screen in pursuit of 'conclusive evidence' to substantiate every decision as players stand by and shiver in the cold as deliberations threaten to interfere with spectators' travel plans as they drag on in the interminable pursuit of truth. Indeed, during a player's period of temporary exclusion on a yellow card, what seems to be something akin to a full judicial hearing can take place. The felon will then learn his fate which could be an upgrade to a red card or perhaps in future, a short custodial sentence.

Back in Billy's heyday, his only recourse to assistance was from his two touch judges who would periodically sprint onto the pitch wildly waving their flags to draw attention to some unsavoury, off the ball misdemeanour. Other than that, the on-field adjudicator of the laws was on his own.

Thompson was a man for the big occasion and he handled over 500 matches. He took charge of 28 finals in major competitions, including Championships, Challenge and County Cups. He was often the go-to official for test matches and he officiated in 17 international matches. In 1973, he refereed all three Ashes tests at Wembley, Headingley and Wilderspool as Australia won the series 2–1. In 1977, he had the honour of refereeing the World Cup Final at the Sydney Cricket Ground when Australia beat Great Britain 13–12.

The Australians must have held Billy in high regard because they invited him to officiate in the first State of Origin game in 1980. The NSWRL insisted on there being a neutral referee in the interstate game which is now such an integral feature of the fixture calendar in Australia. The game was played in Brisbane and Thompson was chosen because of his reputation for letting the game flow and for allowing players to settle differences between themselves in the time-honoured manner.

Queensland won a brutal, physical encounter 20–10 in front of a sell-out Lang Park crowd and the rivalry which boils to this day had been set in train.

In that same year, Thompson had overseen the Anglo-French encounter in Narbonne. He had chalked off a late French 'try' for a forward pass which caused the Gallic crowd to erupt in frenzied anger! The after-match scenes made even the most rabid referee baiting at Odsal seem a veritable cake-walk. Billy and British team manager Bill Fallowfield had to be protected by the Gendarmerie in the dressing room as the home supporters called for their blood. Eventually they escaped in hastily designed disguises via a back door. Fallowfield complained to the French rugby league and refused any further cross channel fixtures until he received undertakings as to future on and off field conduct of 'les Tricolores'.

Billy Thompson took charge of three Wembley finals. In 1971 he earned a certain notoriety as he became the first referee to send a player off in a Challenge Cup final. The circumstances of the dismissal are still hotly contested. Leeds's Syd Hynes reputedly head-butted Alex Murphy, leaving him flat out, or feigning injury, depending on whose version of events you wish to believe. Whatever the reality, Hynes had to undertake the solitary march back to the tunnel. A particular story which Phil Holmes, brother of Leeds legend John, told me, leads me to believe that Billy may have harboured retrospective doubts about the veracity of Alex Murphy's conduct that day.

Phil explained that he was captaining Batley in the first game of the following season in a match which Billy Thompson was refereeing. 'The Gallant Youths' chairman had volunteered them to play in the Lancashire section of the league. Following the Wembley victory the revolving door on Alex's career continued to spin and he found himself as player manager at Warrington. Phil told me that Murphy was working his magic and single handedly ripping their defences apart with his pinpoint passing and kicking game. He turned to Batley's big burly prop Jack Thomas and instructed the forward to 'deal' with the maestro. At the earliest convenience Thomas acted on his skipper's instructions, leaving Alex prostrate, clutching a fractured cheek. Phil Holmes said that he always thought of his teammate Thomas as not being the sharpest knife in the drawer but he was proved wrong on this occasion. As Thompson approached the prop to take action over the incident the forward complained - "Bloody 'ell Billy! It's sodding Wembley all over again!" Thompson barked at the stricken Alex, "Get up Murphy." Talk about 'give a dog a bad name!'

Thompson's second appearance in a Challenge Cup final came in 1978, when Saints registered a try before the scheduled three o'clock kick off when Billy started proceedings a tad prematurely. His final game at Wembley proved to be the last game in a long career. Wigan and Widnes contested the final in 1984 as Billy called time on his refereeing days following injury.

After hanging up his whistle, he became a popular figure on the after dinner speaking circuit. Possessing excellent comic timing and a boundless supply of anecdotes, Billy would have done justice to himself at 'The Wheeltappers and Shunters Club'! He told one story about Castleford's 'Big Dennis' Hartley. In one particularly belligerent encounter, the giant prop felled an opponent with a sweetly timed uppercut and was beckoned over to receive his just desserts. Billy remonstrated with the forward saying: "He wasn't even looking at you Dennis!", only to receive the immediate retort from the big man, "Best time to hit 'em that is Billy!"

In another story, he explained that he had something of a run-in with a steward at Wilderspool. The member of staff appears to have been a bit of a 'Jobsworth' and was insistent that the match official should park his car in the space designated, which was clearly marked by a plaque which read, 'Match Referee's Car.' "Don't be bloody stupid'" said the street wise official, "I'm not going to tell 'em where to find me after the game, now am I!"

There is one story told about Billy Thompson, which although apocryphal, sums up his attitude to a sport which he saw as a man's game where a certain toleration of rough house tactics was part and parcel of what went on. Following an all-in brawl in a Hull derby match he was handling, only the Rovers' full-back kept out of the melee. Eventually Billy, with the help of his touch judges, quelled the disturbance. When order had been restored, he summoned over the last line of defence who had refrained from joining in the violent mayhem. Much to the innocent player's surprise and consternation, the official pointed to the dressing rooms and sent him off. The full-back argued with Billy, asking what was the nature of his crime. "Cowardice!" bellowed Billy.

Billy Thompson was a great servant to rugby league. In 1985 he was awarded the MBE for his contributions to the game. When injury forced his retirement, he was given a testimonial by the RFL in recognition of his tremendous impact on the sport. He worked as an engineer at David Brown's Tractors in Huddersfield for many years and was a regular spectator at Huddersfield Giants' games until his passing at the age of 85 in 2021. The legendary Wigan and Great Britain centre Eric Ashton commented "When the history of Rugby League is written, fitting tribute will be paid to many of the great referees – and foremost among those names will be Billy Thompson."

While Eric Ashton is recognised as a wonderful stylish threequarter who would seldom deal in the more unseemly aspects of the game, Jim Mills was a somewhat different proposition. The Welsh prop was no stranger to a visit to the disciplinary committee. We could be forgiven for assuming that an authority figure like Billy Thompson would be the *bete noire* of a pantomime figure like the giant Widnes forward. Yet following Billy's death, 'Big Jim' added his thoughts, tweeting, "Without doubt, my favourite referee and yes, he did send me off! Rest well Billy." High praise indeed.

25. The road most travelled – Geoff Clarkson

Nigel O'Flaherty Johnson has been one of my closest friends for a quarter of a century. In that time, we have shared life's exhilarating highs and crushing lows. With the obvious exception of my wife with her saintly patience, I would not wish to encounter what Kipling called 'these twin imposters' with anyone else. Nige is a wit, a raconteur, a sage and a special soul. He wears his great wisdom lightly in his personal relationships and in his professional work as the Leeds Rhinos Player Welfare Manager.

A wonderful documentary *As Good As It Gets,* produced by *City Talking Productions*, tells the story of 'the Golden Generation' at Leeds; Kevin Sinfield, Rob Burrow, Kylie Leuluai, Jamie Peacock, JJB et al. With interviews and fly on the wall footage, we get to examine the bonds of brotherhood which made the unlikeliest treble success come to fruition as the final exclamation mark on the careers of these icons. I would be willing to bet that every one of these major protagonists would acknowledge the essential part Nige played for them during any moments of self-doubt in that remarkable 2015 season. I also know that coach Brian McDermott valued his wise counsel in those turbulent times. Nigel personifies back-bone.

The world screeched to a juddering halt in 2020 with the arrival of the Covid epidemic. We all encountered our own private versions of hell as the virus and subsequent 'social distancing' measures visited a plague, both virtual and metaphorical, on all our houses. Some suffered more than others. Nigel's lovely wife Theresa was away in Ireland caring for her elderly, ailing mum when the government announced lockdown measures. The devoted couple found themselves separated for months on end by the Irish Sea. Just prior to the pandemic, Nigel and I had begun preparing resources with a group of former-players who were generously working to put together a project to support a men's mental wellbeing initiative. We didn't want to lose impetus with the important work so we continued as best we could using *Zoom.*

Until this point in my life, the only connotations that the word "zoom" held for me was as a gadget to enhance photography, a 1960s tri-coloured ice lolly shaped like a spaceship from *Thunderbirds* or a catchy musical ditty by *Fat Larry's Band* played on Radio One. As well as saving the *Ahead of the Game* project, *Zoom* now helped preserve mine and Nigel's sanity. We used the virtual medium to set up our own 'Cookery Club.' As politicians partied (as we were to discover subsequently), and as ministers engaged in tongue hockey tussles with work colleagues or advisors drove to Barnard Castle to test their eyesight, those of us further down the food chain stuck assiduously to the new rules.

This is how it worked. We independently sourced some simple ingredients either on-line or within permitted parameters, in-store. We agreed on a recipe and supplemented the food with a couple of unusual guest ales, say Citra Ass Down, Hoppy Ending or perhaps a Smooth Hoperator. At the allotted time we would make contact on *Zoom* (generally after a period of silence and much cussing about mute buttons) and the exercise of the unspeakable creating the uneatable would begin. As we created our culinary delights and discussed the relative merits and subtle undertones of the beverages on offer, we enhanced the quality of our virtual social contact with challenges based on our shared obsession with rugby league trivia and history. Just your typical lads' night out really – only in.

Right: Geoff Clarkson playing for Leeds.
(Courtesy *Rugby League Journal*)

Lists were generally to the fore in the intellectual challenges we set for ourselves. As I outlined some simple culinary techniques and we rehearsed the relative merits of the chiffonade over the julienne, or more likely gave simple instructions like, "don't put the bloody yoke in Nige!" or "not a sodding *tablespoon* of chilli powder you soft sod!", we would consider – players who have played for both Batley and Bradford Northern or Leeds internationals beginning with the letter 'S'. One particular evening when Nige must have been in a particularly reflective, romantic frame of mind, doubtless missing his Irish ailleacht's charms, we even compiled names of players who might make up an *Aphrodisiacal XIII*. From memory some of those selected to represent this love-lorn lot included the Newloves, John and Paul, the Valentine brothers Dave and Rob, from the Scottish borders, Nicky Kiss came in handy for some tongue tennis, Paul Rose and Jamie Bloem provided the floral tributes and Australian hardman from the 1950s, Peter Dimond doubtless wished to show up as a girl's best friend. You get the picture!

As we made one particular gastronomic delight featuring a leg of liver and a whole shoulder of kidney, we set about the challenge of compiling one of our longest catalogues in those monotonous isolating weeks. How many clubs could we name which Geoff Clarkson played for back in the day? As we set about this huge undertaking, we shared what we knew about this itinerant journeyman who epitomised the phrase, "have boots, will travel."

Geoff Clarkson began his rugby career at Wakefield Rugby Union Club in the early 1960s. He was in good company as several other future league men also played in the black and amber of the College Road club. Their officials must have felt a sense of dejection at the constant stream out of their doors of their players into the professional game. Les Sheard was a contemporary of Clarkson and he explained how the club haemorrhaged personnel.

These 'crossdressers' as Wakefield fan David Hinchliffe MP called them included Les himself who initially took the professional bait with Castleford before enjoying his most successful period at Belle Vue. He then saw out his playing days with York. Teammates David Garthwaite, Ray Spencer and John Archer all became Dreadnoughts. Joining them with Trinity was prop David Jeanes who played in the 'watersplash final' in 1968 and later enjoyed great success at Leeds. Jeanes was also in the Great Britain team who drew 10–10 with Australia to lift the World Cup in 1972. Other defectors from Wakefield RFC included Gary van Bellan from the famous clan of giant brothers who represented Bradford Northern with distinction for several seasons, Alan Lownes who enjoyed success with Castleford and David Stevens who crossed the Pennines to join Wigan.

A sporting wag once said of Scottish football manager Tommy Docherty that he had more clubs than Jack Nichlaus. Another notorious nomad in the round ball game was the beanpole striker Peter Crouch who served 10 clubs. The gangly goal scorer was asked by one pundit what he thought he would have been had he not been a professional footballer. Quick as a flash he retorted, "a virgin." Neither of these men from the world of association football though could compete with Geoff Clarkson who made 12 moves in his long career with 10 different clubs.

The tall blonde second row forward had caught the eye of the union county selectors and received a Yorkshire cap in 1965. Shortly afterwards, Wakefield Trinity moved in to take him across the Merrie City to begin his epic rugby league odyssey. Clarkson enjoyed his first taste of silverware by appearing for Trinity in the replay of the 1967 Championship Final. Trinity beat St Helens 21–9 at Swinton following a 4–4 draw at Headingley four days earlier. In the 1967 season he repeated the feat of gaining selection for Yorkshire as he had done at union when he was picked to play in two county matches.

In 1968, Geoff was tempted to join Bradford Northern as my hometown club splashed the cash to recruit some much-needed forward grunt to supply a platform for a glittering array of backs like Berwyn Jones, Ian Brooke and Geoff Wrigglesworth. Clarkson was part of a recruitment drive in a period which saw the likes of Frank Foster, Terry Clawson and Terry Ramshaw beef up a forward pack in need of some grit and heft. In a two-year spell at Odsal, Clarkson made 58 appearances, scoring eight tries.

Alex Murphy had joined Leigh in 1966 in controversial circumstances. 'The Mouth' was as shrewd an operator as the game of rugby league has ever seen and he was assembling a team of journeymen players which would eventually scale unprecedented heights in the game. Murphy recognised the qualities which Geoff Clarkson embodied and he lured the second rower to join his Hilton Park project.

As a forerunner to even greater glory, Leigh lifted the Lancashire Cup in 1970 with a victory over their much-vaunted neighbours St Helens. But Geoff's finest hour came in 1971 when Murphy led his team to Challenge Cup glory in the 24–7 victory over Leeds in one of the greatest David and Goliath showings ever at Wembley Stadium. Tony Barrow played stand-off for Leigh on that famous occasion and recalled that his side had "... Paul Grimes and Geoff Clarkson in the second row – the pair were big and both hard as nails." Along with fellow back row legend, the jovial butcher Peter Smethurst, they provided protection for as Sawyer put it, "If there was any trouble you knew they were at the back of you all the time." It was no coincidence that when the mercurial Murph left for Warrington immediately after this triumph that he persuaded Clarkson to join him at Wilderspool where he made 36 appearances in the primrose and blue.

Clarkson's itchy feet brought him back across the Pennines to his native county in 1972 as he joined Leeds where he remained for a three-year stint making 68 appearances for the club. Pastures new beckoned as Geoff joined the Minster Men at Clarence Street in 1975 and he racked up 36 games for York before moving on to Bramley. In 1978, Clarkson returned to the place where it all began when he rejoined Wakefield Trinity. Shortly after his return, he was approached by Hull Kingston Rovers and duly joined the Craven Park club making 51 appearances for the Robins.

Former Wakefield friend and colleague Les Sheard shared an amusing anecdote about this phase of Geoff's career which also sheds light on the business model adopted by the much travelled forward in playing the system to bolster his earnings from the game to supplement his wages from his successful building firm. The two men were friends who lived in the same village of Cawthorne near Barnsley. Geoff had joined the Robins, but was finding travelling alone on the M62 something of a chore. Les was playing for Trinity at the time and his friend suggested he should request a move to the Rovers. He explains, "Geoff was the consummate operator when it came to chasing the readies." He told Les that the club secretary was known as 'Splattercash' and would turn a blind eye to them claiming individual expenses while sharing the burden of transport with its attendant costs. Les declined the offer, but the refusal to go along with the plan would have implications. "While playing against the Robins in 1978 at Belle Vue," Sheard explains," Geoff exacted his terrible revenge. I ran into one of his tackles during one of my sojourns down the blind-side and he tipped me with a savage spear-tackle (they weren't illegal in those days)" and the resultant inoperable injury to his rotator-cuff limited his effectiveness thereafter. However, Les was to eventually have the last laugh.

While playing for York against Clarkson in an Oldham shirt, Sheard's head collided with his pal's nasal orifice basically rupturing the big man's snout! "While he was lying bleeding and groggy on the ground and I was rubbing my head, I could hear him muttering, "You bastard Les!" It was the ultimate revenge, because no one was more proud of his manly good looks than Geoff!"

Clarkson returned to Bradford Northern in 1980 when coach Peter Fox secured the services of the veteran forward and he played in 21 matches for Northern before leaving for the Watersheddings and his subsequent encounter with Les Sheard. After 11 appearances for the Roughyeds, Geoff re-joined Leigh. Alex Murphy had returned to coach the club and took the old warhorse to help the club to win the 1981–82 Division One Championship for the only time in their history. Clarkson also collected a second Lancashire Cup winners medal a decade after winning his first with the club in 1970. Leigh beat Widnes 8–3 in 1981. Geoff finally called a halt to his playing days with a brief spell at Featherstone Rovers before retiring in 1983. Sadly, this maverick soul with a wanderlust of epic proportions was taken from us in 2001. Geoff Clarkson died from cancer at the age of 57 shortly after enjoying a reunion with the 1971 Leigh squad who were feted by their faithful supporters 30 years on from that unforgettable day at Wembley.

26. Cross code conversions

There is a particular flight of fancy I sometimes allow myself to indulge in. I imagine speaking once again to my dearly departed dad who checked out in 1988. Should some supreme power grant us an hour together in the celestial version of the *Dog and Gun*, how would he view some of the astounding developments of the modern era? Would he believe the toppling of the Berlin Wall or the advent of the internet? Could he grasp the fact that everyone has a computer in their pocket no bigger than the size of a packet of fags? Would his jaw not drop at news of the Covid lockdown, the state of the NHS or the price of a pint? But what I think he would find it hardest to get his head around, would be the reversal of roles between rugby league and rugby union. I can hardly conceive with what incredulity he would receive the news that it is now the XV-a-side code which plunders our talent pool rather than vice-versa.

On the occasion of the opening fixture of the 2024 Six Nations Championship, I was mildly amused to witness the pre Ireland versus France interviews with coaches of the respective teams. Andy Farrell and Shaun Edwards both laid out their game plans in their 'roonded' Lancastrian brogues, having been former colleagues at Wigan in their halcyon days as cup kings and World Club Champions. Yet for how long have the chaps from the other side of the great divide told us that their game is so complex and sophisticated that knuckle scraping northerners could never grasp all its intricate subtleties? To the alicadoos of the 'senior code', league is just a modest little game with much to be modest about. They argue that union is to league, what *chateau neuf-du-pape* is to Tizer or what Jamaican Blue Mountain coffee is to Maxwell House.

However, nowadays it seems a CV including a comprehensive background in the XIII-a-side code is a vital prerequisite to securing a coaching post in union. 'Sir Kev' is the skills and kicking coach with England, Mike Forshaw is in charge of defence in the Principality and, at club level, former Bradford Bulls scrum-half Paul Deacon is the coaching supremo at high-flying Sale.

To this list we may add some of the players who have successfully transitioned to light up the now professional union game. Witness the superstar status to which Jason Robinson was elevated following his conversion. Iestyn Harris see-sawed between the two codes winning caps in both forms of the game. Remember the fanfare with which Twickers hailed the arrival of Sam Burgess at Bath, before throwing him under the bus as the scapegoat for England's slipshod performances in the 2015 World Cup. Nor is the trend to cross code trafficking peculiar to the northern hemisphere. In Australasia, league luminaries like Wendell Sailor, the controversial Israel Folau, Brad Thorn and Sonny Bill Williams were all poached and went to the dark side to ply their trades.

The direction of travel had, for over a century, been in the opposite direction. Prior to the advent of 'open' payments to players, there was an era, sometimes referred to as 'shamateurism', where 'boot money' and 'expenses' were often the order of the day. It was at this time that the union lads were prey for northern clubs. The wages of sin for any player courting approaches from rugby league clubs were akin to a sporting death sentence. Merely speaking to representatives of league clubs could lead to an automatic life 'sine die' ban.

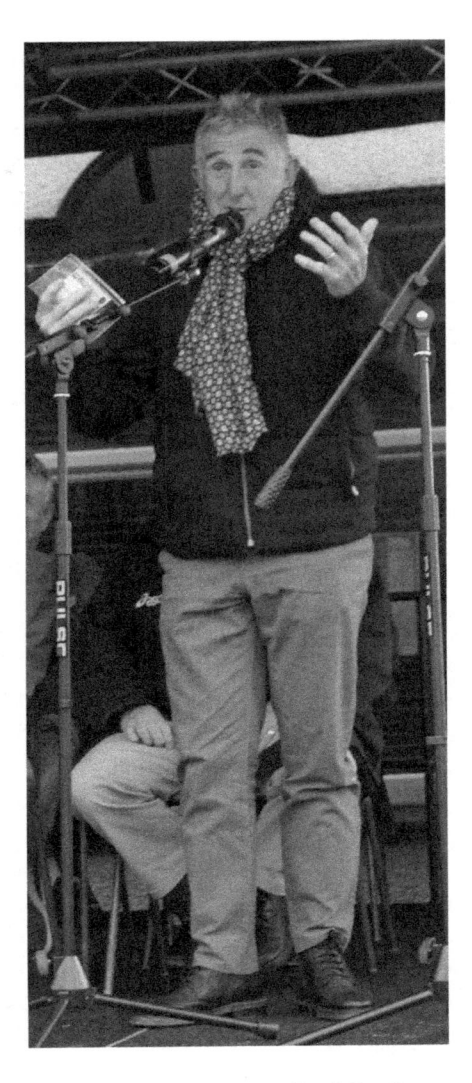

Top left: Terry Price, who signed for Bradford Northern. (Courtesy *Rugby League Journal*)

Top right: Jonathan Davies speaking at the unveiling of the statue of Roy Francis in Brynmawr. (Photo: Peter Lush)

Left: Mike Nicholas, who signed for Warrington from Aberavon and had a successful rugby league career. (Courtesy Gary Slater)

Take the case of Steve Ford of Cardiff in 1985. His brother Phil had embarked on a successful professional career with Warrington in the 1980s and Steve accepted an opportunity to play in a couple of trial games for Leeds. Although he was offered a contract by the club, he decided to return to Wales. However, his appearance at Headingley had been spotted and he received a life ban, even though he had received no money. The banishment was eventually lifted and Steve Ford went on to gain a couple of caps for the national side.

I enjoyed a pint and a chat with Mike Nicholas at the Grand Final some years ago. Like members of my family, he was from Aberavon and he added with a mischievous grin that when he signed for Warrington, the WRU sent him a letter telling him he must never darken their door again! He told me with a mischievous grin that he had it framed and has it on his toilet wall. "They behaved like the bloody politburo back then," he laughed.

Keith Dallimore, a friend of mine from Cardiff, who played club rugby in the early 1970s, told me of one particular incident which reflected the paranoia regarding the contamination of professionalism. He played for his club against a steelworks team based in Newport who included a 'ringer' who had played rugby league. All of the 29 other players who shared the field with the former-league player received a letter signed by the official of the WRU, Bill Clement, telling them that they had compromised their amateur status by sharing the field with this renegade, counselling them against any further misdemeanours.

Given the risks involved, approaches were always clandestine affairs. As a result, the rumour mill was always rife as spectators would tap their noses in a knowing fashion having received a juicy slice of gossip that, "We're getting Barry John" or "Gareth Edwards is in the bag". Clubs would have an elaborate network of agents and scouts with their ears to the ground. Any significant change of circumstances like unemployment, a disciplinary fall out or an unexpected pregnancy of a partner might suddenly render a player to be susceptible to the lure of league lucre. However, scouting was not without its own risks and representatives would run the gauntlet of falling foul of some very physical, summary justice, should their spying missions be discovered.

A big name capture from the union code was always a red-letter day for our game. Wales was the source of the richest pickings. There are far more parallels between the valleys and northern industrial centres where the two codes of rugby thrive and the loam for potential recruitment is thus much more fertile ground for northern scouts. Some English stars did come over however. Salford signed Mike Coulman and Keith Fielding, who went on to star in the successful television contest *Superstars*. Barrow signed international stand-off Tom Brophy and Wakefield secured the services of the chunky scrum-half, Mike Lampkowski.

The Widnes coach back in the 1980s, Doug Laughton, was no stranger to the rugby union market and in 1987 he pulled off a masterstroke with the signing of Hackney born paceman Martin 'Chariots' Offiah. Laughton spotted the flyer playing at Twickenham in the Middlesex Sevens and backed his judgement to take the winger to Naughton Park. Alex Murphy had seen Offiah previously and recommended him to the St Helens board but they rejected the proposal deeming him to be "unco-ordinated." Martin Offiah became one of the game's greats, winning the Lance Todd trophy twice after transferring to Wigan. On the second occasion he did so, it was in the 1994 Final when he went 90 metres to touch down in one of the greatest tries ever seen at Wembley. Sinking to his knees in celebration, his gesture is captured for posterity on the Wembley Statue immortalising Offiah kneeling, head gazing to the heavens with hands outstretched, as if in prayerful contemplation. He played 33 games for Great Britain and famously scored 10 tries for Wigan in a single match against Leeds.

Rochdale Hornets adopted a novel approach to recruiting players from rugby union. Their Chairman, Arthur Walker, was visiting Australia in 1960 when he decided to take in a game involving the Fijian union team who were on tour. Two players, who were cousins, caught his eye. They were centre Orisi Dawai and winger Josefa 'Joe' Levula, who was also the Fijian sprint champion. The players were invited to sign for the club and the pair arrived in the Lancashire cotton town in 1961, but only after the King of Fiji, fearing a talent drain from the island, initially denied consent for them to leave. On his death the pair were allowed to pursue their new life. Levula enjoyed great success scoring 37 tries in 80 matches before transferring to Bradford Northern for £1,500 when the Yorkshire club reformed in 1964. Sadly, Dawai was tragically young when he died suddenly in Birch Hill hospital in the town in 1966. On his headstone in Rochdale Cemetery, 9,000 miles from his homeland, he is described as, "Fiji's greatest sportsman."

Rochdale continued to encourage players from the island to join them and in 1962 they signed forwards Laitia Ravouvou and Voate Druie. Two years later they brought over their most successful convert Aspai Toga, who formed a barnstorming second row partnership with Ravouvou. Toga's talent brought him to the attention of the star-studded St George in Australia. He joined them, but sadly died as the result of coral poisoning contracted in a pre-season swim. In 1965, winger Mike Ratu became a favourite at the Athletics Ground and 20 years later his son Emon appeared in over 100 matches for Hornets.

But it was the players from South Wales who were the richest seam of talent. Robert Gate did a splendid job in cataloguing the exploits of the many Welshmen to turn professional in his two volumes entitled, *Gone North*. Bradford Northern enjoyed a purple patch in the 1940s, reaching three consecutive Wembley finals. Their Welsh manager Dai Rees built a side blending local talent like the Ward brothers, Ernest and Donald and former union players from Wales, including Willie Davies, Trevor Foster, Frank Whitcombe and Emlyn Walters.

Frank Whitcombe was a larger-than-life character in every sense. A huge man weighing over 20 stone, he was one of 10 children raised in the working-class area of Grangetown in Cardiff. He played at London Welsh while serving in the Army. He signed for Northern for £100 and two suits. However, in order to commence his league career, he had to buy himself out of the forces which cost him £90. The story is told that on the way to Wembley in 1947, the bus driver got lost and so Frank took the wheel himself and drove the team to the stadium. In 1948 Whitcombe gained a double distinction of becoming the first forward and first member on the losing side, to receive the Lance Todd trophy as Northern lost to Wigan.

William Thomas Harcourt 'Willie' Davies was something of a teenage prodigy in union. He partnered his cousin Haydyn Tanner at half-back when both were still sixth formers at school and was a member of the Swansea team which defeated the touring All Blacks in 1935. The New Zealand captain, Jack Manchester, speaking to members of the press after the 11–3 reversal, famously said, "Tell them back home we lost, but please don't tell them we were beaten by a pair of schoolboys!" After graduating from Swansea University, Davies attended Carnegie College and played at Headingley Rugby Union club. He then signed for Bradford Northern and won the Lance Todd trophy in his side's 8–4 victory over Leeds in 1947.

A few years later, just down the road in Leeds, the Headingley board pulled off an enormous coup by signing Lewis Jones who was dubbed 'The Golden Boy of Welsh Rugby.' Born in Gorseinon in 1931, he was hardly more than a boy of 18 who had not long left school, when he made a spectacular Welsh debut against England at Twickenham in 1950. So impressive was his performance that he gained selection for the British Lions tour to Australia and New Zealand later that year, albeit as a late injury replacement. In 1952, on his return home, he stunned the nation with a shock transfer to Leeds for a £6,000 fee. He remained loyal to the Loiners in a 12-year career at the club. During this time, he amassed a points total of 2,920, a figure only bettered in recent times by Kevin Sinfield. Jones played in the 1952 Challenge Cup victory over Barrow and in Leeds's first ever Championship win in 1961 over Warrington. Everyone at Leeds mourned his loss when he died aged 92 in 2024.

The Wigan club have long been associated with players from Wales. Two players who gave them excellent service, playing in over 700 matches between them were Bert Jenkins and Johnny Thomas in the years before the First World War. Later, in the 1920s, a plethora of players from the valleys joined the Central Park outfit. George Owens, Syd Jerram, Danny Hurcombe, Wilf Hodden and Johnny Ring were just some of the Welshmen who wore the cherry and white with distinction. The player who dwarfs the achievements of any of his countrymen though, was the maestro that was Jim Sullivan.

He was born in Cardiff and by the age of 16 was playing full-back in their first team. He became the youngest player to represent the Barbarians at the age of 17 in a match against Newport. His prodigious talent drew the attention of clubs including Huddersfield, Wakefield Trinity and Hull FC. Sullivan though decided to accept Wigan's offer of £750 – over £300,000 today – and put pen to paper in June 1921. The club website describes him as "the ultimate rugby league player" and Eddie Waring's verdict is simply that he was, "the greatest Welshman ever to be signed."

Sullivan played in 28 games for Great Britain and 26 for Wales. He has the distinction of being a dual international, because he also represented the Principality at baseball. His numbers alone are mind boggling. In a career stretching from 1921 to 1945, he made 774 club appearances, scoring 83 tries and kicking 2,317 goals, amassing a total of 4,883 points. In 1925, in a Challenge Cup match against the wonderfully named, Flimby and Fothergill, who sound more like a music hall duo than an amateur rugby league club, he landed a remarkable 22 goals. In his time in a Wigan shirt, he won three League Championships, two Challenge Cups, including the first to be played at Wembley, and three Lancashire Cups. When he retired, he took on the coaching duties at Central Park, leading them to Championship glory five times and to two further Challenge Cups. In 1952 he moved on to enjoy further success with neighbours St Helens, where he played a pivotal role in the development of a certain young teenage prodigy by the name of Alex Murphy.

The 1960s marked a turbulent time in Welsh rugby union. The days of the great players such as JPR, Gareth Edwards and Barry John had not yet arrived. 1967 marked two defections to rugby league as Terry Price, who no lesser judge than Phil Bennett felt would have been better than John 'JPR' Williams were it not for injuries, joined Bradford Northern in a great fanfare of publicity. Meanwhile at Salford, flamboyant Chairman Brian Snape was assembling a marvellous array of talent at the Willows. In that same year he paid David Watkins £16,000 to join the club.

Left: The Rugby Codebreakers statue at Cardiff Bay. The players are Gus Risman, Billy Boston and Clive Sullivan. Other players named on the statue are: William 'Wax' Wiliams, David Willicombe, Dennis Brown, Gerald Cordle, Joe Corsi, Colin Dixon, Norman Fender, Roy Francis, Johnny Freeman, Jim Sullivan and Frank Whitcombe.
(Photo: Peter Lush)

Dai Watkins MBE made his Welsh debut against England aged 20 in 1963. The Newport stand-off was the poster boy of the Welsh game in the swinging 1960s. He captained the British and Irish Lions in two tests in New Zealand in 1966. Shortly after moving to league, I saw him as he came to watch his new teammates take part in a sevens competition at Fartown, Huddersfield and was struck by his diminutive stature, standing just five feet six inches and weighing just over 10 stone. Fears that the physicality of our game would be too challenging were swiftly set aside as he made a great success of his new career. Keith Mumby, a former schoolmate and brilliant full-back once told me that of all the players he encountered, only Watkins made him look pedestrian when he 'did him' with a change of pace in a game at Odsal. Suffice to say, Watkins was inducted into the Rugby League Hall of Fame in 2022, a year prior to his death. He became the sixth Welshman to be so honoured.

1967 threatened to mark an all-time low in Welsh rugby union as they entered the final match of the Five Nations without a single win. The English, from across the Severn Bridge, were in pursuit of a Triple Crown and Championship and few Welsh supporters held out much hope of victory in the Easter Saturday fixture. The WRU selectors lost faith with Terry Price and brought in 18-year-old Newport centre Keith Jarrett, playing him out of position at full-back. Much to the crowd's delight, their new 'Wunderkind' gathered a ball, which had bounced almost vertically near touch, arriving to snatch it out of the air with perfect timing before sprinting off down the sideline to score one of the great tries at the Arms Park. In all, Jarrett contributed 19 points in a famous 34–21 victory. He went on to gain another nine caps for his country and was selected for the 1968 British Lions tour. On his return, the sporting all-rounder who had also represented Glamorgan at cricket on two occasions, signed for Barrow for £14,000.

One thing that all new arrivals had to contend with was the resentment which was often felt by opponents and even teammates who could be jealous of the, to them, eye-watering, tax free sums these union boys were banking with no guarantee that they would add to a team's success. Shortly after Jarrett's arrival, I was part of a group of kids who were the guinea pigs for players and officials who were taking their coaching badges at a session at Odsal. One of them was high profile referee Fred Lindop. He officiated in one of the Barrow player's early games and told us of the verbal stick Jarrett took regarding his price tag and the value for money this represented, as his opponents mocked him throughout the game.

Forays into the union market always represented something of a gamble. There are no sale or return clauses and it is certainly a case of 'buyer beware.' Sadly, although he played 92 matches for the Cumbrian club, Keth Jarrett's career was brutally cut short after he signed for Wigan. Before he had chance to play for his new club, the Welshman suffered a stroke which ended his playing career at the tender age of 25.

The 1980s were hard times in Wales. In post miner's strike South Wales, in Thatcher's Britain, whole communities sank into dereliction and despair. Shell suited young men hung around on street corners and drug dealers moved in to mop up the last financial dregs of any redundancy money which might still be left. Rugby was at least a distraction from the grim realities of post-industrial decline and defections to rugby league only added to the sense of depression.

Terry Holmes had replaced Gareth Edwards and was one of the hottest properties in the game. He played 25 times for Wales, winning a Triple Crown and going on two Lions tours. Tall and powerfully built for a scrum-half, Holmes was unfortunate to be plagued by injury. He received serious shoulder damage in South Africa necessitating surgery.

Shortly thereafter, he tore his anterior cruciate ligament and again went under the surgeon's knife. So, it was with a degree of scepticism Bradford Northern supporters received the news that the club had signed the Cardiff player for £80,000. In his first outing at Swinton, with the whole media circus looking on, he was led from the field with a dislocated shoulder by physio Ron Barritt. Injury problems continued to beset Holmes, who cannot be blamed for cashing in when the opportunity arose. He said years later, "It was an opportunity to get a bit of financial stability behind me," adding, "It's just a shame I was never really fit up there."

A story with a happier ending relates to one of Terry Holmes' half back partners from that era. Jonathan Davies may well be, given the current financial turn of events, the last truly great Welsh superstar to grace our game. He signed for Widnes in 1989 for £230,000 and went on to become a legend of rugby league. Among all the glittering highlights in his time with the Chemics and later with Warrington, I prize one particular piece of Davies magic above all others. In 1994, I organised a school trip for the rugby mad kids of Wyke Middle School where I worked. One of them was a young Mark Dunning, who many years later was to become Head Coach at Bradford Bulls. The occasion was the first test at Wembley against the touring Australians. Midway through the first half, the ball travelled through several pairs of hands before Davies entered the line from full-back. Taking the ball on the fly he made an arching run at blistering pace. The Australian last line of defence, Brett Mullins was as fast a player as I have seen but 'Jiffy' put on the afterburners to dive over at the corner. It is a memory I shall always treasure.

In the new age of the game, perhaps the powers that be will have to address their thoughts on how the production-line of future talent can be refreshed and replenished. Relying on converts from rugby union will certainly be a thing of the past.

27. Tom and Ralph Winnard

In 2005 a young primary school teacher came for an interview at Holybrook Primary School. The governors and myself were very impressed by his obvious passion and enthusiasm and he was duly appointed. I was aware that he was Sam Gardner who was making a name for himself locally as a winger for Keighley Cougars. Our school had a strong rugby league tradition and I knew Sam would make a great contribution. Thankfully he was a good English and drama teacher too!

In Sam's time with Keighley, he played 95 games and scored 26 tries. He eventually drew down the curtain in his final match in 2009 in the biggest game of his career. He scored the opening try as Keighley overcame Oldham 28–26 in the Championship Play-off Final at Warrington. Alongside him that day was teammate Danny Jones, who tragically died in a match in London shortly afterwards, leading to the amazing efforts of his wife Lizzie in raising funds and awareness for a defibrillator charity for which she received a richly deserved MBE. In a typically generous gesture, Sam had his shirt from the final framed and awarded it to the pupils for being his inspiration.

Shortly after joining the staff team, Sam mentioned in passing that his grandad had been a professional player. Now I wish I had a quid for every time someone had claimed to have a relative who had 'played for t' Northern'. Indeed, in my years living in Wales, I seldom had conversations about rugby with anyone who did not claim that some manner of representative honour was held by them or one of their kin. There must have been countless thousands of Welsh schoolboy caps awarded to legions of would-be Gareth Edwardses. I was curious about Sam's relative's credentials and enquired who he was. My scepticism was immediately mollified when he said, "He was called Tom Winnard." To a rugby league anorak like me, this was tantamount to telling an Evertonian that your grandad was Dixie Dean.

Tom Winnard initially joined Wigan Highfield in 1930, but later that year he transferred to St Helens. He went on to make 102 appearances for the club, scored 55 tries and kicked 115 goals. His highest honour for Saints came in the 1931–32 season when he scored a try in the 9–5 Championship Final victory over Huddersfield at Belle Vue, Wakefield.

In 1933, Bradford Northern were making plans to move from their dilapidated, ramshackle Birch Lane home near the present Dudley Hill amateur ground, to the vast bowl of the newly constructed Odsal Stadium. The directors were keen to strengthen the side to accompany this upgrade in accommodation. Consequently, in December of that year they splashed out £385 for Tom Winnard as a statement of their ambitious intent.

The momentous move to the new ground came in 1934 and it is interesting to reflect on what a different world this was by noting some of the contemporaneous events of that time. Hitler had recently declared himself Fuhrer in Germany and Stalin was beginning his barbaric programme of massacres in the Soviet Union. In the USA, Bonnie Parker and Clyde Barrow were gunned down by the FBI and Donald Duck was making his first appearance in a short film entitled *The Wise Little Hen*.

On 1 September 1934, an estimated crowd of 20,000 saw a Bradford Northern team of Pilling, Bradbury, Winnard, Walker, Marsh, Hayes, Green, Cotton, Collins, Morgan, Parr and Sherwood, go down 31–16 to Huddersfield.

Tom Winnard playing for England against France at Halifax in 1937. England won 23–9. He scored two tries and a goal. (Courtesy Alex Service)

Ralph Winnard playing for Bradford Northern against Keighley. (Courtesy *Rugby League Journal*)

This was a foretaste of things to come as settling into their new surroundings proved rather difficult. Winnard and his teammates lost their first 10 games before beating Featherstone Rovers at home on 17 November 1934.

The term 'one cap wonder' is, I always feel, rather an unkind sobriquet to bestow on someone who has scaled the heights within their chosen sport, albeit on just the sole occasion. Tom Winnard won his only cap for England in a European Championship match against France in 1937. The game was initially scheduled for Odsal, but the pitch was unplayable so it took place at Halifax's Thrum Hall on 10 April with England winning 23–9. *The Glory of Their Times,* edited by Phil Melling and Tony Collins, catalogues the important contribution of black players in the game and it highlights this match as the occasion which saw the Broughton Rangers' winger Jimmy Cumberbatch become the first black player to win an England cap. Both he and Winnard bagged a brace of tries with Tom landing a goal for good measure. Interestingly, two of his international colleagues that day, full-back Belshaw and prop Woods, were from Liverpool Stanley, thus reflecting how less 'traditional' clubs provided players at the elite level, unlike today.

Tom Winnard remained at Bradford Northern for 11 years before retiring in 1944. Our game has a rich tradition of sons following in their father's footsteps – Gus and his sons Bev & John Risman, Albert and Stan Fearnley, Allan and Richard Agar and Eric and Steve Prescott (of Man of Steel fame), spring to mind. Tom's own son Ralph also followed his father into the professional game. Ralph Winnard gave sterling service to Bradford Northern in the mid-1950s as a period of unprecedented success, a veritable golden age in the 1940s, came to an end. Ralph joined the club from West Bowling amateurs – where I cut my own rugby teeth many years later – on 16 March 1955. On his debut he scored a try in the 26–4 victory over Batley under the Odsal floodlights. It is testimony to Ralph's durability that he was ever-present in the 1959–60 season when he captained the club and played in all 42 fixtures. In his nine years with Northern he played 162 games and scored 31 tries before a knee injury caused his retirement in 1962.

Tom Winnard passed away in 1986 and his son Ralph died in 2018 at the age of 83. I was privileged to meet Sam's mum Marg and her twin Linda to talk about their family members. Tom Winnard's dad, also named Tom, had a fruit and vegetable stall at Wigan market and as children they remembered their father returning home from Lancashire bearing mountains of fresh produce. Grandad Tom had played for Wigan in 1913 having signed following a trial 'A' team game in which he scored 13 tries. I was interested to discover that Tom Jnr. and his wife Agnes had seven children in all and that Ralph's brother Alan also played in the professional ranks with Bramley. The twins recalled their father coaching them in athletics on a field near their Bankfoot home which is now the site of a large supermarket. They had obviously inherited the Winnard gene as both went on to have long and distinguished careers as PE teachers.

I gained some valuable insights into the family's life outside the world of rugby league. Tom had served during the Second World War in the Italy campaign with the Green Howards. Like so many of his generation he was loath to talk about his experiences, but his daughters thought that their father was probably suffering from what would now be termed PTSD. He had poor mental health as a consequence in his later years. A positive wartime memory for Alan and Ralph was captured in a photo of the two young boys proudly holding the

Championship Cup from the 1940–41 season which their father won alongside such immortals of the game who played in the two-legged victory over Wigan, including Stan Brogden, Ernest Ward, Gus Risman and Trevor Foster.

The family shared with me a document produced by local sports historian Nigel Williams in 1987. It catalogued Tom Winnard's scoring exploits in his days with Bradford. His research uncovered a fact which may come as a surprise to students of the game. Williams compares club legend Ernest Ward's 1,428 points from 392 games at an average of 3.64 per game with Tom's record of 1,055 in 253 appearances at an average of 4.16 per match concluding, "...in my mind, Tom Winnard was the better of the two players from a scoring point of view."

In later life Ralph Winnard suffered with Alzheimer's dementia, but Sam Gardner recalled that his uncle had been able to witness his Championship victory in 2009 on television and had been able to discuss the game with him. The family can be proud of three generations of players who have graced the professional ranks.

28. Retiring to Blackpool

They say that youth is wasted on the young. Some things like cheese and fine wine improve with the passing of the years. As a 15-year-old studying English Literature for 'O' level, I was introduced to a poem by Philip Larkin, who although a resident of Hull for many years, was not, I believe, an aficionado of rugby league. The poem we studied with our teacher Alan Hall – known to us sniggering schoolboys as Albert for obvious reasons – was called *At Grass*. I didn't, or possibly more accurately, couldn't get it at that tender age when life is all before you and reflection is for the oldies. As far as I was concerned it was a poem about some horses in a field.

With the passing of time I have come to understand the melancholic message which Larkin's poem conveys. As the poet views the once fabled thoroughbreds as they graze in a paddock he asks: "Do memories plague their ears like flies?" These formerly magnificent beasts have now aged and "slipped their names and stand at ease." Once household names, they are now anonymous, hidden away from the public gaze, known only to their grooms and carers. It is a commentary on how we disregard the past and there is a sadness in its tone as it muses on the transitory nature of all past glories. Ultimately it brings into focus the inevitability of our own mortality. And also, yes, it is a poem about some horses in a field.

Folklore has it that swans reserve their most beautiful song until just before they die. This romantic and rather tragic notion gives us the phrase 'swan song', which is often applied to singers and creatives in the arts world, as well as to sports stars. It derives from ancient Greek and Roman sources, but Shakespeare too quoted it centuries later – never too proud to indulge in a bit of creative plagiarism, 'Our Will', for as George Bernard Shaw quipped about 'the Bard', he told a good tale as long as somebody else had told it first.

Like those other twin certainties in life, death and taxes, getting old and taking retirement comes to us all. Nothing lasts forever and rugby league players have to come to terms with this reality and give in to *Anno Domini* at some point. Many athletes say that the realisation hits them suddenly, in a damascene moment of clarity, as they somehow instinctively know that they need to call time on proceedings. Others like all-time record breaking fast bowler Jimm Anderson need the proverbial 'tap on the shoulder'. Some struggle to recognise that while the spirit may be strong, the flesh is weak, as they seek one last season or one more tour or one final fight. It can end well. Witness the heroics of say, Frankie Dettori in horse racing, Stanley Matthews in his famous Cup Final of 1953 or grandpa George Foreman regaining the world heavyweight crown at the age of 45. More often than not though, it tends to end rather sadly and can diminish the achievements of the stars of yesteryear and tarnish our memories of these athletes as we see them brought down to the level of other mere mortals by the passing of the years.

Retirement to some idyllic coastal resort to live out our dotage in a little bungalow after years of hard toil is a dream which many of us share. Blackpool, as Stanley Holloway noted in his monologue about the ill-fated Ramsbottom family, is "noted for fresh air and fun". The town's one time football manager Ian Holloway though took a side-swipe at the west coast resort, saying, "I love Blackpool. We're very similar. We both look better in the dark". Another wag recently quipped that Blackpool is what Walt Disney would have built if he only had a fiver! Whatever your view of the place is, however, it is remarkable how many rugby league stars performed their swan song in a tangerine, black and white kit at Borough Park as they took a seaside retirement.

Blackpool Borough first applied to join the RFL in 1950, but membership was not granted until the 1954–55 season. Initially, the new club played its home fixtures at the Blackpool Greyhound Stadium before moving to its new Borough Park home. Given the restrictions which the ground's size imposed, the more attractive fixtures were taken to the Bloomfield Road ground of their footballing neighbours and it was there in 1955 that a crowd of 12,015 saw their team draw 24–24 with the touring New Zealanders. Two years later they drew a record attendance of over 22,000 for a third round Challenge Cup match against near neighbours, Leigh.

One can only imagine the excitement felt by the Borough faithful when they learned that the legendary Brian Bevan would be joining them from Warrington as player-coach in 1962. The Australian try scoring machine had represented the Wilderspool side in 620 matches. During his time at the club, he had crossed for 740 tries in a glorious career. Now the ageing superstar would bring his talent and expertise to the fledgling club. He appeared in 42 matches for Borough contributing 17 tries for the perennial strugglers. While at Blackpool in 1964 Bevan, then aged 40, was selected for Other Nationalities in an end of season sevens tournament at Halifax after he had officially retired. Perhaps this ploy by the board to employ former rugby league royalty, provided the blue-print for other forays to secure the services of the great and the good, however fleeting or short-term their plans might be.

Brian McTigue was recognised as one of the most skilful ball handling forwards of the 1950s and 1960s. I recall seeing him throwing a lateral pass almost like an American football quarter-back on the one occasion I watched him play for Wigan. The man who went on to star against the Australians and win much silverware at Central Park, had almost taken a different route into the world of professional boxing. In the 1950s he took part in some exhibition bouts with the great American light-heavyweight Joey Maxim who boasted victories over Freddie Mills and Sugar Ray Robinson among his conquests. Maxim, who chose his ring name in reference to the machine-gun of that name as a result of the power and rapidity of his jab, was so impressed with the young McTigue that he offered to take him to the States to pursue his pugilistic career. Thankfully for rugby league fans he stayed in the north of England. He played 422 games for Wigan and 25 for Great Britain. Somehow the Blackpool board lured the man known as 'The Wizard' to Borough Park. However, the experiment was not a success and the now veteran McTigue represented the club just once.

A fellow Wigan stalwart from the same era was stand-off Dave Bolton. He had clocked up over 300 appearances at the club before embarking on a career in Australia with Balmain where he enjoyed great success and was included in the Tigers' Hall of Fame. His international career spanned a period between 1958 and 1963 and saw him play 23 times for his country. After returning from Australia, Bolton too was signed by Blackpool, but again this turned out to be a short-term move as he only made five appearances for them.

As the swinging 1960s progressed, so this trend of mopping up former Wigan players continued. Keith Holden was a tough, fair-haired centre who signed for the club on the banks of the River Douglas from Leigh. He played in over 150 games in cherry and white in two periods at Central Park. Holden played left centre and scored a try in the classic 1965 Cup

Final against Hunslet. Later his own son followed him to Wigan where he played scrum-half in the 1980s and Keith Holden Snr. was also the father-in-law of Terry Newton. By the late sixties, Holden was player-coach at Borough, where he made 29 appearances.

It was at this point in 1969 that the Seasiders made their greatest coup in the form of the Tiger Bay icon, Billy Boston. He had been awarded a second testimonial when he retired at Wigan and consequently Blackpool had to seek permission from the RFL for Billy to come out of retirement to join them. In his biography of the great man, Robert Gate explained that his wife Joan explained that Boston had become bored and this led to his comeback. The proliferation of former Wiganers who all travelled together to ease transport to training and his existing relationship with coach Holden may well have been factors which influenced Billy's choice as he had also been offered deals by Oldham and Warrington.

Billy Boston made his Blackpool debut on Boxing Day 1969. With him that day against Rochdale Hornets were former teammates Terry Entwhistle and Ray Ashby. Another Wigan lad and son of a famous father, Joe Egan played at hooker. In that game, a fellow Great Britain international colleague of Boston's, John Stopford, who was also coming out of retirement, played on Borough's opposite wing.

He had been a member of the last great Swinton team to win the First Division Championship in two consecutive seasons in 1962–63 and 1963–64 under their inspired coach Cliff Evans. The former Station Road man had been part of the star-studded back unit which included Ken Gowers, John Speed, Bobby Fleet and Alan Buckley, who helped him score a record breaking 42 tries in 1963–64. Stopford was a member of the 1966 Great Britain tour to Australia, in which he scored 16 tries in 15 games. On that Boxing Day, Stopford clashed heads with a member of his own side in a 'friendly fire' incident which resulted in the winger requiring nine stitches. Blackpool lost 20–6 to the Hornets.

Robert Gate points out that the problem for the two star wingers was that their teammates didn't have the skill and guile to move the ball out wide to provide them with the ammunition to damage the opposition. Boston in particular had to come in field in search of the ball in order to use his power and bulk. But while victory eluded Borough, in terms of attendance, the acquisition of the veteran stars had paid dividends. In the game prior to the one against Rochdale, 250 spectators had watched the match against Workington Town. On Boxing Day, the attendance had been 3,447 which is an increase of some 13-fold, thus vindicating the directors' recruitment policy. However, over the festive period, matters off the field did not go well. Gate explains, "Just how precarious things were at Blackpool was shown when there were just a handful of players at the training session prior to the New Year's fixture at Salford". Boston was absent with 'flu and on matchday the club drafted in two local amateurs.

By the end of the season, Keith Holden resigned as of head coach, although he stayed on as a player. Johnny Stopford took over as the coach and was pleased to learn that Boston intended to continue with his comeback the following season. Billy trained throughout the summer months and on the evening of 25 August turned out in the second row against Huyton at Borough Park. Blackpool lost to their fellow strugglers from Merseyside 10–5 and Billy decided to finally retire. He had played 11 matches for Blackpool and scored five tries.

For a number of years there were no high-profile signings at the club. Then in the early 1980s the directors seemed to revert to type with the recruitment of a St Helens legend and two members from Great Britain's 1972 World Cup winning squad.

Top: Billy Boston playing for Blackpool.

Left: Brian Bevan being treated for an injury while at Blackpool.

(Both photos courtesy *Rugby League Journal*)

John Mantle was a former Welsh rugby union international who taught at Rivington Road School in St Helens, which my wife attended. He made 435 appearances for the club and played in 19 major finals. The powerful back rower was a much respected and feared opponent whose ability to break the line and vigorous defensive capabilities earned him 13 caps for Great Britain and eight for Wales in his 11 years at Knowsley Road. When Mantle left the club, he spent one season at each of his next three clubs, Salford, Leigh and Barrow before very brief spells at Keighley and Oldham. In 1982, Blackpool were in dire straits and reached out to Mantle to join them as coach. He took charge for five games which all ended in defeat as Blackpool lost to Doncaster, Halifax, Carlisle, Bramley and Oldham. He played in the game against Bramley which ended 26–22 to the Yorkshire team. The ignominy of the final defeat to Oldham, 66–7, led to Mantle and the club parting company.

Bob Irving was a second row forward at Oldham who, although small for his position, was an elusive runner who went on to win a place in the club's Hall of Fame. Despite Oldham experiencing some lean years during Irving's time at the club, he nonetheless gained international recognition. In 1967 he played against France and Australia and secured a place on the 1970 Ashes tour. He played in the first test in Brisbane. He was in the 1972 World Cup winning squad and joined Wigan the following season before subsequently spending time at Salford and Barrow. Blackpool signed Irving as player-coach for the 1981–82 season and during his six months stay at the club he played in 16 matches, scoring four tries. He was eventually sacked after a run of poor results and moved on to Swinton.

In his retirement he lived in Blackpool where he ran a hotel before graduating and becoming a Senior Lecturer in Business Studies at Blackpool and Fylde College. Irving was a devout Roman Catholic who volunteered at a soup kitchen for homeless people in the town. Sadly, he died of a heart attack at the age of 51 in 1999.

A teammate of Bob Irving's in that 1972 World Cup squad was Paul Charlton. The Whitehaven born full-back, who began life as a hooker, joined Workington Town in 1961. His attacking prowess, safety under the high ball and resolute defence brought him international honours. This was in an era where there were many talented full-backs, such as Hull's Arthur Keegan, Castleford's Derek Edwards and Bev Riman at Leeds, all vying for the Great Britain number one jersey. His courage and non-stop energy gained the attention of Brian Snape at Salford who was building an all-star outfit from both codes at the Willows. Charlton signed for them in 1969 and they reached Wembley, only to be thwarted by a Castleford team inspired by the Lance Todd winning Mal Reilly. This was special to me as I made my first visit to London to watch that game with my father. Following a six year stay with the Red Devils, he returned to Workington Town for a second stint before leaving in 1980. By now an elder statesman of the game, Paul Charlton joined the ranks of Blackpool's former greats as he turned out for Borough, playing 11 matches before hanging up his boots.

We could imagine the fantasy team we could pick from this roll call of some of the game's finest players. They saw out their time on the west coast, like old thoroughbred horses in Larkin's paddock having "slipped their names". Sadly for Blackpool Borough, they did not have them in their pomp or the club's fortunes may have been very different. Unfortunately, they eventually went out of existence in 1994 as another example of a heartland club that could not survive harsh economic realities.

29. Seeing double – twins in rugby league

There are two different types of twins. Fraternal twins are born when two different eggs are fertilised by two different sperms at the same time and they are consequently not necessarily identical in appearance or gender. Identical twins, also known as monozygotic twins, occur when one sperm fertilises just one egg which then divides into two foetuses. It is estimated that there are about 11 million identical twins in the world today.

Twins have had some profound influences on history. Romulus and Remus were reputedly suckled and raised by wolves and were the founders of the city of Rome. In ancient Greek mythology, Apollo and Artemis were the son and daughter of Leto and Zeus. Apollo became the God of light and Artemis the Goddess of wild things and hunting. In the Bible, in Genesis, the twins Jacob and Esau fought in their mother's womb and thereafter beget nations which incessantly war against one another.

In sport there have been some famous twins who have scaled the heights in their chosen fields. In cricket, Craig and Jamie Overton have both been included in the England squad in recent times. They follow in the footsteps of the Bedser twins, Alec and Eric, who were notoriously close in an almost telepathic sense. It is said that they often turned up in identical outfits even though this was unplanned and they routinely finished one another's sentences. Both of the Bedsers were evacuated from Dunkirk and were teammates for Surrey in the 1940s and 1950s. Australia benefited from the hard-nosed competitors Steve and Mark Waugh. Dutch football unearthed two jewels in the De Boer twins, Frank and Ronald who wore the orange shirt of Holland in several glorious campaigns.

In boxing in the 1960s there were two quite different sets of twins. Henry and George Cooper were lads who came from Bellingham in London. When I was a youth worker there in the 1970s, we had a sports ground near their childhood home and the old groundsman Fred Belcher used to tell me with great pride how he often chased them off his precious, manicured and much-loved cricket square. 'Our 'Enery' went on to be a 'national treasure' with his knock down of the then, Cassius Clay, soon to be Muhammed Ali. Two other boxing twins from the metropolis were far less loveable characters who took to the ring – Ronnie and Reggie Kray.

I recall one afternoon when working at a school on a Bradford estate that a man with two powerfully built pit-bull type dogs had come onto the school grounds and let them off their leads. Given the potential for this to end badly, I went out for a word. Composure was the key I felt, as the guy looked like he could have sorted me without any canine assistance! In a firm but non-confrontational voice I asked, "Excuse me sir, but could you take your dogs away as we must keep the children safe?" Though he looked a bit fierce he turned out to be perfectly reasonable and apologised before calling his dogs: "C'mon Ronnie! Here Reggie". Talk about smile sweetly and carry a big stick.

So, since we are on the subject of scary twins, let us consider our first rugby league siblings, the Drake twins of Hull. The stories of the toughness of the Hull pack in the 1950s and early 1960s are legion. Few sides relished a visit to the Boulevard and this was in no small measure due to the prospect of an encounter with the brothers Drake. Black and white photos of the pair reveal faces that only a mother could love. Thick, dark swept back hair, bushy eyebrows and gap-tooth smiles conveying more malice than warmth, belie the fact that those who knew them swore they were lovely gentle souls – off the pitch. On the field of play it was something of a different matter. A recurrent adjective which crops up when their contemporaries speak of the pair is, 'naughty'.

The twins were of the non-identical variety. Jim was shorter, stoutly built and one of the hardest props in the game at a time when every team had, what are now euphemistically termed, 'enforcers'. Bill, who began life as a long-striding winger, stood some six feet two inches and became a fast, ball handling second row. Like his brother, he too was adept at the dark arts and was not a man you would wish to meet down a dark alley at the blind side of the set piece.

They were born in Workington in 1931, but at the age of 14, their family relocated to York. Jim originally favoured the round ball game at which he excelled earning him a place in the Yorkshire county trials. However, before he could take part in the game, he injured his knee playing rugby and following this missed opportunity he switched to playing rugby league. Both Drake boys learned the game at the Heworth amateur club in York. Jim signed for Hull as a full-back, but shortly after he contracted rheumatic fever and in his enforced period of inactivity, he piled weight on. Doctors predicted an end to his rugby days, but he defied their prognoses and returned to the Boulevard. His increased bulk and girth now fitted him more readily to the position of prop forward. He made his debut at loose-forward when the great Johnny Whiteley was stuck in traffic, but eventually moved to the front row.

Jim was sadly plagued with injuries and a knee problem deprived him of a Championship Final appearance and a place on the Lions tour to Australia in 1958. Nevertheless, he did play in the 1959 Cup Final and represented Great Britain against France in 1960. He played for his native Cumberland on five occasions before leaving Hull in 1961 having made 243 appearances for the club. His next move took him the short distance from west to east in Kingston upon Hull where he became one of that select band of men to play for both clubs in the city, making 64 appearances for the Robins before retiring in 1965.

Bill Drake followed his brother to Hull FC in 1952. The other half of 'the Terrible Twins', as they came to be known, made 294 appearances for the black and whites. His scoring record for a forward is quite remarkable as he racked up 101 tries including five hat tricks as well as kicking 53 goals. When the pioneering coach and arch innovator Roy Francis left for Leeds in 1963, he wasted no time in signing Bill for the Loiners because he knew he could help him deliver the fast-flowing brand of rugby he wished to see at Headingley. He made 32 appearances in the famous blue and amber shirt before moving to his hometown club York prior to his retirement in 1965. After his footballing career, he earned a living in the building trade before becoming a pub landlord in York. Bill died on 8 October 2012, exactly four years to the day after his twin brother Jim. Both brothers are members of the prestigious Hull Hall of Fame.

When thinking of durable, combative, feisty players, the Marsh twins from Thornhill spring to mind. David and Paul Marsh were identical twins who played for over a decade from the late 1990s. The identical pair plied their trades at various Yorkshire clubs, mainly as hookers but also in half-back roles. David played for Wakefield, York, Hunslet and Keighley in 386 professional appearances. Brother Paul also played the majority of his career at Belle Vue, but he then developed as a coach with York, Hunslet and Keighley.

I heard Paul March interviewed on local radio during his days at Hunslet on several occasions and he seemed to be a man of forthright views who tended not to mince his words. At that time, my colleague Sam Gardner, the grandson of former great Tom Winnard, was playing for Keighley and one Monday morning following their game against the Hawks he showed me a sheet of paper which he had found the previous day when he had been playing for Keighley against a Paul March coached Hunslet. The sheet was a set of coach's notes, a mini-dossier of sorts, which he had found on the visitors' changing room floor when helping tidy up after the match. It contained information for his players on each of their opposite numbers. Coincidentally, the previous week I had completed Sam's teaching appraisal which covered strengths, areas for developments, training needs and targets for the forthcoming year. It ran to a side and a half of A4 paper and was a detailed analysis of his professional performance. Paul March's appraisal of Sam as a player was less detailed and much more succinct. "Fast, steps well off his left, safe under the high ball, soft as s..t," it read. As Rabbie Burns said, "Oh to see ourselves as others see us."

'The Tiger Twins', Kevin and Bob Beardmore, were fixtures 'down t' lane' at Castleford in the 1980s. Kevin was a hooker who made 247 appearances for the club. Bob was a goalkicking scrum-half who played 293 times for Castleford scoring 99 tries and kicking 518 goals. Kevin won county and international honours and represented Great Britain 14 times. The brothers played together at Wembley in 1986 in the narrow 15–14 victory over Hull Kingston Rovers. Bob was instrumental in earning the victory and was awarded the Lance Todd trophy on the strength of his performance. Both Beardmores were rewarded with testimonials by the club in 1988 and both are in the Tigers Hall of Fame.

Interviewed by Richard de la Riviere for *The League Express* in 2022, shortly before Kevin's death at the age of 62, the pair were asked about 'the twin thing' of having some kind of telepathic understanding. Kevin said, "It might sound daft but there was definitely something there. There was some sort of psychic power there. Sometimes without looking for Bob, I knew he'd be there. We scored a lot of tries off each other that we probably wouldn't have done otherwise."

Kevin and Keith Rayne both enjoyed long and successful careers which often took them down similar routes. The twins, who were both hard working forwards, spent the lion's share of their careers at Wakefield Trinity and Leeds in the 1970s and 1980s and both were awarded Great Britain caps. Kevin played his only international against France at Central Park in 1981 while Keith played two games for England, also winning four caps for Great Britain. Kevin Rayne finished his long career with Bramley in 1993. Keith tried his hand at coaching with Batley in the 1990–91 season before finishing at Doncaster in 1992.

There have been some famous rugby league clans over the years. The Goldthorpes at Hunslet in the 'All Four Cups' era, the Arkwrights at St Helens and the farming Fairbanks brothers, with dad Jack, being three examples of family dynasties in the game. In more recent times the highest profile set of super siblings have been the Burgess boys. The Dewsbury born lads followed father Mark into the professional ranks. Mark Burgess was a durable prop who played for Nottingham, Rochdale, Dewsbury and Hunslet. Tragically he was stricken by Motor Neuron Disease and died at the age of 45 leaving behind his teacher wife Julie and four sons.

Sam was the first to rise to prominence with Bradford Bulls and has gone on to have a stellar career with South Sydney Rabbitohs and on the international stage. He switched codes but was treated terribly by the chaps at Twickers after England's debacle in the 2015 world cup. He became Warrington Wolves' head coach in 2024. Next off the rank came eldest brother Luke who had spells at Harlequins RL and Doncaster before signing for Leeds and winning the Super League Trophy with the Rhinos in 2009 prior to joining Sam at South Sydney in 2011. A friend of mine on the Bulls staff, Nigel O'Flaherty-Johnson, a craggy faced former professional player with Batley and a former miner, who possessed a wonderful broken nose which looked as if it were making every effort to smell his own left ear, said to me at the time of Luke's departure, "There's twins as well and they're going to be every bit as good!"

Tom and George Burgess are those twins and Nige's prophecy did come good. Tom made his debut for the Bulls in 2011 against Halifax and played 45 games for them. George was coming up through the ranks, but Russell Crowe snapped him up for the Rabbitohs in 2013 before he had graduated to the first team and Tom joined him to reunite all four brothers later that year. Like Sam, the twins have won many international honours in the game. Both of them stand six feet five inches and weigh in at 19 stones.

Martha Kelner of *The Mail on Sunday* interviewed George and Tom Burgess before the 2013 Rugby League World Cup. Tom explained how the impact of losing their father to MND when they were only 14-years-old had a huge effect on them and served to bond the twins even more closely. In the same interview they did admit to taking advantage of being identical to switch places at school if things got boring.

Finally, the Rugby League World Cup in 2022 proved to be something of a double bubble-fest as Wales included two sets of twins in Ben and Rhys Evans – who also featured in the 2013 competition – and Bradford's Conor and Curtis Davies. Included in Ireland's ranks were fellow wingers Louis and Innes Senior who both had Super League experience with the Huddersfield Giants.

30. Roy Kinnear

When we think of union players 'Going North' it is because the majority of converts to the XIII-a-side code come from the valleys of South Wales. Far rarer beasts are those men from north of the border, 'Coming South'. In the entire history of the game, only six players from Scotland have played at international level in both forms of the game. Probably the most famous is Dave Valentine who joined Huddersfield and led Great Britain to success in the inaugural Rugby League World Cup in 1954. Coincidentally, in the final 16–12 victory over France at the Parc des Princes, a fellow Scot, David Rose, who is a member of that rare group of dual internationals, played on the wing. In more recent times Alan Tait, who enjoyed great success with Widnes, is one of the higher profile players to leave his native Caledonia to become a member of this exclusive club.

Other Scots have joined the professional ranks and the majority of those have hailed from the Scottish borders. For example, Hawick born Rob Valentine joined big brother Dave at Fartown who also had Ally Ford and Billy Hollands, both Scots borderers, on their books in the 1960s. Leeds had Selkirk men Ron Cowan and Drew Broach in their ranks. Broach was the nephew of Alex Fiddes who played for Huddersfield and Castleford in the 1930s and 1940s. Another uncle and nephew who both came from north of the border were Billy and Charlie Renilson from Jedburgh. Billy played for Halifax from 1925 to 1928 and nephew Charlie went to Thrum Hall in 1957. The back row forward gave 12 years service to the blue and whites, winning eight Great Britain caps and inclusion in the Halifax Hall of Fame.

It was certainly true that men from the borders, from clubs like Hawick, Jed-Forest and Gala, often felt that the players from the rather better-heeled clubs of Edinburgh were far more likely to represent their native land at Murrayfield. Some doubtless concluded that league was their best option. One such player was George Fairbairn who left Kelso to sign for Wigan and later joined Hull KR, winning international status and the Man of Steel Award in 1980.

Robert Muir 'Roy' Kinnear was rather an exception to this geographical rule. He was born on 3 February 1904 in Edinburgh and later attended the prestigious George Heriot School in the city. Like many pupils from the renowned educational establishment, Roy went on to play for the 'Old Boys', Heriot's Former Pupils. A centre for the club, he caught the eye of the British Lions' selectors and was picked to tour South Africa in 1924. He played in all four tests against the Springboks. However, Kinnear had to wait a further two years before being awarded a Scottish cap and he played in three games against France, Wales and Ireland.

In 1927, Kinnear was approached by Wigan and made what must have been a shock move to Central Park. During his six years with the Lancashire club, he scored 81 tries in 182 appearances. In 1928, Kinnear was a member of the team which beat Widnes 5–4 to lift the Lancashire Cup. His annus mirabilis came in 1929 when the Scottish centre played for Other Nationalities against England before being picked for Great Britain later in the season. It was in that same year that he made Challenge Cup history with the cherry and whites.

Wembley Stadium was built in 1923 to showcase the British Empire Exhibition which made a huge loss and it was feared that it would become something of a white elephant. While the event had been a flop, the stadium found its true worth as a sports venue when the Football

Association took the FA Cup Final there. Bolton played West Ham United in what has gone down in history as 'The White Horse Final' as PC George Scorey and his white horse Billy cleared the huge crowd which had spilled onto the pitch as the authorities vastly underestimated the numbers who would turn up to the unticketed event. Estimates of the attendance for that 1923 encounter are around 200,000.

Six years later, the RFL made the monumental decision to take the Challenge Cup to the capital city. The idea initially came from Kinnear's fellow Scot, John Wilson, who had become Secretary of the RFL in 1920. He visited the Empire Stadium and on his return north, he recommended the move to the full governing body. The ensuing vote was a close affair with the 'ayes' winning narrowly 14–10.

On 4 May 1929, Roy Kinnear and his Wigan team lined up to face Dewsbury in front of a 41,500 crowd in that first Wembley showdown. The Yorkshire side was a homespun outfit with all but one of their side hailing from east of the Pennines. Wigan were a much more cosmopolitan bunch with five Welshmen, including legendary full-back Jim Sullivan, two New Zealanders and Scot, Kinnear in their team.

A London correspondent of *The Manchester Guardian* was very impressed by what he saw. He reported that the game made the average match between union sides seem "rather weak and watery". He wrote that "It showed the possibilities of intensive training, hard running and the closest possible marking". The most surprising feature to the reporter was, "the terrific speed at which it was fought out."

On the day, Wigan won 13–2. The glory of scoring the first ever try at Wembley fell to their youngest player, 22-year-old Syd Abram, who along with John Bennett and Jack Sherington, were the only native Wiganers in the team. Roy Kinnear contributed to the historic win when he scored the third and final try of the match. A rather sad footnote to the historic occasion was that Dewsbury's winger that day Henry Coates sold his loser's medal two days later for £4 – probably about two weeks wages – reflecting the harsh economic climate of those times.

Kinnear hung up his league boots in 1933 and worked as a car salesman in Wigan. When war was declared in 1939, the 35-year-old volunteered and joined the RAF. For the duration of the Second World War, there was an armistice in the conflict between the codes which saw league players like Trevor Foster and Earnest Ward playing alongside union men like Hayden Tanner and Bleddyn Williams. However, the apartheid like policies of the union authorities were not entirely set aside. In 1940, *The Scotsman* newspaper carried the headline, "SRU seven-a-side ban on RM Kinnear" and it reported: "An attraction has been lost to the Gala seven-a-side rugby tournament today by the Scottish Rugby Union's ban on Heriot's fielding their former international three-quarter Roy Kinnear. At the moment he is in the Edinburgh district … and it was hoped his appearance would swell the attendance at a tournament which is raising money for Red Cross funds." Not even the fight against fascism nor the needs of much needed help for war charities could sway what Duncan Smith writing in the same newspaper in 2020, referred to as "the Scottish blazerati".

The RAF did not ban Roy Kinnear from representing them at rugby union, but sadly his contribution to their team had tragic consequences. On 22 September 1942, at the age of 38, Roy Kinnear collapsed and died of a heart attack in a match. He was one of 13 former

Scottish rugby players to die in the service of the country, albeit on the sports field rather than the field of battle. He is buried with a military headstone in Uxbridge.

There have been many famous rugby dynasties where sons have followed famous fathers into the game of rugby league - the Winnards, Rismans, Bridges and most recently Sinfields come to mind. Roy's own son gained fame, but not in his father's sporting footsteps. Roy Kinnear junior's talent lay in the field of acting. He was initially a comedian and appeared regularly in the 1960s show, *That Was the Week that Was*. Indeed, when making the box office success *Zulu*, Stanley Baker is reputed to have wanted him in the role of the VC winning Private Hitch. The story goes that Baker spotted the actor from the weekly satirical show but only knew his name began with 'K' - and thus in a case of mistaken identity, David Kernan got the gig. Nevertheless, Roy became a very successful character actor in film and television. Sadly, in 1988 he was filming in Toledo in Spain when he fell from a horse during shooting and broke his pelvis. He died the following day of a heart attack brought on by the injury, at the age of 54.

Roy was married to the actor Carmel Cryan who plays Brenda Boyle in the television soap 'Eastenders'. Their son Rory is maintaining the thespian tradition. Born in 1978, the actor and playwright performed with the Royal Shakespeare Company and Royal National Theatre. He is famous for playing 'M's' sidekick Bill Tanner in the Bond films *Quantum of Solace*, *Skyfall* and *Spectre*.

31. The 'Dad's Army' test

Dad's Army was a successful comedy series which ran for nine seasons with 80 episodes produced between 1968 and 1977. Sadly, the last remaining member of the crew, Ian Lavender died in February 2024. The "Stupid boy" of "Don't tell him Pike" fame has now joined the rest of the gang in that great drill hall in the sky. The series spawned a film version in 1971 and another quite dreadful homage for the big screen in 2016. Written by Jimmy Perry and David Croft, it follows the exploits of the pompous Captain Mainwaring and his band of men in their varying degrees of decrepitude as the Walmington-on-Sea branch of the Local Defence Volunteers. The LDV were nicknamed the 'Dad's Army' and some unkindly attributed the initials of their organisation to, 'Look, Duck and Vanish', claiming this would be their response in the event of a German invasion.

In 1978, the 14th touring side in Australian history came to Great Britain under the management of Frank 'Biscuits' Stanton. Their skipper was Bobby Fulton who was born in England but whose family emigrated when he was four. Fulton's birthplace was Stockton Heath in Warrington and this led Eddie Waring to come up with another of his commentating faux pas as he announced, "Bobby Fulton, born in Warrington as a youngster."

The tour began at Blackpool Borough where the game ended with the unusual scoreline of 38–1 to the tourists. They then disposed of Cumbria, Great Britain Under-24s and Bradford Northern before suffering their first reversal to Warrington in a midweek fixture at Wilderspool. The Kangaroos beat a strong Wales team 8–3 and warmed up for the opening test by defeating Leeds.

A crowd of 17,644 gathered at Central Park for the first test. Entering the last quarter, the home side led courtesy of a John Bevan try when he beat Graham Eadie to a ball which had been slid into the in-goal area. However, two late tries by Kerry Boustead and Bobby Fulton saw the Australians rally to win 15–9. In a feisty affair, the two bantamweight scrum halves, Steve Nash and Tommy Raudonikis, were dismissed for fighting.

In the run up to the second test at Odsal, the tourists beat Hull and Salford, but suffered their second defeat of the tour to Widnes who were emerging as a real force in the domestic game. Peter Fox was the Great Britain manager in the series and he had come in for a good deal of criticism for his selection in the first test. The wily Fox was a master tactician and the ultimate motivator. He inspired great loyalty from players and he obviously communicated what he required from those he picked in the clearest of terms. His ability to create an 'us against the world', siege mentality was second to none.

Fox wielded the axe after the Central Park defeat and brought in John Joyner, Les Dyl and John Atkinson for Eric Hughes, Eddie Cunningham and John Bevan–- three Yorkshire based players for three from across the Pennines. Whether this was a result of Fox having greater trust in those players from the white rose county as a consequence of him coaching in several 'Roses' clashes, who can say? But it was in the pack that his selections caused the most raised eyebrows.

The coach had made an obvious decision that he wanted men with experience in his ranks. The entire front row was changed. Jimmy Thompson and David Ward were dropped and Paul Rose was demoted to the subs' bench in place of Len Casey. Fox brought in Jim

Mills, Tony Fisher and Brian Lockwood. These gnarled old warriors were all over 30 and entering the veteran stage of their careers. In the second row, Hull Kingston Rovers' Phil Lowe replaced clubmate Len Casey.

There were some derisory remarks from the Australian camp who swiftly dubbed Peter Fox's men 'Dad's Army'. How wise this was is certainly questionable. 'Big Jim' Mills, whose authorised biography by Peter Lush and Maurice Bamford was published in 2013, was a giant of a man, standing six feet four inches and weighing in at 18 stones. Sent off 20 times in his career, one story of his antics certainly bears repeating. I heard Jim give a very amusing after-dinner speech some years ago. He signed for North Sydney and flew out to Australia to join his new team. He said that he could not believe the waiting crowd at the airport. Jim said that he believed he bore a resemblance to Burt Reynolds, the American actor and wondered if the throng was due to mistaken identity. He later realised it was just a reflection of a league mad population and the incredible profile of the game there.

He admitted to extreme nerves on his debut as the crowd were baying to see the big Brit cut down to size. Early in the piece Mills decided to show his detractors just who was the boss and received his marching orders for his troubles. An early meeting with the disciplinary committee awaited him. He took a taxi to their headquarters and worked out a defence strategy of throwing himself on the mercy of the court and pleading mitigating circumstances. He told the beaks, "I was extremely nervous and unused to the extreme heat and this led to my behaviour which was totally out of character." The committee were obviously minded to give Jim the benefit of the doubt and counselling against any further misdemeanours they gave a verdict of "sending off sufficient." The big man was delighted and he left, thanking them for their understanding. Sadly, soon after his debut, another game saw 'Big Jim' dismissed for a second time. The same taxi driver delivered him and the sheepish prop took a seat before the committee, with the words, "Bloody hell it was hot again, wannit!"

Tony Fisher was one of the hardest men I ever saw on a rugby pitch. Anyone who ever met him commented on the size of his huge hands. I remember as a kid that my dad's mining workmate Albert, whose son Mike Stephenson was the Dewsbury hooker, had been told by his coach that Fisher would punch him in the first scrum and that he must return the blow to show he was not intimidated. He later told his father it was the daftest thing he ever did.

The second test took place on 5 November 1978 at Odsal Stadium. No doubt there would have been a whiff of gunpowder in the air in advance of Fireworks Night. Sadly, I was not present at my boyhood haunt to witness it. By then I was a student at Bangor University in North Wales. None of my mates from the rugby club were interested in the XIII-a-side code so I cut a lonely figure and went to my then girlfriend's to watch as we had no television in our digs. The one silver lining was that she was the landlord's daughter at our local, 'The Albion', so I got to watch it with a pint in the bar. I was the sole spectator as Wales on Sundays was 'dry' back then and the pub was shut.

Watching the game back recently I was struck by the lack of formulaic tactics and the variations in play. For instance, the tourists kicked early on in their sets to gain territorial advantage and the ball was thrown out wide by both sides when the opportunity arose. The tackling was fierce and the tourist's second row, Rod Reddy, did not endear himself to the home crowd by flattening both Steve Nash and Brian Lockwood in two separate incidents. Eventually Jim Mills took matters into his own hands – or rather head, as he butted Reddy.

Referee Mick Naughton could easily have sent him off, but he must have taken the Australian player's previous actions into account believing he had it coming. The green and golds certainly meted out some rough treatment to British skipper Roger Millward who was forced to leave the field to be replaced by John Holmes in the second half.

The fear which was felt in many a British fan's breast was that the ageing legs of the 'Dad's Army' might eventually be exploited as the game entered the closing stanza. But the gallant Lions stuck to the task and with Widnes flyer Stuart Wright scoring two tries and Wigan's George Fairbairn contributing six goals, they emerged victorious 18–14, much to my joy watching in splendid isolation in Wales. An important ingredient in the victory was the contribution of the old heads in the front row. Tony Fisher out-hooked Max Krilich, winning the scrums 19–12 and Brian Lockwood received the Man-of-the-Match award. Sadly, this was to be the last British victory against their Ashes rivals for 10 years.

Prior to the final test, the tourists gained relatively easy victories over Wigan, Saints and York before travelling to Headingley for the decider. Fox made two changes with Bevan coming in for Dyl and Vince Farrar winning his first cap replacing the star of Odsal, Brian Lockwood, who was forced out by injury. Australia brought in George Peponis to replace Max Krilich who had come off second best to Tony Fisher, and Rod Morris replaced Craig Young at prop. Les Boyd, who went on to become a legend at Warrington, was brought in for Rod Reddy, who had certainly dished out some punishment in the previous test. The game proved a bridge too far and Australia gained a 23–6 victory and the Ashes in front of a 30,604 crowd.

There is one final and somewhat controversial footnote to the eventful 1978 tour. In the week prior to the third test, an incident occurred, the ramifications of which, should it have happened today where everyone has a camera in their pocket, can hardly be imagined. This was the era of punk rock and the world was certainly in a state of cultural flux. The tourists always stayed at the Queens Hotel in Leeds when they had fixtures nearby. Eddie Waring famously had a suite on the hotel's top floor from which he held court and conducted his business affairs. Also staying at the hotel were the band, 'The Jam'. Apparently, the Australian manager Jim Caldwell and lead singer Paul Weller got into an altercation when Caldwell accidentally bumped into the band member's chair. Weller allegedly hit Caldwell with a glass and Australian reinforcements arrived and became involved in a melee which resulted in one of 'The Jam's' members being treated for broken ribs at Leeds Infirmary.

Paul Weller was arrested and appeared at Leeds Crown Court on a charge of wounding which was later dismissed. The band were asked to leave the Queens for their own safety and Paul Weller references the evening's events on the album notes for 'Dig the New Breed' writing, "A night in the nick in Leeds! Paul Weller's innocent chalked on the steps of Leeds Court. God bless you girls."

The police did visit the hotel later in the week, but the Australians were exonerated of any wrongdoing and though the matter received minor coverage in the press here and in Australia, it was largely swept under the carpet. My, how times have changed. Still, "what goes on, on tour, stays on tour", as they say!

32. Alf Meakin and Berwyn Jones

Writing in *The Independent* in March 2008, the late, much-lamented Dave Hadfield derided the then attempts by Castleford to lure the 'disgraced' 30-year-old indoor European sprint champion Dwain Chambers to join the Weldon Road outfit. He poured scorn on the idea and argued, "If Cas are as crass as it appears, the game will be asked to accept the proposition that a pariah from another discipline, with no knowledge of rugby league whatever, is capable of making the transition to Super League at this stage." He thought that the venture had about as much chance of success as Phil 'The Power' Taylor becoming the next Castleford scrum-half. Highlighting other high profile 'flops' such as Macdonald Bailey's one "petrified appearance" for Leigh in 1953, Hadfield acknowledged that Berwyn Jones and Alf Meakin were "the exceptions to the rule" that sprint specialists were doomed to fail in our game.

What I was intrigued to learn is that there were some interesting details to connect the two former athletes who made a relative success of building careers in rugby league. Berwyn Jones and Alf Meakin had experienced success on the track as teammates in 1962. In that year they were members of the Great Britain sprint relay team which took the bronze medal at the European Championships in Belgrade alongside Ron Jones and David Jones. Meakin must have felt a bit like the odd-one-out as he was quite literally 'keeping up with the Joneses'.

Berwyn Jones was certainly the more successful of the two converts. Born in Rhymney, South Wales, Thomas Berwyn Jones occasionally turned out on the wing for his hometown club and was the son of a village postmaster. After school, where he met his future wife Ann, he trained to be a teacher at Monmouthshire Training College and later at Loughborough. Brian Anthony, a student pal from his Monmouth days recalls, "I only realised he was a good sprinter one day when we had to run like hell to catch a bus – Berwyn ran like a bat out of hell!"

His innate speed brought him to the attention of the athletics authorities and in 1963 he was part of the four-man team to defeat the USA at the White City Stadium. In doing so they equalled the, then, world record time for the 4 x 110 yards distance. The Tokyo Olympics of 1964 beckoned, but Berwyn's next move shook the athletics world to the core.

Having secretly played in two games against Doncaster and Huddersfield for Wakefield Trinity under the wonderfully ironic alias 'Walker', he was signed by the club for a reported fee of £6,000. Given that the average price of a semi-detached was probably half that amount at the time, the financial attraction of the move is obvious. At a reception for the relay team at Buckingham Palace, hosted by the Duke of Edinburgh, shortly after signing the deal and thus relinquishing his amateur status, Berwyn said, "I feel extremely guilty at letting the boys down but it was an opportunity that I could not turn down as it gave financial security for my wife Ann and I."

Once he had crossed the Rubicon, Jones was gambling his sporting future. However, any second thoughts must have been short lived as he had almost immediate success when he contributed two tries as Trinity defeated Leeds 18–2 in the Yorkshire Cup Final at Fartown. He continued to enjoy success at the club and went on to play in three international matches, all against France and the Welshman scored a try in each game.

Berwyn Jones playing for Great Britain. (Courtesy *Rugby League Journal*)

In 1966, Berwyn was selected for the Great Britain tour to Australia and New Zealand and although he played in 15 games and scored 24 tries, he was unable to displace Barrow's Bill Burgess or Geoff Wrigglesworth of Leeds who held onto the wing berths in the test matches. Between 1964 and 1967, the Welsh speedster made 189 appearances for the club from the Merrie City scoring 47 tries before transferring to my boyhood heroes and joining Bradford Northern.

I recall that our Odsal pitch in the 1960s was something of a quagmire necessitating the players changing into clean jerseys on the pitch at half-time as they did not repair to the changing rooms up the steps at the top of the stadium at the break. The only corridors of green were to be found down the touchlines, but Berwyn Jones still managed to excite the faithful with his exhilarating bursts of pace down the flanks. He was aided and abetted by his centre Geoff Wrigglesworth with whom he had competed for the wing spot on the recent tour before the Leeds centre was signed to make a formidable partnership which led to Berwyn scoring 26 tries in his opening season.

Jones left Bradford for St Helens in 1969 and made his debut at Knowsley Road against Castleford, but his stay was short-lived. He played only four games for Saints with the last being against Warrington before the flyer hung up his boots. He taught for some years in Herefordshire and retired with his wife to their home in Ross-on-Wye. Sadly, Berwyn was stricken by Motor Neuron Disease which has focused the modern generation of supporters' thoughts as we have watched the heroic struggles of Rob Burrow against this cruel condition, prior to his passing away in June 2024. Berwyn died in January 2007 and the long-serving former director at Bradford, Jack Bates, paid tribute to the man he recalled "could run away from birds."

Alf Meakin did not quite scale the rugby heights of the man he ran with in Yugoslavia, winning bronze together in 1962, but he does have the distinction of being an Olympian over his former relay colleague. In the week prior to the Covid delayed games in Tokyo in 2021 *Blackpool Gazette* reporter Andy Moore invited Alf to recall his own involvement in the 1964 Games in the Japanese capital. Having won a Commonwealth gold in Perth in 1962 he became part of the British relay team in Tokyo. Meakin told the reporter that his outstanding memory was meeting an ageing Jesse Owens who had spoiled Hitler's party at the 1936 Olympic Games.

Alf was born in Swinton on 30 August 1938, but his family moved to Blackpool when he was eight. As a teenager he won county and national honours in sprinting and when he joined the RAF for National Service he was posted to the south east where he joined Thames Valley Harriers. Later he was made an honorary life member of that famous club.

Returning to Blackpool after his RAF experience, Alf worked in various jobs including car sales, as an estate agent and even selling premium bonds. After his Olympic appearance he was approached to have a trial at Headingley with Leeds, but the club did not retain his services. Alf decided to monetise his athletic prowess by signing for his adopted town team Blackpool Borough. He told Andy Moore: "I'd never played the game before but I could beat people one-on-one, though I quickly realised there was much more to the game than that and I didn't stay for very long. Some players would tell me what they were going to do to me when they tackled me, but I just told them they'd have to catch me first!" Given that two future members of the Hall of Fame, Brian Bevan and Billy Boston, enjoyed brief swan songs in the tangerine, white and black of the seaside club in the 1960s means Alf Meakin can count himself to be in good company in the list of former Borough wingers.

Blackpool Borough operated until 1993 and then experienced a nomadic existence under various guises as Springfield, Chorley and Trafford until they returned to the town as Blackpool Gladiators before folding in 1997. Statistical information on Alf's career at the club is scant, but Ray Connolly, the Chair of the Blackpool Rugby League Supporters Club, which stoically battles on despite the demise of their 'parent' club, offered what he knew of Meakin's time at Borough Park. Ray told me: "What I mostly remember is how fast he was. Give him the ball in a straight line and nobody could catch him. He didn't seem to find it easy to go round anybody however, but he could score tries in the right circumstances. I have a Supporters Club handbook covering the 1965–66 season and he was there in the first match, a friendly against Bradford Northern. He played 27 league and cup games scoring 12 tries."

Alf Meakin's final claim to fame is perhaps the most important one. In 2013 he became the oldest recipient of a bone marrow transplant to successfully treat leukaemia so that he can continue to enjoy life into his eighties. Some things really are more important even than rugby league.

33. Geoff Fletcher

I think that the term, "He's a bit of a character," can be something of a euphemism. It has been applied regularly to public figures like Boris Johnson, Nigel Farage or say, Piers Morgan, to whom I could substitute other more fitting epithets. But when we describe Geoff Fletcher as "a bit of a character," the phrase is bestowed with nothing short of awe and wonder at the exploits and achievements of a man steeped in rugby league. The great American basketball coach, John Wooden, who died at the age of 100 in 2010, stated, "Sports do not build character, they reveal it." Geoff Fletcher's actions in single-handedly keeping the game going on Merseyside reveal him as a stoic of epic proportions and a man of huge determination and commitment to the cause of progressing our game.

Geoff was widely nicknamed 'Piggy' on account of him running the family's pig farm, Holme Farm, just a short distance from the old Knowsley Road ground in his hometown of St Helens. He began his amateur career with Thatto Heath and Pilkington Recs winning international and county honours, before being signed by another former Saints' great, Alan Prescott, at Leigh. He went on to have three stints at the Hilton Park club in a professional career spanning 23 years in which he played 559 games.

Fletcher also played for Oldham, Wigan and Workington Town. While at Central Park he narrowly missed out on a Wembley appearance when he was absent from the 1970 Final against Castleford with a broken elbow. Incidentally, I attended this game as a pupil of Wibsey School in Bradford on a Wallace Arnold Coach trip. When we reached Newport Pagnell on the way back home, the teachers realised they'd left one kid back at Wembley! Talk about 'the good old days in education.'

Leafing through some old programmes I found one of a visit by Oldham to Odsal in the second round of the Challenge Cup in 1968. In the notes welcoming the visitors, Fletcher is described as: "Pack leader and club captain, a fine player who has blossomed forth this season and is being freely tipped to make the World Cup squad." The piece also comments on the positive impact which his ball playing prowess had on feeding the speedy 19-year-old international Bob Irving, noting that the "powerful runner is thriving on the Fletcher distribution."

However, this phase of Fletcher's career was to be a mere proving ground in preparation for the trials and tribulations he was about to encounter on joining Huyton in 1977. Rugby league on Merseyside was forever destined to be something of an endangered species. From its earliest incarnation as Liverpool Stanley, 1934 to 1951, to its emergence as Liverpool City, 1951 to 1968 at Knotty Ash, with all the connotations of Ken Dodd and his Diddy Men, to its eventual emergence as Huyton, life was always an uphill struggle. Following his death at the age of 74 in 2017, *The St Helens Star* paid tribute to Geoff Fletcher saying that while St Helens and Huyton might be but a "stone's throw" away geographically, they were lightyears apart in terms of their sporting heritages. The passage added, "Alas some of the locals took the 'stone's throw' term too literally and vandals with no respect to the club's Alt Park home or the code that played there, routinely smashed anything – windows, fences and even concrete terracing. Anyone visiting there in the early 80s would have been forgiven for thinking they had walked onto the set of *Play for Today*."

Geoff Fletcher playing for Huyton. (Courtesy *Rugby League Journal*)

I am aware that in painting a picture of a community, we can easily cause offence to residents who hold the vicinity in which they dwell in high regard. Liverpool generally has suffered some dreadful barbs from high profile figures who have seemingly queued up to put the boot in when the city has suffered some tragedy or other. In 2004, following the appalling death of Ken Bigley in Iraq, Boris Johnson, back then a mere hack for *The Spectator*, made an excoriating attack on Liverpudlians for their, to his view, perennial tendency to claim to be victims. *The Sun* newspaper was, and is, boycotted for its portrayal of Liverpool FC's supporters after the disaster at Hillsborough. Murdoch's more up market rag, *The Times* joined in this theme in the aftermath of the tragedy when columnist Edward Pearce referred to the city as "the capital of self-pity."

We can all be blinkered about our own communities and guilty of 'boosterism' in claiming accolades for the places in which we live beyond that which might be deemed justified by outside observers. Huyton certainly has its cheerleaders. Writing in *The Liverpool Echo* in September 2019, journalist Jess Molyneux said, "…it is hard not to smile when you think of all Huyton has to offer." She goes on to catalogue its charms as the friendliness of the locals and its huge branch of Asda.

The town, which was mentioned in the *Domesday Book* in 1086, certainly has had some famous residents and associates. Former Labour Prime Minister Harold Wilson – who incidentally closed more pits than Maggie Thatcher – represented the constituency from 1950 to 1983. It is the birthplace of association football stars like Stevie Gerrard, Peter Reid and Joey Barton, as well as being home to the original Beatle Stuart Sutcliffe. In the world of the arts, it has given us writers of gritty northern drama, like Alan Bleasdale with *Boys From the Black Stuff* and Phil Redmond's works for television such as *Hollyoaks*, *Brookside* and *Grange Hill*. Perhaps more surprisingly Sir Rex Harrison, who starred in *My Fair Lady* as Professor Henry Higgins, was born there. It is remarkable that given his roots, it was not Eliza Doolittle giving him lessons in elocution rather than vice-versa: 'Know warra mean liyk'.

Geoff Fletcher stuck with the Huyton project through its years by the River Alt, to its incarnation as Runcorn Highfield, then Highfield and finally as the Prescott Panthers. He finally called a halt when the club folded in 1997. In all these years, he fulfilled about every official, informal and ad-hoc role, from player, coach, director, chairman, kitman, bar tender, odd-job-man, general dogsbody and tea lady. I recall the former York, Castleford and Wakefield Trinity full-back Les Sheard recounting how he and his team-mates had to clear dog muck, broken glass and other debris from the playing surface before one particular match at Huyton.

In delving into Geoff Fletcher's contribution to his beloved club I came across a Bradford Northern programme of a visit from Huyton to play in a club fixture in a match which was designated a testimonial game for Johnny Rae. Our loose-forward was returning from surgery to a serious medial ligament injury and was training on Odsal Rec which was a notoriously boggy stretch of turf next to the club car park. To this day I boast a blue scar from diving on a house brick concealed in the murky depths in one area of swamp on that pitch. Rae collided with Terry Ramshaw – who bore more than a passing resemblance to Desperate Dan! – and his knee 'went' again causing his premature retirement and the consequent testimonial. How delighted must he have been to be awarded the Huyton game as the occasion of his reward for his services to the club? Perhaps this is indicative of the parsimonious nature of our board giving away their generosity with all the largess of a latter-day Ebeneezer Scrooge, knowing receipts from the encounter would mark an all-season low!

In his programme notes, manager Albert Fearnley paid "...tribute to all who have been concerned with the affairs of Huyton over the years that they have continued to flourish in such a soccer stronghold as Liverpool and district." One can only suggest that the use of the word 'flourish' might have been gilding the lily a tad. In the programme for their visit some four winters later, a more accurate summary of affairs was offered. It read: "They have weathered all kinds of storms during their chequered history and have always come up smiling against odds that would have sunk most clubs." Perhaps it would have been fairer to say, Geoff Fletcher had single-handedly weathered said storms.

In 1982, Geoff's services were rewarded when he was voted winner of the Rugby League Writers inaugural award. He was presented with the Arthur Brooks Trophy named in honour of *The Daily Mirror* journalist. In his acceptance speech, the unassuming hero had the gathered newspaper men in stitches with his typical gallows humour. He explained how some lions had escaped in Huyton en-route to the venue for a nearby circus. "The poor lions were petrified," sympathised Fletcher.

I am reminded of a story which the wonderful raconteur Maurice Bamford, the former Great Britain coach, told at a dinner in honour of a boyhood teammate of mine, Keith Mumby. Maurice was giving the diners an insight into the behind the scenes difficulties in the game's lower echelons. Maurice explained that at Huyton, they needed to make ends meet on crowds of about 250 per home match, so money was always too tight to mention. Geoff Fletcher was a director at Alt Park and one particularly wet and windy night on Merseyside, after training, he donned a stylish camel coloured coat he was particularly proud of in preparation to attend the directors meeting to be held that night.

Geoff was follicly challenged from a relatively early age and he wore a wig. Indeed, there had been a national news coverage of a confrontation which ensued when Huddersfield's Graham Swale hid Geoff's 'syrup' – but that is to digress. Having spruced himself up, Geoff made his way across the dimly lit carpark with its rutted surface and deep muddy puddles. Out of the gloom emerged a large figure of one of Huyton's pack saying, "I want my money Fletch. I've not been paid for weeks and you owe me." Geoff explained that cash flow concerns prevented him from settling up with the disgruntled employee and following a 'full and frank exchange of views', a melee ensued. Blows were struck and both men ended up rolling round in the mud before Fletcher eventually emerged victorious. He straightened his filthy wig and entered the meeting in his blood and mud splattered light coloured overcoat. The chairman challenged his fellow board member regarding his tardiness, to which Fletcher replied, "Sorry Mr Chairman but I've just been outside negotiating a contract."

Recently I rewatched the documentary *Another Bloody Sunday* which was shot in 1981 and directed by Barry Cockroft for the Yorkshire Television series *Once in a Lifetime*. It follows the fortunes of fellow strugglers Doncaster who until the final game of the season were vying for bottom spot with Huyton. The YouTube footage is well worth a watch. It begins with testimony from the curmudgeonly General Manager of the Dons, Tom Morton, delivering a eulogy about the state of affairs at Tattersfield which would have done the late Les Dawson credit. The playing scenes are slowed down and accompanied by Prokofiev's *Dance of the Knights*, from the opera of Romeo and Juliet – or I as call it, the music from *The Apprentice*.

It has a strange melancholic beauty as the great hulks collide and the anguish and exhaustion are palpable. The star performer is the Cockney Tony Banham, who confounds his racist detractors to emerge as the hero of the piece. He grew up in Hull where he was a publican in Hessle Road before becoming a bouncer in Doncaster, where he also volunteered working with kids with disabilities. The other standout performance in the documentary comes from Geoff Fletcher himself. In this fly-on-the-wall film, the rugby league spectator probably gained the most telling insight as to what the man who could have been dubbed Mr Huyton brought to the party.

His team talk in rousing his men for the final game of the season is hardly a cry for "England and St George" or a plea to "plug the wall with our English dead", but it is stirring stuff. Sadly for Fletcher, Doncaster lowered their colours on the day but thankfully we have something of the man's inspirational presence to remind us of this true character of the game. An ancient anonymous sage once said that, "Adversity introduces a man to himself." If this is so then Geoff Fletcher must have been profoundly self-aware. In a world where kids all want to support Manchester United or Arsenal, no matter where they come from, or where we only bother to study the fortunes of the top Super League clubs and ignore the minnows, we would do well to remember unsung heroes like Geoff Fletcher who make up the base of the sporting pyramid. As Dr Martin Luther King Junior put it, "The greatness of man cannot be seen in the hours of comfort and convenience, but rather in moments of conflict and adversity." Geoff endured and enjoyed everything that was thrown his way and we should honour men of his quality.

34. Remembrance

Archduke Franz Ferdinand and his wife Sophie, Austro-Hungarian heirs to the throne, were gunned down by a Serbian assassin on Sunday 28 June 1914. This act set in train the first truly industrial war, as the various squabbling factions of Queen Victoria's numerous progeny fell in one behind the other into their pre-war alliances. The die was cast. The 'Triple Entente' of Great Britain, France and Russia lined up against Germany and Austria-Hungary in a grudge match which would condemn, in Wilfred Owen's words, "half the seed of Europe" to an early grave.

Probably the best-known former player who lost his life in the war was Hull's Jack Harrison. I recall that as a child, my father took me to the Boulevard to watch Bradford Northern and he bought me a paperback history of the 'Airlie Birds'. On the coach journey home I read how the former teacher, who scored a record 52 tries in the 1913–14 season, including one in the 6–0 Challenge Cup Final victory over Wakefield Trinity, became the only rugby league player to be awarded the Victoria Cross. He received it posthumously after being killed at Oppy Wood near Calais. The citation in the *London Gazette* read: "2nd Lt. Harrison led his company against the enemy trench under heavy rifle and machine gun fire, but was repulsed. Reorganising his command as best he could in No Man's Land, he again attacked in darkness under terrific fire, but with no success. Then, turning round, this gallant officer single-handedly made a dash at the machine-gun, hoping to knock out the gun and so save the lives of many of his company. His self-sacrifice and absolute disregard of danger was an inspiring example to all. He is reported missing, believed killed."

Jack Harrison's name is listed on the Thiepval Memorial to the 72,195 missing soldiers who have no known grave. Visitors to Hull FC's KCOM Stadium will see the excellent memorial which has been erected by the club to this fallen hero whose own son was killed at Dunkirk in the Second World War.

But why was there such a paucity of information regarding Northern Union men who joined the Great Fallen in the First World War? The historian, Professor Tony Collins, explains how social class attitudes contributed to the recording and memorialising of the victims of war. Many of the manual jobs which working men undertook before 1914 were dangerous. Employers often viewed workers who were injured or killed as a fact of life and merely an inevitable by-product of the industrial process. These attitudes to death in service were unsentimental, at best and callous at worst. For example, in 1913 there were 1,149 fatal accidents in the British coal industry. This is shocking, but in 1910 it had been even higher with a record 1,818 deaths. In that same year there were 178,962 non-fatal injuries.

The daily familiarity with the brutal realities of tragedy and death bred a fatalistic attitude to the harsh facts of life for those who favoured the Northern Union code of football. Tony Collins explains "The sport's annual handbook 'the Official Guide' for the first season after the war did not even mention it. Wakefield Trinity's annual report for 1918–19 not only makes no reference to the War, but does not refer to the death of its captain, WL Beattie, in action in France in 1917. The minute books of the Yorkshire Society of Referees contain not a single reference to the War at all between 1914 and 1918."

Collins points out that while no official figures for Northern Union players, amateur and professional, were ever officially compiled, a correspondent for *The Athletic News* in 1919 suggested that of the clubs who responded to his enquiries, he was able to gather that of 760 league players who served, 103 lost their lives. We know that Widnes lost 13 men, Swinton nine and at Hull 11 colleagues of Jack Harrison also made the ultimate sacrifice.

Given the scant nature of contemporary record keeping regarding deaths of Northern Union players, we are hugely indebted to the magnificent research undertaken by Jane and Chris Roberts in 2018. Their book *The Greatest Sacrifice - Fallen Heroes of the Northern Union* published by Scratching Shed Publishing, puts a wrong to rights. It sets out to catalogue the brave contribution of the players whose ultimate sacrifice had been hitherto untold. The authors believe that the Northern Union Ruling Council, which in 1914 had encouraged its players "to think first of the nation's honour and needs", was at the end of the global conflict, taking a view that they should draw a veil over the game's players who were killed and look to the future. Thankfully the extensive research of the couple has gone some way to filling this lamentable vacuum.

My own initial research into losses from the Bradford Northern club had revealed no results, but I did discover that nine Bradford City association football players were killed – including one named Harry Potter. The Roberts' impressive research did uncover details of some Bradford NU players who were lost of whom I was unaware and I am very grateful for the information which their diligent work has uncovered.

At the start of the War, the government could call on 90,000 men who made up the British Army, Reservists and members of the Territorial Army. This group formed the British Expeditionary Force (BEF) which was dispatched to France in an attempt to halt the German Schlieffen Plan to march into France via Belgium. This would be in advance of Lord Kitchener training volunteer soldiers to bolster the war effort. The BEF encountered the enemy in the first battle of the War at Mons on 23 August 1914. The Battle of Mons gave us the great myth of 'The Angel of Mons', when stories spread of the fallen being gathered up by an angel and carried into the clouds. No doubt this was an early indication of the way in which a traumatised nation would seek solace and even look for supernatural explanations for the carnage which was to follow.

St Helens half-back Eddie Toole was the first rugby league fatality at Mons. Bradford Northern had two reservists who had served together in the Army in India who fought in the battle. Rumours emerged at Birch Lane that both James Simpson and Ralph Laycock had perished. However, it transpired that Laycock had been taken prisoner and he subsequently returned home in 1918. Laycock played his only game for Northern at home against Halifax the following year. Sadly, James Simpson was less fortunate and was reported missing presumed dead. His name is recorded on the Menin Gate.

Harold Ruck was born in Stroud in Gloucestershire. A huge man by the standards of that era, he was six feet tall and tipped the scales at over 14 stones. He had joined the Grenadier Guards and was selected to play in the second-row for The Army against The Navy where he caught the eye of Bradford scouts. He was enticed north in 1913 and made his debut in a 13–0 defeat to Barrow. Ruck played in 38 of the club's 39 matches in the 1913–14 season, helping them win through to the Yorkshire Cup Final. As a reservist, his rugby career was interrupted and Harold rejoined his old regiment and was posted to France in March 1915.

He survived for 18 months in which he saw a great deal of action before he was killed at the Battle of Morval in September 1918 as part of the Somme offensive. Sadly for his parents, he was the second son they had lost because his brother Francis had died in France seven months earlier.

Fred Longthorpe was born in Laisterdyke in Bradford in 1889 and attended Belle Vue School in the city. He joined the family greengrocery business prior to joining up in 1907. By 1912 he had moved through the ranks to reach the position of Corporal. However, shortly after gaining this promotion, Fred opted to buy himself out of the forces and returned to work in the greengrocer's shop. He played amateur rugby for Westfield Albion before signing for Bradford Northern. He was a centre who *The Telegraph and Argus* described as "... a player of great promise, a very steady and tricky man, and a fearless tackler who is expected to prove a rare acquisition to the club."

Having played several matches, Longthorpe applied for a Commission in 1916 and was granted one to become a 2nd Lieutenant in 1917 and was sent to France. In the same month as his arrival, he received a gunshot wound to the thigh and died of his wounds the following day on 20 September 1918. Fred Longthorpe is buried in Beaulencourt in France.

The last NU player to be killed in the First World War was also a Bradford player. Harry Basil Wray was a 32-year-old Company Sergeant Major who died only a fortnight before the Armistice was signed. Wray was part of an Anglo-French force sent to reinforce the Italian front in a battle against Austro-Hungarian forces in the Battle of Vittorio Veneto. Wray had signed for Northern in 1914 and played six games for the club before being called up for military service. During his time in France, he played against the New Zealand Army for the Yorkshire Army NU who emerged victorious against a side containing several All Blacks in a game to raise funds for the War effort. He was killed on 29 October 1918, just six days before the cessation of fighting in that arena of the conflict. Harry Wray is buried in the Tezze British Cemetery in Italy.

The gaps in evidence as a result of the lack of record keeping at the time make the contributions of heritage groups on this matter all the more admirable and remarkable. At the centenary anniversary of the First World War, I was invited by Andy Harland, a lifelong friend and former captain of Dudley Hill when they won the BARLA National Cup, who had worked at the RFL, to spend a day with him at Rochdale Hornets where he was working on a part-time basis. The experience provided me with a valuable insight as to the uphill struggle to keep clubs from outside Super League going on shoestring budgets. I looked on as Andy and his only other colleague ordered programmes, tried to secure the services of ball boys and girls and paid the local butcher for the half-time pies. Andy showed me around and I was most impressed to see the work of their local history group and to discover their findings regarding the Great War.

They discovered that 25 Rochdale players enlisted to serve and that three of them were killed in the subsequent fighting. Sergeant Twigg and Archie Field died at Arras in 1917. Walter 'Rattler' Roman was the most famous of the three and something of a Hornet's legend. In November 1911 he played for Wales and the West of England against Australia at Bristol as the tourists won 23–3. In February 1914, he played for England against Wales in a 16–12 victory at St Helens. Subsequently Roman was selected for the 1914 tour of Australia which immediately preceded the outbreak of war. Although born in Somerset, after joining

Rochdale, he settled in the town and became the landlord of the Beehive Hotel only half a mile from the club's Athletic Grounds. Walter Roman died on 28 July 1916 in Cheltenham as a result of injuries sustained on the first day of the Battle of the Somme. The heritage group produced a special commemorative tee shirt in honour of the fallen players and I was proud to sport mine at the gym thereafter.

It was at Headingley though that I found the most comprehensive research on player fatalities. The city of Leeds has a unique and poignant connection to the Great War as the very last soldier to be killed in combat hailed from the city. Private George Ellison was killed by a sniper's bullet on the morning of 11th November – just 90 minutes before the signing of the Armistice.

Merely a month after war was declared, the Leeds Pals Battalion had recruited 1,275 soldiers and some 20,000 people cheered the men, whose average age was 21, as they left Leeds Station. Tragedy awaited them at the Somme. Local historian Stephanie Webb has undertaken extensive research on Leeds's contribution to the war. She explains: "On 1 July 1916, 24 officers of the Leeds Pals took their men over the top into No Man's Land. At the end of the first day of the battle, only 17 of 900 men answered a roll call. 750 of their number had lost their lives and the Battalion was all but decimated. Across the city, hundreds of families closed their curtains in mourning. It is said that after the Somme, every street in the city had at least one house with curtains drawn."

One of the men who met his end on the Somme was Samuel William 'Billy' Jarman. Like Walter Roman, the Leeds back-row forward was selected to tour Australia with the England Northern Union side led by the great Harold Wagstaff. Only a serious injury, incurred the week before in the second test 12–7 defeat, prevented Billy from playing in the historic 'Rorke's Drift' victory. As a reservist, Jarman was called up to serve in the Scots Guards on his return home but the knee injury sustained on the Australian tour prevented his involvement in active duties at the start of the war. He was assistant groundsman at Bramley Cricket Club until, with his rehabilitation complete, Guardsman 6295 was posted to the Western Front in August 1915. He was killed almost exactly one year after his arrival. Like Jack Harrison his body was never recovered and he too is recorded on the Thiepval Memorial.

In 2016, the Leeds Rhinos Foundation Heritage Committee researched and collated a full list of Leeds former players, both first and second team, who made the ultimate sacrifice. In the summer of 2017, a special commemorative stone was unveiled to remember all those men. In total 51 players from the club enrolled to serve their country. Sixteen of the men died in the hostilities. They were (with Heritage Numbers);

First team: Samuel William Jarman (225), Jimmy Sanders (231), Leonard Leckenby (267), Sidney Clifford Abbott (269), Joseph Henry Hopkins (286), Arthur Llewellyn (287), Belfred Ward (289), David Harkness Blakey (290), John Robert Pickles (295)

Second team: HE Bannister, J Harkness, L Farrar, B Thorpe, N Parker, George Pickard and GR White.

Thanks to the painstaking research of the Leeds Heritage volunteers - "We **WILL** remember them."

35. Jimmy Birts and Keith Mumby

Looking back, schools in the late 1960s and early 1970s could be quite brutal places and I sometimes wince to hear people bang on about 'the good old days in education'. We were only allowed footballs on the playground at lunchtime at the primary school I attended. Morning and afternoon breaks were ball-free affairs so we adapted to this by kicking stones or each other. If we improvised and used someone's school cap as a ball, we were caned.

At secondary school, while there were teachers who could be quite caustic and intimidating, there were others who, like Colin Welland's character in *Kes,* were on the side of the underdog. I was lucky that we had one such teacher in the form of Mr Philpott, a French master. Barry Philpott used to watch Bradford Northern and while he was by no means an expert on the game, he agreed to start a school rugby team after a good deal of pleading. Following a trial for would-be players, he picked a team, and set up some fixtures. I was awarded the captaincy on account of being what could be termed 'vocal'. From then on, school became bearable, indeed almost worthwhile, so in a sense the game saved my educational bacon. Things got even better when we were given the opportunity to play with other like-minded lads from other schools in city representative teams.

Recently I was thumbing through back issues of *The Rugby League Journal* which does such a splendid job of highlighting the history of the game "for those fans" (like me) "who don't want to forget". The editor, Harry Edgar, does a splendid job in paying tribute to former players, referees and other officials who have passed on and it is to his great credit that he is so respectful in acknowledging their part in our shared heritage. In my sojourn down memory lane, I found Winter 2014's edition (Number 49). I recalled how saddened and shocked I had been to learn of the sudden passing of one of my schoolboy contemporaries, Jimmy Birts, at the tragically young age of 57. I always enjoy the section in the *Journal* devoted to 'Unsung Heroes'. Jimmy was one such – a full-back who never let anyone down.

I first met Jimmy in 1971 when we were both selected as members of the Bradford Schools Under-15 squad to attend a week-long coaching course at Bisham Abbey in Berkshire. It is now one of three National Sports Centres run by Sport England. This was a huge honour and an opportunity to learn from coaches of the calibre of Albert Fearnley and Laurie Gant as well as former players in Paul Daley and John Sykes.

One of the other lads on the course was Keith Mumby who went on to become one of the game's greats. Both Jimmy and Keith were full-backs and this fact would be a salient factor in Jimmy's future career. I first played against Keith as a 12-year-old when he starred for Drummond Road School as they hammered our Wibsey Junior School side. He graduated to Rhodesway Comp and I went to Grange where our paths crossed regularly. Later we played together in some Bradford Boys games and other youth representative teams. From the outset his greatest attribute was his flawless tackling technique. Many thousands of fans would later witness his impeccable defensive work as he would languidly cover across to cut down any breaks with a copybook tackle around the legs. Jimmy was a tall willowy kid with a shock of vivid ginger locks who attended the non-rugby league playing Eccleshill Upper School, but such were his obvious talents that he was identified and selected for the city's representative side.

Left: Keith Mumby playing for Great Britain. Right: Jimmy Birts playing for Carlisle.
(Both photos courtesy *Rugby League Journal*)

When we arrived at Bisham Abbey, we were shown around the ancient manorial building which was a former monastery dating back to the 13th century which stands on the banks of the Thames. To us unsophisticated Bradford lads, it looked pretty posh and really spooky. This impression was reinforced by our guide who informed us that the building was host to a well-documented ghost or two.

Apparently, an over-zealous governess had beaten one of her pupils to death for making blots on their school work. One or both of them, we were told, now wailed as they roamed the abbey's byways by night. Having been regaled with this story in an obvious ploy to discourage nocturnal meanderings, we were sent to our collective dormitories for our first night. Unable to sleep, in the early hours Mumby and I decided to explore. After a few minutes, we heard footsteps and hid behind the towering stone pillars of a gothic archway in the corridor. In the dim light it was possible to identify the footsteps as belonging to Jimmy as his flowing ginger locks gave him away even in the dim light. To our schoolboy mirth we jumped out at him almost causing him to answer his nocturnal call of nature before he reached the facilities!

Just over 12 months later, both Keith and Jimmy were signed by Bradford Northern while I and most other lads from that course graduated to amateur clubs such as West Bowling, Queensbury and Dudley Hill. In 1973, Keith Mumby found himself catapulted into the first team when Eddie Tees decided, without further notice, to hang up his boots after the side was hammered by the touring Australians. Keith was pitched in against Doncaster which I am sure was a short-term fix for the club who doubtless planned to seek a less callow last line of defence in the weeks ahead. The rest, as they say, is history.

Mumby broke the record for points in a debut which had been held by the legendary John Holmes of Leeds by registering 12 goals and a try. The full-back berth was his own and he went on to give the club many years of flawless service. In a 17-year career with Bradford Northern, Keith made 645 appearances with 73 tries, 783 goals and registered 1,856 points. He won nine caps for Yorkshire, represented Great Britain on 11 occasions and was included in the 1984 tour squad to Australasia. In 2020, he was afforded the honour of being appointed as the first honorary president of the Bradford Bulls.

An assessment of Keith's capabilities was inadvertently shared with me in a chance encounter as I queued up with fellow fans to enter Odsal for a home game in the early 1980s. In an adjacent line for OAPs and kids I overheard an old chap who was of a vintage to remember the halcyon days of the 1940s and early 1950s speaking about our current full-back. We are all aware of the beer goggle effect of nostalgia on our judgements and assessments of the modern players against those "in my day". This old sage stated simply to his mate that Keith was the finest he had ever seen. High praise indeed, given the quality of previous full-backs at Odsal from Billy Leake in the 1940s, Kiwi Joe Phillips in the 1950s and Terry Price in the 1960s.

So for Jimmy Birts, the path to first team rugby at Bradford was barred by his brilliant mate Keith Mumby. He did play in one first team match on the left wing but he would need to seek pastures new and opportunity knocked when Maurice Bamford – not a bad judge of rugby calibre – stepped in to take Jimmy to Thrum Hall.

In his wonderful love letter to his hometown club, Robert Gate compiled his own 100 Thrum Hallers in *Halifax Heroes 1945–1998*. To his credit Jimmy makes the cut which is testimony to his ability and longevity. In statistical terms, Gate records that Jimmy made 102 appearances, scored 15 tries, 272 goals and 15 drop-goals, thus amassing 604 points. He describes him as: "Red-haired, six feet tall but slimly built and as good an all-round full-back as has been seen at Thrum Hall. He was capable of landing goals from half-way and beyond and was adept at dropping goals, while his tackling was of the textbook variety. His attacking style was exciting, his long dashes being executed at considerable pace and he registered some spectacular tries."

When Maurice Bamford left for Wigan in 1981, it is illuminating that he had his new club fork out £22,000 to take Jimmy with him. Injury and loss of form restricted him to only 11 appearances for the 'Pie Eaters' and Jimmy ended his career with the new Carlisle club.

For many years, schools traditionally favoured rugby union and rugby league was often excluded in schools even in the heartlands of our game. Educators and administrators seemed determined to ape the public schools and the selective grammar schools in their traditional commitment to the union code and the almost spiritual belief in the values of 'rugger' in building character in the young gentlemen who attended these rather elitist establishments. I for one am pleased that some of us were allowed, and indeed encouraged, to play the more proletarian game *we* loved. It enriched our lives and helped forge memories and friendships which endure to this day.

RIP Jimmy Birts – gone but never forgotten.

36. Alex Givvons

Many rugby league supporters will have memories of experiencing the extreme weather conditions of a visit to the Watersheddings ground in Oldham. The ground seemed to have its own unique micro-climate. Standing 770 feet above sea level, it was the highest ground in rugby league. The clue to this fact is that the name of the town derives from the old Norse word 'holmi' meaning "promontory or outcrop", describing the town's lofty hilltop position.

My first visit there was in February 1968 on a freezing night with rain of almost biblical proportions lashing down, for a Challenge Cup replay involving Bradford Northern. I recall that our star full-back, Terry Price, was replaced at the 11th hour by Jimmy Russell, an acquisition from Huddersfield. It later transpired that Price had arrived at Odsal displaying signs that he might have taken a drink and a pushing and shoving session with manager Albert Fearnley, himself no stranger to the charms of John Barleycorn, had ensued. My introduction to Watersheddings thus ended in a drenching and a defeat.

Oldham RLFC played at the ground from 1889 until 1997 when it was demolished to make way for a housing estate. In the following years the club endured rather a nomadic existence and a rebrand as Oldham Bears before going out of business for a time in 1997. They now play in the third tier of the game, but 'the Roughyeds' are aiming high with the appointment of Sean Long as manager for 2024. Their nickname is a reference to the rough felt used in hat making which employed many people prior to the proliferation of cotton mills in the town.

The fact that Oldham is a true centre of rugby league excellence is shown by the pedigree of the famous players who hail from the town. Greats of the modern game who can lay claim to be Oldhamers include Barrie McDermott, Kevin Sinfield, Iestyn Harris, Kyle Eastmond and Paul and Danny Sculthorpe.

In October 2023, I was delighted to hear that Oldham were renaming the club, not with some futuristic or Americanised moniker like the Oldham Orbits or Ocelots, but rather by a name referencing their proud heritage. Oldham have rebranded themselves as Oldham RLFC 1876 Ltd. The club was one of the original members of the Northern Union and were at the inaugural meeting at the George Hotel. Chairman Bill Quinn explained the thinking behind the change saying, "It is an insult not to celebrate our rich history and not to honour those who went before us. Many of them did great things and the club has a very impressive honours board." "Hear, hear!" to that sentiment say I.

One man who certainly did great things for the club was Alex Givvons. He was born in Pillgwenlly, Newport in Monmouthshire in 1913. Alex (pronounced 'Alec') was the son of a Welsh mother and a West Indian father who was a merchant seaman from St Thomas. He was one of two brothers and he also had a step brother, Trevor Williams, from his mother's second marriage. He began his rugby playing career at Holy Cross Roman Catholic School in Emlyn Street under the tutelage of Father Hanon. One of his classmates and fellow future rugby league star was Trevor Foster, with whom he maintained a lifelong friendship. Alex was nine years old when he joined the school team and he went on to captain Monmouthshire schools. Father Hanon encouraged the young scrum-half to join the Pill Harriers as the local Pillgwenlly side were known.

Givvons did train with Newport, but never played with the Rodney Parade club. In an interview he gave to Oldham rugby league historian Michael Turner later in his life, he explained that many of his own age group at the club were students who turned out for them when home in their holidays. Cash strapped Alex was from much humbler stock and couldn't afford to socialise with them. Consequently, Alex joined the Cross Keys club where he soon caught the eye of journalist Clem Lewis who had been outside-half for Wales immediately before and after the First World War. In a copy of the *Daily News* in 1932, Lewis wrote, "he is the biggest discovery I have seen since the war."

However, it was not only those in his own community who were taking notice of the new rising star. Givvons had come up on the radar of league clubs in the north of England. Oldham sent scouts to Aberavon to sign Tommy Egan. Turner explains what happened next. "During their stay, the Oldham delegation took in another match involving Cross Keys and were immediately impressed by a young man at scrum-half. On their return, the full committee were informed of the discovery and when they learnt that Huddersfield were also in the hunt for his signature, a decision was taken to offer terms to secure the Welshman's services without further delay." Writing in *The Dictionary of Welsh Biography*, Rebecca Eversley-Davies explains: "As other codebreakers made their way north from Wales, it became important to Givvons that people knew his leaving Newport was not a result of racism." Later he did convince his step brother Trevor Williams to join him at the club, but he failed to settle and Alex did attribute racist attitudes in some quarters to have contributed to his leaving.

Alex Givvons signed for the Roughyeds on 19 January 1933 on the same day that the England cricket team were concluding their Ashes test in Adelaide in the infamous 'Bodyline' series. He made his debut just two days later against Barrow, having had no time to acclimatise to his surroundings or the new game's challenges. Nevertheless, Givvons became a success and three years later he became only the second black player to represent Wales at rugby league. Coincidentally, the first person of colour to have done so was a fellow Newportonian from Risca, George Bennett, who had joined Wigan as a 17-year-old. Bennett made his international debut in 1935 which was 49 years before a rugby union cap was awarded to a black player by the WRU. In all Alex Givvons played six times for his country and they won on every occasion in which he wore the red jersey.

In his career with the east Lancashire club, Givvons made 241 appearances scoring 54 tries. He left for Huddersfield, the club which had shown their initial interest in his Cross Keys days. While at Fartown, he was a member of the Challenge Cup winning team which defeated Bradford Northern in the two-legged final in the 1944–45 season. But in 1948 he returned to his adopted home of Oldham this time as a loose-forward prior to his retirement in 1949.

One of Alex Givvons' two sons, also Alex, followed in his father's footsteps and played professionally with Halifax, Swinton and Blackpool Borough. His major claim to fame while with the Seasiders was that he was centre partner to the great Brian Bevan as he drew down the curtain on an illustrious career. In the 1970s and 1980s, Alex Jnr, became a top rugby league referee.

After hanging up his boots, Alex Givvons Snr. served the club until he was in his 80s in various capacities. He was 'A' team coach, kitman and dressing room supervisor. Fittingly, he and his wife Eunice lived in Watersheddings Street a mere stone's throw from the ground prior to its demolition.

When Michael Turner interviewed him in later life, he revealed that "a trace of Lancashire had seeped into his Welsh accent." Former players told Turner that Alex was "well liked, highly respected and a real gentleman" and they described him as "a courteous, almost fatherly man who demanded high standards." So widely respected was he that the town council voted to name a street near the site of the old ground in his honour. Givvons Fold provides a permanent reminder of the high esteem in which this adopted Roughyed is held. In 1995, Oldham unveiled its own Hall of Fame and Alex Givvons was invited to open it. Some years later he was added to the roll of honour to join other greats such as Bob Irving, Rocky Turner, Terry Flanagan and Bernard Ganley.

Writing in *The Rugby Paper* in 2020, Peter Jackson reflects on the longevity of Alex Givvons' service to Oldham RLFC. He points out that when he arrived in the town there had been 360 mills in the locality. In the intervening years, the town's economic fortunes had plummeted from the halcyon days when it had earned its reputation as 'Cottonopolis'. Jackson states that, "Elk Mill, the last cotton-spinning factory built in Lancashire, had been in production for fewer than five years when Givvons arrived in the town. When it closed in 1998, he and the Roughyeds were still a going concern."

Alex Givvons died in 2002 at the age of 88. He was a fine servant to a club which is rightly determined to honour those who have contributed to its proud heritage.

37. Featherstone Rovers – 1983 The last hurrah

Whenever I see a building bearing a plinth of stone declaring its origin to be 1913, a certain feeling of melancholy seeps into my bones as I wonder whether the stone mason who inscribed that number could have conceived what horrors which were to follow. I must admit to feeling that way about 1983.

In that year I had attended a family funeral in Caerau, near Maesteg in South Wales. During my stay I drove my Uncle Gerry, a huge jovial man with a handlebar moustache which the Australian fast bowler Merv Hughes would have envied, who had been a miner all his life, over the top of a mountain which dominated the little square of houses which made up their pit village. 'The Bwlch' as the summit was known, looked rather different to me. As we stood together taking in the panoramic views, I asked what the huge mountains of coal which filled the valley were. "That's for the war, Dai", sighed the old collier.

1983 had seen Mrs Thatcher return to government on the back of her victory against 'The Enemy Without' in the Falklands War. Now the 'Iron Lady' set about preparing a plan of action to defeat 'The Enemy Within'. Her Chancellor Nigel Lawson likened the plans to train and equip the police to confront and beat the NUM and to stockpile coal supplies to supply power stations and thus defeat striking miners as being as necessary as had been "rearming to face the threat of Hitler." Now that's fighting talk!

Featherstone is synonymous with two things. Those are rugby league and coal. The small town's very *raison d' etre* is based on the black gold which fuelled the industrial revolution. Pits like Acton Hall and Sharlston employed generations of men who made their living underground and recreated themselves playing and watching rugby league. The sport held an almost religious significance in the life of this closely knit community. Just how close were the bonds of kinship became clear to me when I had the opportunity to get to know Stuart Dickens, a goalkicking prop who made over 400 appearances for the Post Office Road club before retiring in 2012 who is a member of the Rovers' 'Hall of Fame'. I recall Stuart telling me of the reception he received from behind the posts when he scored a try shortly after being bereaved by the loss of his mum. They are a supportive and tight breed in Featherstone.

"Close the coalhouse door dad, there's blood inside," goes the song by Alex Glasgow, a pitman's son from Gateshead which featured in the 1968 stage musical he wrote with Alan Plater which examines the brutal history of the industry via one family's reminiscences of life in the mines. Long before the bitter yearlong dispute of 1984, Featherstone bore the scars of previous struggles between the workers and the forces of 'the Establishment'.

On 7 September 1893, an event known locally as 'The Featherstone Massacre' took place. Following a sharp decline in the price of coal, the mine owners stayed true to form and proposed a 25 percent cut in wages which the Miners' Federation, which had been founded in 1888, opposed. A lockout ensued which led to 80,000 men being denied work in 253 pits in the West Riding region. In Featherstone, miners learned that coal from Acton Hall was being loaded onto wagons on the orders of the pit owner Lord Samuel Cunliffe Lister to be taken to Manningham Mills, his imposing monolithic textile factory which stood as a monument to the wool baron's vast wealth which dominates the Bradford skyline to this day.

As workers went to confront the owner, local magistrate Bernard Hartley read 'The Riot Act' to the gathered protestors. Since most of the local constabulary had been deployed to control crowds at Doncaster Racecourse where the St Leger was taking place, the powers that be brought in the local Army militia. Rather than aiming over the heads of the protestors in warning as the law required, the soldiers fired into the throng. Eight people were seriously wounded and James Gibb, aged 22, and James Duggan, aged 25, were killed. A hastily convened inquest at the Railway Hotel the following day expressed regret that Gibb had died as he was declared "a peaceable man", but it deemed Duggan's death to be "lawful".

The first rugby club in Fev was established in 1902 and it joined the Northern Union in 1907, playing in the local district leagues. In 1921 they graduated to playing at semi-professional level and seven years later tasted success when they reached the Championship Final. They lost 11–0 to Swinton. In the year when the Second World War broke out, the club won its first silverware, the Yorkshire County Cup. In 1951, Featherstone played a masterstroke when they appointed the legendary Eric Batten as player-coach. The great man led the club to their first ever Wembley Final the following season. Rovers lost 18–10 to Workington Town in the first Final to be shown on BBC television. Even when not making finals, the small, unfashionable club generally responded well when the Cup came round. Prior to reaching Wembley in 1983, Featherstone had appeared in 10 semi-finals in the previous 25 years. In 1967 they won the trophy under coach and former referee Laurie Gant when they beat Barrow 17–12. In 1973, Peter Fox led them to repeat the feat as they hammered Bradford Northern 33–14 in a one-sided affair. The following year saw Rovers return to the capital, but they could not repeat back-to-back victories as they were undone by Alex Murphy's Warrington.

When local man Allan Agar arrived at Post Office Road in the 1982–83 season, the team in the famous 'butcher's apron' kits were having a thin time of things. They had hit rock bottom when Alex Murphy's Warrington smashed them 45–0.

Rovers were always something of a 'selling club', who supplied other well healed neighbours with the talent they had nurtured in order to keep the financial wolves at bay. Agar marshalled his forces, the majority of whom worked locally in mining, and embarked on an adventure which led all the way to the Twin Towers. En route, Fev beat Batley and Salford in the opening rounds before registering a famous victory at St Helens in the third round. In the semi-final they overcame Bradford Northern despite a breathtaking solo try by a young Ellery Hanley which will live long in the memory of those who witnessed it.

Featherstone's opponents at Wembley were the star-studded Hull FC led by former player Arthur Bunting. The Boulevard club were in the process of recruiting a galaxy of stars in the form of domestic internationals like skipper Dave 'Toppo' Topliss, Steve 'Knocker' Norton and ferocious front rower Trevor Skerrett. These high profile acquisitions were blended in with future stars such as 19-year-old Lee Crooks in a pack which also included former Featherstone stalwarts like Charlie Stone and Keith Bridges. Alongside these household names, Hull added spice with the inclusion of the New Zealand trio, James Leuluai, Dane O'Hara and Gary Kemble. Given the imbalance of resources the two clubs could call upon, it is no surprise that the bookies made the Humberside club 5/1 on favourites while Fev were 4/1 against in the betting. Such were the odds that in the week running up to the final some bookies refused to take punters' bets at all.

Of the Hull side, only Kevin Harkin had not yet won international honours. In Featherstone's ranks only Ken Kellett had experience of a Wembley final, a decade earlier.

My own recollections of the 1983 final are rather strange. Sadly for me, I was denied the opportunity of watching the match live as I was tutoring on a Youth Workers' course at Hazlewood Castle near York for the Bradford Youth Service. The establishment was run by Carmelite Monks and they hired out the venue for educational courses. Thankfully, there was a bar and television lounge and I sweet talked one of the staff to tape the match for me on a newfangled piece of kit called (apparently) a VCR. That night after lectures concluded I repaired to the lounge and having acted like one of *The Likely Lads* to avoid the score, I settled down in eager anticipation, expecting a Hull victory. The others had all set off out so it was just me and the barman. Like all true speccies, I get carried away and despite my Methodist upbringing I can revert to rather profane expletives during a game. The barman in his jeans and sweater seemed an ordinary guy so I saw little need to moderate my vocabulary. It was only the following morning when said barman served the students and me our breakfasts in his monk's garb that I felt a degree of deferred embarrassment.

Re-watching the game on YouTube was really interesting. In *Grandstand's* preamble to the main event, all the well-worn phrases about 'the tiny pit village' were trotted out. Magician David Copperfield conducted the community singing in a costume in a half-and-half style involving the kits of both teams in the interests of impartiality. The guest of honour was Lord Gormley of Ashton. Joe Gormley as he was prior to being ennobled and welcomed into the House of Lords, had been the President of the NUM. He was seen as a benign trade unionist that the establishment were prepared to countenance and even accept into their bosom, unlike his successor who was to become the nation's bogey-man a year later for daring to suggest that the government had a pit closure plan. Arthur Scargill would not be handing over the Challenge Cup anytime soon.

Prior to kick off, the players peeled off and were announced individually, receiving their own cheers from the public in another time-honoured ritual long since jettisoned by the modern code. BBC commentator Ray French declared the game one of the greatest 'David versus Goliath' affairs in the game's history. And yet it was Rovers who opened the scoring as second row David Hobbs spotted an opportunity to beat the Hull defence by bouncing off James Leuluai and scoring his 17th try of the season which Steve Quinn could not convert.

Shortly afterwards, a pivotal moment occurred when Rovers' captain Terry Hudson missed an attempted kick at a loose ball from a scrum, only to make contact with a diving Steve Harkin's jaw. This led to the Hull scrum-half's departure on a stretcher with concussion. Hull reshuffled, moving Topliss to scrum-half and substitute Terry Day to stand-off. This limited 'Toppo's' effectiveness to link with the star studded threequarters and at half-time Arthur Bunting replaced Day with forward sub Mick Crane going to scrum-half. This improved Hull's attacking options, but perhaps came a little late in the day. 19-year-old Lee Crooks's nerves were apparent as he fluffed an early drop goal attempt and missed two kickable goals from close range. After Gary Kemble was deemed to infringe by holding down in the tackle, Quinn registered a goal and stretched Rovers' lead to 5–0.

As half time beckoned, Wembley witnessed another first as speedy Fev centre John Gilbert embarked on a pacy, jinking run, only to be felled by a vicious swinging arm from Hull's Paul Rose. The result of the altercation was that Gilbert was carted off with concussion while Rose became the first player to be sin-binned at Wembley. Most pundits agreed that referee Robin Whitfield, himself a former player, had 'bottled it' and used the new dispensation to avoid making the right decision to send the player off. How often would this tendency for the man in the middle to take the soft option manifest itself in the years ahead?

One of the features of the game which strikes the modern spectator is the relevance of the scrum in shaping the outcome of the game. Hull had coaxed 31-year-old Keith Bridges out of retirement in the hope of gaining dominance in the battle for possession. But it was Featherstone's own experienced rake, Ray Handscombe, who came out on top. Hull found themselves having to defend 18 tackles as Rovers won three successive scrums late in the first half. I found it refreshing not to witness the airborne battle of the modern game as the last tackle brings the inevitable lottery of the high ball as both sides kept the ball in hand preferring to try to win scrum possession after the sixth tackle.

The introduction of Crane seemed to breathe new life into Hull as they dominated the early exchanges in the second stanza. Referee Whitfield again found himself at the centre of things as Charlie Stone attempted to play the ball forward and was impeded by David Hobbs leading to the referee awarding a disputed penalty try to tie affairs at 5–5. As the Humbersiders mounted more pressure, Leuluai rounded off a smart move involving Crane and Topliss to cross and give the black and whites the lead for the first time, 10–5. Many of the fans would have shared the sentiment expressed by Alex Murphy that "the floodgates might open." This perception was compounded still further as Fev's talismanic leader 'Tex' Hudson was invited to cool his heels for 10 minutes for using Dave Topliss' head as a football. This followed a few fiery encounters between the two half-backs. Crooks slotted the resultant penalty and the lead was extended to 12–5 with 12-man Rovers running out of time.

In the 64th minute, Rovers mounted an attack into the Hull 25. They continued to enjoy the lion's share of possession and the favourites could not shake them off. Gary Kemble, who had conceded a first half penalty near his own line, now repeated the offence. This gave Steve Quinn the chance to cut the arrears to just one converted try. This the tall marksman duly did and hope sprang eternal for the Featherstone faithful.

Again, the momentum shifted to the men in blue and white and the sense of a side united by privations and the vicissitudes of communal suffering and hardship seemed to galvanise Featherstone as they attacked the enemy lines with ever greater vigour. The crowd watched in disbelief as David Hobbs sealed his Lance Todd trophy winning performance and crossed for his second try of the afternoon. With the score standing at 12–12, Hobbs knocked over a drop-goal only to see Robin Whitfield chalk it off as 'touched in flight'. But Rovers would not be denied and when the linesman intervened to point out a foul on star loose-forward Peter Smith, Quinn knocked over the penalty to send the Featherstone fans into paroxysms of delight at their team's 14–12 victory. As the hooter sounded, Ray French hailed the victory as "one of the greatest triumphs of all time" as he lauded the efforts of the men from "the brave little mining village." As their heroes ascended the Wembley steps, their adoring neighbours bestowed scarves and hats on the players as they approached Lord Gormley to receive the Challenge Cup. Legend has it that as he handed it to Terry Hudson, the former miner's leader said, "What shift is thy on on Monday?" and Hudson replied, "Nights, can tha' do owt abart it?"

The writing though was on the wall. 1984 may not have been the Orwellian nightmare of totalitarianism dreamt up by Eric Blair, but for communities like Featherstone it was no less apocalyptic. The year-long miners' strike and its financial and social impact sounded the death knell for northern towns dependent on the mining industry. Families who were reliant on the pittance of strike pay and handouts from supporters of the beleaguered strikers were hardly able to continue to attend matches.

To their credit, the board at Post Office Road did introduce a season ticket scheme whereby supporters could attend on a watch-now-pay-later basis, but hungry children and mounting debts do tend to shift people's priorities. The travails of the pitmen were eventually to end in bitter defeat and the pit head gear at Acton Hall was demolished with such haste after the strike that one elderly lady likened it to knocking the crown off a dethroned monarch as King Coal was consigned to the dustbin of history.

Once proud men whose sinewy strength stood them in good stead at their place of work and on the sports field now stood idle as they watched their compensation payments disappear as their high streets were boarded up and housing estates became no go areas.

In his wonderful speech to the audience at the Albert Hall in the 1996 classic *Brassed Off* Pete Postlethwaite's character, bandleader Danny, sums up how many must have felt in towns like Fev: "If these men were seals or whales, you'd all be up in bloody arms. But they're not, they're just common-or-garden human beings."

In rugby league too, the brave new world ushered in Murdoch's millions and clubs like Featherstone were deemed too small, unimportant or unfashionable. The mega rich tycoon attempted to impose mergers including bringing together Wakey, Cas and Fev under the umbrella of a team to be called 'Calder'. This would have been to destroy the tribalism which is at the very core of our game and all three clubs howled their protests. When Super League handed out the spoils in 1996, Featherstone did not make the cut and another nail was hammered into the coffin of this once great club. The mastermind behind Rovers' last hurrah, Allan Agar deserves the final word. "When Sky came they said it would be the making of the sport. I said it would be the ruination of some clubs as well. Well, we've seen some clubs go under. There's something wrong in sport if that happens. In rugby now, you've got to be in a city to be a big success. The days of small-town romance have gone. What we did in 1983, you'll never see again."

Left: Featherstone coach Alan Agar with the Challenge Cup. (Courtesy *Rugby League Journal*)

38. Rugby league in the Second World War

In 2018, Jane and Chris Roberts produced the marvellously comprehensive record of professional Northern Union players who joined the fallen in the Great War. *The Greatest Sacrifice* catalogues all the players who died in action between 1914 and 1918. This important piece of research filled what had been a gaping vacuum in telling the stories of those who gave their all in the cause but who hitherto been forgotten by the game's leaders.

Although Nigel McCrery has attempted a similar task for the union code in the Second World War in *The Final Scrum* (2018), there has been no comprehensive equivalent undertaking to pay respect to the rugby league players who died in that second global conflagration. Once again, this reflects how the XV-a-side folk memorialise their own in a more thorough fashion than our game. Perhaps this is due to rank and social status and the fact that given its roots in the public schools, union men tended to be of officer rank and deemed 'more worthy' of remembrance.

McCrery's book is an excellent contribution in honouring those union men who made the ultimate sacrifice in that war against the forces of fascism. He highlights some fascinating and courageous athletes who laid down their lives for King and country. While Roy Kinnear, who played for Wigan in the first Wembley Challenge Cup final, gets a mention – largely as a Scotland, British Lions and Heriot's Former Pupils man – the others are all from the amateur game. Some are high profile figures like Russian Prince Alexander Obolensky of Oxford University and England and Eric Liddell of Chariots of Fire fame, who died in a Chinese Internment Camp.

The story of the Reverend Christopher Tanner is particularly poignant. The former wing who gained five caps for England, was serving as chaplain on the battle cruiser HMS Fiji when she was torpedoed off the coast of Crete. Tanner repeatedly entered the water to save stricken sailors, eventually rescuing some 30 men before collapsing and dying of exhaustion. His heroic and selfless action earned him a posthumous Albert Medal.

It is estimated that some 384,000 service personnel perished in the Second World War. Furthermore, with the rapid technological developments in aviation and the investment in arms capabilities, devastation could be visited on British industrial centres so that 70,000 civilian fatalities ensued. Nor should we forget that the British bombing of German cities like Dresden and Berlin wrought carnage of unimaginable horror as the government fought terror with terror.

But what of those former players from rugby league who fought around the globe in the various theatres of war? This brief piece is by no means exhaustive, but their stories are worthy of record and hopefully go some small way to honouring their memories.

In 1938, Wigan had a staggering 16 Welsh players on their books. The ties between the Lancashire coal mining town and the valleys of South Wales have always been strong. One of 'the Wigan Welsh' in the immediate War years was Percy Leslie Moxey who had been selected for several Welsh trials prior to coming north. Born in Pentre, on 1 January 1915, he moved to Llanelli in 1937, where he became a policeman and joined the Stradey Park club as a second row forward. The following year Moxey moved to Central Park to join the veritable gaggle of his countrymen at the illustrious club. His family relocated to East Anglia and settled in Great Yarmouth and Percy married Barbera Reynolds from the town in 1941. He joined the RAF and trained as a navigator on bombers. On the night of 7 August 1942, Pilot Officer 121570 and two colleagues took off on a training exercise from Upper Heyford airfield. Their Wellington bomber collided with a barrage balloon and the plane crashed to the ground killing all three occupants. Percy Moxey's body was recovered and he is buried at Gorlston Cemetery in Great Yarmouth.

Gwyn Williams was a teammate of Moxey's at Wigan. Although he was not killed in the conflict, his combat injuries ended his rugby career. He was a member of a truly remarkable family of brothers from South Wales. In all, there were eight boys who all played for the Cardiff club. Along with their parents and four sisters, they lived in a tiny rented house in the village of Taff's Wells and their story was told in full by Terry Breverton in 2022 in his book *The Blue and Black Brothers.* Gwyn was the eldest boy and remarkably at least one of the brothers represented the Cardiff team in every season from 1934 to 1974. The most famous sibling was Bleddyn who played for Wales and the British Lions and became a household name in the world of rugby union. It was in order to send Bleddyn to the prestigious Rydal School in North Wales, that Gwyn signed for Wigan in 1938, to help with the cost of his younger brother's schooling.

In his first season at Central Park, Gwyn Williams demonstrated his versatility playing in various positions in the backs and in the pack. He made 32 appearances in cherry and white and scored four tries. He tasted silverware with the club in the Lancashire Cup Final as Wigan defeated Salford 10–7 at Station Road. At the outbreak of the Second World War, Gwyn joined the Welsh Guards, while Bleddyn trained as a fighter pilot. Both were selected to play in a Combined Services fixture, but Gwyn declined and opted to join his military comrades as they headed to North Africa. During the campaign in the desert, he received a gunshot wound to the head. This ended his rugby career and although he returned to civilian life he lived, as Breverton put it, "in uncomplaining pain for all his days."

Wigan's arch rivals, St Helens, also lost two players in combat. Harry Briscoe was a tricky scrum-half with the Knowsley Road outfit. Like a future superstar of the club Alex Murphy, he made his debut as a 16-year-old on 6 March 1937 in a home fixture against Swinton. At that point he was the youngest player to have ever represented Saints. The former Parr Central pupil is described on the club's website as "an elusive customer around the scrum base, with excellent handling skills." In 85 appearances for the club, he scored eight tries. Briscoe also shares the distinction of being a member of the last Saints team to play in a derby against St Helens Recs when they defeated their neighbours 5–3 on 2 January 1939 at their City Road ground. He joined the Royal Service Corps and also served in the Number 2 Commando unit. Harry Briscoe was killed in action in Italy on 17 April 1945 aged 26.

Patrick Dullard also represented St Helens, making 22 appearances as a hooker during the mid-1930s. During the War, he became a member of the Irish Guards and served in the 'Market Garden' campaign which is remembered in the film *A Bridge Too Far*. Rising to the rank of Sergeant, Dullard was killed on 25 October 1944 as he was attempting to secure the town of Nijmegen from the Germans. He is buried in Jonkerbos War Cemetery, at Gelderland in the Netherlands.

David Morgan Evans was born on 21 April 1911 and was a powerfully built prop forward who played for Neath before venturing north to join Huddersfield in 1936. During his time at

Fartown, he was selected to play for Wales on three occasions against England, France and a Rugby League XIII. He was a member of the Huddersfield team that lifted the Yorkshire Cup in 1938 when they defeated Hull 18–10 in the Final.

Evans joined the Royal Navy and was a stoker on HMS Hood. The huge vessel was involved in one of the most disastrous episodes of the entire conflict. Built during the First World War, 'the Mighty Hood' remained the world's largest warship for 20 years. She had seen action in the Battle of Jutland in 1916. The ship was an Admiralty-class battlecruiser, the only one of four which were planned to be built to ensure that Britannia did indeed rule the waves. On 24 May 1941, at shortly before 6am at the Battle of Denmark Straits, HMS Hood, already damaged in the action, received a direct hit from the Bismarck. The Hood sank in less than three minutes, with only three crew members surviving the disaster. David Evans perished along with 1,414 comrades. He left behind a wife and a daughter he would never see as she was born on the same day as her father's death.

Les 'Juicy' Adams was born in the Hyde Park area of Leeds in 1909. At junior school he was spotted on the playground by his teacher who was impressed by a slip of a kid giving the runaround to the bigger boys. GA Davies, who encouraged his pupil to take up the oval ball, was a veteran of the 'Rorke's Drift' test of 1914 so he would doubtless have been a shrewd judge of talent. Adams eventually joined Leeds in 1926. The Rhinos website describes him as having 'rubber ball-like qualities' and he rapidly graduated to the first team. The club gave themselves something of a selectorial headache by also signing the great Australian half Joe 'Chimpy' Busch. Perhaps competition spurred Les Adams on because he continued to experience success. He won his first Challenge Cup winner's medal in 1931–32, when Leeds beat Swinton 11–8. He was also selected to tour on the 1932 trip to Australia and New Zealand where he played in the Brisbane test. The following season however, he grew tired of playing second fiddle to Busch and opted for a move to Fartown. He took Huddersfield to the Twin Towers where they won before moving on to Castleford where he repeated the feat. This meant that he could claim the remarkable achievement of having won three Challenge Cup winner's medals on three occasions with three different clubs.

Adams became a pub landlord in Leeds, but when War was declared in 1939, he joined the RAF as a rear gunner. He did appear again for Leeds when he guested at Headingley in 1942. In his military career he rose to the rank of Flight Sergeant and continued to carry out his hazardous duties in the War effort. Les Adams was undertaking aerial reconnaissance over Rangoon in Burma when his plane was shot down on 31 January 1945. Of the crew of nine, the three members at the plane's rear, including Les, were killed. The six survivors became prisoners of war and two were subsequently tortured then beheaded by their captors. After the war, the Japanese officers who had overseen the barbaric treatment of the captives were placed on trial and executed for war crimes. Les Adams' body was never recovered.

Oliver Morris played rugby union for Llanelli and Pontypridd and was spotted by Hunslet and signed for the Parkside club. Weighing just over nine stones, doubts were expressed over his suitability for his newly chosen sport but he proved his detractors wrong. He won five caps for Wales in rugby league. In 1938 he was a member of Hunslet's triumphant Championship winning side which overcame Leeds 8–2 in the Final at Elland Road. The dream derby final to ascertain which of the city of Leeds's clubs would claim local bragging rights was attended by a huge crowd of over 54,000. Morris obviously impressed the Leeds directors who signed him shortly afterwards for the then, hefty fee of £450.

In his career at Headingley, the diminutive stand-off made 61 appearances and scored 44 tries and 33 goals. Morris played in two victorious wartime Challenge Cup finals for Leeds in 1941 and 1942. Both games were against Halifax and both took place at Odsal Stadium. In the second of these finals, Oliver Morris partnered Les Adams who guested as scrum-half for Leeds. Sadly, both men suffered the same fate. Morris was killed near Rimini in the Italian campaign on 20 September 1944 at the age of 27.

Bradford Northern lost two playing members in the Second World War. Unfortunately, my research drew a blank on one player save that his name was Charles Freeman. His teammate, John William 'Jack' Moore was a loose-forward who made 189 appearances for the club in a career spanning 1935 to 1942. He made one international appearance for England against Wales at Oldham in 1940.

On the afternoon of 27 February 1942, Moore was a member of a crew of 173 onboard the E-class destroyer HMS Electra which was involved in fierce fighting against Japanese naval forces in the Battle of Java Seas. She received several hits before eventually sinking. 119 men, including Jack Moore, died in the action. Of the 54 survivors who were rescued by a US submarine, one subsequently died of wounds and 10 who were seriously injured were handed over to a Japanese vessel and subsequently became POWs. The remaining survivors were taken to hospital in Australia.

Given its coastal location and important role as a major port, Hull as a city was a prime target for enemy bombers. It was the second most bombed city outside London. Hull FC even had a wartime fixture abandoned during one particular air-raid. Players from the club also became part of the sad roll of honour who lost their lives in the service of their country.

Jack 'Dolly' Dawson joined Hull from Warrington in 1942. Born in Grimsby, Dawson eventually moved to Merseyside to pursue a career in the concrete industry. He joined the Sefton club to play rugby union before signing professional forms for Warrington. In 1932, he moved back to the east coast when he was recruited by Hull FC. The loose-forward made his debut in black and white against Bramley to mark the start of a career in which he made 239 appearances, scoring 26 tries. Dawson was an active member of the Hessle Church and Scout group and was also an accomplished baseball player. He volunteered to join the RAF where he trained to become a fighter pilot. Flight Sergeant Dawson was on a training flight piloted by 20-year-old William Brettell, when their B25 Mitchell Bomber crashed, killing both men on 23 June 1943.

Another star of the Boulevard who enlisted for military service was Ernest Herbert. The stand-off signed for Hull in 1934 from Ossett RUFC in the West Riding. This talented half-back was capped by England in two games against France in 1936 and 1938. He was a member of the Hull team which lost to Huddersfield in the Yorkshire Cup Final in 1938 in which David Evans, who perished when HMS Hood sank, was in their opponent's ranks. Herbert became landlord of the Falcon Inn in Leeds and served in the army. When he was home on leave in Leeds, he was taken ill with glandular fever and died aged just 28.

Interestingly, two teammates from the Airlie Birds shared a similar wartime experience. Ernie Lawrence was a local Hull man who made his debut against Widnes on 24 September 1938. The half-back joined the Royal Artillery and saw active service in Europe. Lawrence was taken prisoner in Italy, but managed to escape before being recaptured and sent to a more secure facility than the one at which he was previously held. Nevertheless, he escaped again and this second break for freedom led to Ernie safely reaching neutral Switzerland. He was mentioned in dispatches in *The London Gazette* on 11 January 1945 for "gallant and distinguished service."

Lawrence returned to Hull FC after the war and became club captain. His teammate, Fred Sillito, was also captured by the Italians. He too enacted a daring escape in which he hid from the enemy in a hollow tree before safely reaching British lines. Shillito too returned to Hull's ranks before a serious shoulder injury, sustained in a match against Bramley, ended his rugby career.

Albert Edward Allen was a centre who joined Hull in 1938, making his debut that year in the fixture against Oldham. He went on to make 131 appearances and scored 31 tries. He was selected for a Rugby League XIII against a Combined Services side which included the great Roy Francis which was played at the Boulevard to raise money for war charities. Allen joined the Royal Air Force Volunteer Reserve and was killed on active service on 28 May 1944. Aircraftman Allen was just 22 and is buried at Hull Eastern Cemetery.

It is estimated that during the Second World War, almost 40,000 Australian troops were killed in fighting across the various theatres of the conflict. New Zealand lost a further 12,000 service personnel in the global conflagrations.

Details of some of the Australian combatants who were lost are quite sparse. For instance, we know that St George's Johnny Holliday was killed in Timor in 1942 and Newcastle Wests' Sidney Welshmen died in the Italian Campaign in 1943. Peter Hickey, who played in 14 Grade One games having joined Toowoomba in 1935, served in the Royal Australian Air Force (RAAF). He was killed when his aircraft was shot down over France on 8 January 1942.

David Middleton writing in *Big League* draws attention to one particular player who has not had much attention for his contribution to the war effort. He refers to Fred May as 'The Forgotten Soldier'. May played five-eighth (stand-off) for Eastern Suburbs and along with his half-back partner Sel Lisle, he enjoyed a successful career with the club. Both starred in the 1940 Premiership Final 24–14 victory over Canterbury. The following season they reached the final again, but were beaten 31–14 by St George. Fred enlisted on 24 May 1942 and served in New Guinea on the Aitape-Wewak campaign in the mountainous, heavily forested terrain in the north of the island. Corporal FR May was killed when his platoon was ambushed as they were cut down by Japanese machine gun fire on 13 March 1945.

Powerfully built prop Spencer 'Sam' Walklate was a policeman who joined St George in 1942, but whose career was cut short by a knee injury. Lance Corporal Walklate who had enlisted in 1943 was part of the top secret, elite Z Force tasked with disrupting the Japanese as they occupied New Guinea. The eight-man mission's boats were swamped on the attempted landing and 27-year-old Walklate and Private Ronald Eagleton found themselves pursued by a thousand Japanese troops. The two Australians were eventually captured, tortured and killed. For decades, the military authorities searched for their bodies. Eventually, in 2014, their remains were found and identified on the remote island of Kairiru and their families were able to attend their internment at Port Moresby Cemetery. Sadly, Spencer Walklate's brother Eric was also killed in action in the Second World War.

William Joseph 'Bill' Ryan was born in Petersham on 24 September 1919. In 1941, Ryan played 12 matches for Newtown and was selected to play centre for New South Wales. His brother Bruce was also a gifted player who enjoyed success with Leeds in the 1947–48 season and went on to be an Australian selector in the 1970s. Bill Ryan served as a lieutenant in the 55/53 Infantry Battalion of the Second Australian Imperial Force. He was killed near Sanananda in New Guinea on 7 December 1942.

Another former Australian first grade player to die in that Pacific arena was Alan Keato. The son of William and Annie Keato, he was born in Liverpool, New South Wales on 7 September 1920. He made five appearances for Western Suburbs in 1943 and his brother Bill, a goalkicking full-back, became the Wests' all-time greatest points scorer and died in 2012 aged 93. Alan Keato joined the Australian Army on 10 February 1943 where he rose to the rank of Lance Bombardier. He was killed at Lae in New Guinea on 16 December 1943.

John Patrick 'Jack' Lennox was born in Mudgee in New South Wales on 21 March 1907 and began his first-class career with St George. He played 40 times in the red and white jumper at centre before joining South Sydney in 1933 where he made 15 more appearances, having moved to the second-row. He enlisted in 1941 as a gunner in the 2/15th Field Regiment. He was involved in the defence of Singapore in 1941 as the Japanese forced the allies back into the city. He was captured and became a Prisoner-of-War on the Fall of Singapore. He died in a POW camp on 7 December 1943 as many thousands of Commonwealth troops did in the inhumane conditions imposed by their captors.

Len and Joe Brennan were brothers. They were a pair of fleet footed wingers who starred for St George. Len played for the club on 40 occasions including the 1933 Grand Final. He joined the RAAF in 1941 and rose to the rank of Flight Sergeant in 104 Squadron. On 8 June 1943, the 32-year-old was co-piloting a Vickers Wellington bomber when it was shot down in the Mediterranean off the coast of French Tunisia. The only member of the crew to survive was Pilot Officer FE McLaren who was picked up by a Royal Navy vessel the following day.

Harry Allwork was born in Eastbourne, East Sussex on 22 April 1909 to parents William and Edith who emigrated to Australia. He became a carpenter and joined North Sydney in 1933 where he made 16 appearances in the pack. On 15 July 1940 he enlisted with the Second Australian Imperial Force. The following year Allwork was posted to Egypt where he was killed in the Second Battle of El Alamein on 31 October 1942.

Prior to the Second World War 'The University' (Sydney University) played in the First Grade competition. The student amateurs struggled to compete with the campaigners from the professional ranks and the venture was eventually abandoned in 1937. John Robert Walter 'Jack' Redman played for 'The University' 10 times and when he concluded his studies in 1934, the former centre joined Balmain. Moving into the back row, Jack made 87 appearances for the club, scoring 41 tries. In 1939 he was in the Balmain side which triumphed 33–4 over Souths in the Premiership Final. His talents were recognised when he was selected for New South Wales in that season. Jack joined the RAAF in 1941 where his obvious capabilities earned him the rank of Squadron Leader. The 30-year-old lost his life when his plane was shot down over Borneo on 5 July 1940.

Another member of the Balmain club who paid the ultimate price was Maurice Fitzgerald who made three appearances as a loose-forward for them in 1936. He joined the RAAF on 3 February 1941 and in May of that year, Leading Aircraftman Fitzgerald was involved in training Canadian fliers before being attached to the RAF arriving in England in November 1941. On 1 June 1942, he boarded the Vickers Wellington Z1311 aircraft with five other comrades at RAF Breighton to take part in 'the thousand bomber raid' on Essen, as part of the night bombing raids on German towns which was the brainchild of Arthur 'Bomber' Harris. When their plane was over Hainaut in Belgium, it was shot down by an enemy Messerschmitt, killing all on board. The airmen's bodies were eventually recovered and they were buried in the cemetery at Charleroi.

Examining the heroics of this handful of rugby league men puts into sharp relief the debt of gratitude which we future generations owe to that band of brothers who defeated the forces of evil in the Second World War. To paraphrase the epitaph on the Kohima Cemetery in northern India, where 1,420 British and Indian soldiers lay at rest, having repulsed the advancing Japanese forces on the brutal Burma campaign, they indeed gave *their* tomorrows for *our* todays.

Wartime Services Rugby Union: Army versus RAF: Trevor Foster, Ernest Ward, Roy Francis and Jim Stott – all rugby league players in the Army side, before the game at Richmond.
(Photo: Courtesy Simon Foster)

39. The Indomitables

I count myself to be hugely privileged to have had the opportunity to meet and spend time with a man who was a true icon in rugby league. Trevor John French Foster served Bradford Northern and then Bradford Bulls in various capacities over a 67-year period, from player to timekeeper, from coach to youth development officer and eventually to saviour in 1964. A true gentleman to the core, Trevor was never cautioned or sent off in his long and illustrious career having signed for Northern in 1938 for £400, making his final appearance at the age of 40. He was awarded an MBE in 2001 for his tireless work on behalf of various charities in his adopted city.

I first encountered the great man when I was a teenager and he coached me as a youth learning the ropes of the game. When I applied for a lottery grant to construct a floodlit all-weather facility for the school and community I worked at, I asked Trevor to open it and he was so humble in accepting it being named in his honour. I delivered him back home afterwards and we chatted about the highlights of his achievements in the game. I gave him a copy of his testimonial brochure from the 1950s which I had and he said he'd pass it on to one of his grandkids.

The Newport born legend played in four Wembley finals in the years immediately after the Second World War and my old man regaled me with wondrous tales of his exploits describing him as the greatest player he ever saw. I was deeply honoured when I was asked to write his obituary in the Bulls programme when he passed away in 2005. In that piece I borrowed from an article written about the great cricketer and Arsenal footballer Denis Compton. His eulogy had included a reference to the manner in which he brightened up the world of post-war austerity and I likened this to the way Trevor played the game saying, "there was no rationing in a performance by Trevor Foster."

When I asked Trevor what he felt was the pinnacle of his achievements, he did not hesitate in his response. "Without doubt it was the 1946 tour to Australia and New Zealand," he told me and he showed me a boomerang which he had brought home as a memento. Simon, Trevor's son, explained that he had suffered a bad knee injury in a country game in Wollongong early in the tour which kept him out of all three tests in Australia. He stayed with the side, although the management feared he might need to return home. Trevor selflessly remained with the squad setting his own disappointment aside to play a pivotal role in preparing the team and running errands. This would have been so typical of the man who always preached the importance of the team over the individual.

He was one of 11 Welshmen on the trip, but ironically, the tourists were routinely referred to as England both at home and in Australasia. In fact, the tour almost never happened at all. Transport was the stumbling block. Every available seagoing vessel was pressed into service to repatriate allied troops from the various theatres of war in which they had been fighting. The Second World War had ended just the previous year and international sport was not a priority. But the Australian government were keen to satisfy a sports-starved, war weary public and thus dispatched a Minister in the form of Herbert Evatt to negotiate with the British authorities to send a team to satisfy his nation's cravings and it was the RFL which stepped up. However, unless transport could be sorted out then this would not happen.

The HMS Indomitable (Courtesy Simon Foster)

Writing in *The New European* in 2021, Mick O'Hare explained how the matter was resolved. The 23,000 ton aircraft carrier HMS *Indomitable* which had survived torpedo strikes and kamikaze attacks during the conflagrations, was docked at Plymouth. The ship was scheduled to deliver 2,000 Australian servicemen back home and so it was decided that the 26 strong touring party should be added to the list of passengers. It was fitting that the ship's name should confer on the touring party a sobriquet, in 1946, which has gone down through the ages for that group of players who would return home as the only ever touring team to be unbeaten in all three Ashes tests, having drawn one and won two matches. Truly they exhibited an Indomitable spirit.

The team was captained by the great Gus Risman of Salford. He and his vice-captain, Tommy McCue of Widnes, were the only players who had been on the previous Ashes tour in 1936. Interestingly, the two second rowers who played in the test team following Trevor's injury, Les White (York) and Doug Phillips (Oldham) along with Northern's Ernest Ward, were still serving soldiers. Special dispensation had to be sought for their release. Initially this was denied for White and Phillips, but after the intervention of the Secretary of State for War, Jack Lawson, this decision was reversed.

The ship set sail from Devonport on 3 April 1946. As a former Physical Training Instructor during the war, Trevor had been entrusted with the task of keeping his teammates fit on the arduous journey. He set about his keep fit schedule with his fellow players on the ship's deck. Some of the squad suffered from sea sickness and put in extra yards to run to the side of the vessel to throw up. They had only been provided with three rugby balls to train with. Mick O'Hare in his excellent account of the journey highlights how Bradford's Eric Batten, famed for his unique ploy of hurdling would-be tacklers, threw himself overboard, dropping 20 metres into the shark infested waters off Port Said to retrieve a ball which had ended up in the sea, earning him a severe reprimand from the captain. This episode makes Manu Tuilagi's 2011 stunt of jumping off a ferry in Auckland during England's abortive rugby union World Cup campaign seem more like a case of jumping up and down in muddy puddles.

It was agreed that the players would receive 30 shillings a week while at sea and 50 shillings a week on land. Wives were awarded £3 a week and seven shillings and sixpence a week per child. On completion of the tour, the players would receive a proportion of any profits which might accrue.

O'Hare explains: "Team captain Gus Risman recalled the players were afforded petty officer privileges meaning they had bunks and a mess hall, use of which was later restricted when officers discovered how much rugby players ate." Trevor told me that following the privations of rationing, the availability of food on board was a highlight. His teammate, Welsh prop Frank Whitcombe, was fabled for his huge appetite. My dad was friendly with the jovial giant who would come to our home bearing steak which he would get my mum to cook, telling her to take some for the family. Frank's grandson Martin has collaborated with Huw Richards to write an excellent book, *The Indomitables* (2024) which provides a comprehensive record of the whole tour. This adds to the book of the same title by Colin Thomson (2009), a fellow Bradfordian now living in South Wales.

HMS *Indomitable* was originally scheduled to dock in Sydney but a logistical issue prevented this and the passengers disembarked at Fremantle on 30 April. This necessitated a six-day train journey across the red hot, arid Nullarbor Plain. Players slept on the carriage floor or if they could squeeze in, on luggage racks. Bryn Knowelden of Barrow describes that overland section of the journey in *No Sand Dunes in Featherstone*. He said: "We just slept as we were in our suits and we had meals by the side of the train just sat in the sandhills. We got good food and as soon as the train stopped, the Aboriginals came out from all over. They got what was left of the meal."

Eddie Waring was a cub-reporter with *The Sunday Pictorial* and he had paid for his own passage to be with the team. Later he wrote, "No team ever travelled so frugally. No luxury hotels for these globetrotters." Simon Foster reminded me what a pivotal role 'Uncle Eddie' played. When his dad was injured at Wollongong, it was Waring who administered the magic sponge. The resourceful journalist also organised a Welsh male voice choir from the squad, which the English players could join to maintain team solidarity and prevent cliques. Concerts were performed to boost the coffers for a few little extras like soap for the players. Waring even organised a change of accommodation when a rat infestation was discovered in the tourists' hotel. Other journalists who shared the tourists' hardships were Ernest Cawthorne of *The Manchester Evening News* and Alfred Drewery from *The Yorkshire Post*.

Eventually the team arrived on the eastern seaboard and following some provincial matches. including a game at Toowoomba. A stand roof collapsed due to spectators climbing on it to gain a better view, causing some to need hospital treatment. Then the test series commenced. The first was played on 17 June at the Sydney Cricket Ground. The enormous interest in the series is reflected in the fact that the ground was full by 11.30am for a 3pm kick off. 64,527 spectators crammed into the ground in eager anticipation. The game ended in an 8–8 draw. Ron Bailey and Lionel Cooper, who later became the darling of the crowd at Fartown, scored tries as captain and centre Joe Jorgenson added a goal. Frank Whitcome powered over from short range for the visitors and Willie Horne added a second try. A Gus Risman goal completed the scoring. A pivotal incident occurred on the half hour. The Bradford centre Jack Kitching was sent off for punching his opposite number, Joe Jorgenson.

Great Britain versus Combined North Coast XIII at Grafton on 16 July 1946. Great Britain won 53-8.
(Photo: courtesy Simon Foster)

Later the Englishman claimed he had been bitten. Eddie Waring said, "Kitching tackled Jorgenson and ... he felt a sharp pain in his side. He pushed Jorgenson off, got up and immediately put his hand to his side. Referee McMahon thought he had hit Jorgenson and ... he had to walk." There was much heated debate between both teams' management groups after the game and Jorgenson demanded a hearing to clear his name, but this was denied.

Given the drawn first test, the second match of the series was eagerly anticipated. It was played at the Exhibition Ground at Brisbane on 6 July. The gates were opened at 7am and by 10am it was full for a 2.30pm start. 40,500 were in the ground as the turnstiles were locked. Thousands were locked out and the gates were crashed. Many present believe that the actual crowd was nearer to 60,000 including the gatecrashers. The England team had to have a police escort to get through the vast crowd. They emerged victorious, 14–5, as Halifax winger Arthur Bassett bagged a hat-trick of tries.

For the second time, the tourists were down to 12 men when Joe Egan received his marching orders. He took exception to a particularly heavy tackle on Ernest Ward by Arthur Clues, who would have many battles royal with Trevor Foster when he later joined Leeds. Egan took retribution and was sent off by referee Stan Chambers. But England had now retained the Ashes so it was mission accomplished.

It was back to the SCG for the third test on 20 July. England gained victory by 20–7 in front of 35,294 spectators. Perhaps there was an element of poetic justice as Arthur Clues was sent off for a swinging arm against victorious English captain Gus Risman.

Following the Australian leg of the tour, the party was flown in batches to New Zealand on three consecutive days between 22 and 24 July. The test was played there on 10 August and Trevor Foster joined eight other Welsh players in a match which took place at a sodden

Carlow Park. Sadly for the tourists, they suffered a 13–8 reversal against the Kiwis. The game was played in cloying mud like a scene from Passchendale and Trevor told me that he had seldom played in worse conditions. Eddie Waring wrote: "It was the first time I had seen seagulls at a football match, but there they were with the teams in one half of the field and the 'gulls in the other." But Trevor did not allow weeks of almost persistent rain to dampen his enthusiasm for the wonderful hospitality he and his teammates received in 'the land of the long white cloud'. He described the Maori people as some of the most generous he ever met.

The team sailed home on RMS Rangitiki and arrived at Tilbury docks some 174 days after their departure, having clocked up 40,000 miles on their epic odyssey. Each player received £123 as their share of the proceeds of the tour. Their nickname, 'The Indomitables', is a fitting epitaph to these brave men who represented their country with such distinction. And what of the vessel which bore them so nobly on their adventure? She was decommissioned and eventually sold for scrap. She arrived at Faslane to be broken up on 30 September 1955, but HMS Indomitable will always be remembered in the annals of rugby league folklore.

Recently I was contacted by Simon Foster and invited to be part of a steering group tasked with planning an event to mark the 80th anniversary of 'The Indomitables' epic odyssey to be held in 2026. The commemoration will take place at Odsal Stadium which is apt given the inclusion of six Bradford Northern players on that record breaking tour. His father's memorabilia from his trip to Australia and New Zealand will form an important part of the evening which will serve to keep the candle of those intrepid travellers alight in the hearts of we members of the rugby league community.

40. Mr Dudley Hill – Andy Harland

Being something of an old sentimentalist, I am quite partial to a certain ballad by the late Kenny Rogers which he sang with his great pal Dolly Parton. *You Can't Make Old Friends* is an acknowledgement of friendships which have stood the test of time. It reminds us that we should cherish and nurture our relationships and understand that their longevity makes the special bonds irreplaceable. No journey down Memory Lane would be complete for me were I not to drop in, metaphorically speaking, on one of my oldest friends, Andy Harland at the Neil Hunt Stadium in Bradford, where the amateur side Dudley Hill play their home games.

The club has its own family connections for me, even though my amateur allegiances were to West Bowling where I played as a teenager. My dad coached Dudley Hill when he first moved to Bradford after the Second World War. Back then, the club operated out of the De Lacy pub where the old man would share a pie, a pipe and a pint with 'his lads' after training or on match days. Leisure opportunities were far more restricted than in our modern era and the players in the 1950s no doubt welcomed the chance to let off steam at the weekend as a break from their hard yacker in manufacturing, textiles or engineering.

Andy Harland *is* Mr Dudley Hill. As a former President, his love affair with the club is exemplified in a true anecdote which takes us back to the year 2009. It was as we approached the May Bank Holiday of that year that I received a phone call from Andy. "We'd like you and your lass to come along and celebrate our 25th anniversary," he said and I was pleased to confirm we would be attending. The 'do' was to be staged at the Dudley Hill clubhouse and I would have expected nothing less. Andrea, his wife and he, had met when her father, Frank Hodgson talked Andy into playing for the club and therefore it had been the guiding force in bringing about the silver wedding they were about to mark. My other half put on her best party frock and dancing heals and I donned my best bib and tucker. Armed with a suitable card and a flouncily wrapped *silver* picture frame as a present, we went along in eager anticipation. Our initial doubts were raised when we entered the clubhouse to see a mainly male gathering. Most of the guys were quite follicly challenged and a tad rotund suggesting that athletic pursuits were no longer a major feature of their lives. The dress code was decidedly casual with jeans and tracksuit being the order of the evening. We proffered our gift and mumbled "Happy silver wedding." "Don't be bloody daft," said Andy, "It's anniversary of us winning t' BARLA National Cup!" This was a reminder that along with his beloved wife, Dudley Hill was also the apple of his eye!

On being challenged about his relationship with whisky, Winston Churchill said that he had taken more out of it than it had taken out of him. When I consider my mate Andy, I think that much the same can be said of him and rugby league. Looking at his craggy features and rolling gait, the game has left him with some physical reminders of ancient battles on long forgotten fields. But for every creaking joint and teeth which have much in common with the stars, coming out at night as they do, Andy is more than recompensed with a treasure trove of memories which the game has given him and which he would not trade for the world.

Men like Andy are the very fibre and backbone of community rugby league. What always amazes me is the sheer volume of people he knows in the game. Whenever I am privileged to be in his company at events, meetings or matches, I am blown away by the number of contacts he has which to modern business gurus would make him a true 'rainmaker'. People from both the grassroots and the professional game go out of their way to catch up with him. I recall coming back from a visit to Wembley together when a tall elderly gentleman made a bee-line to embrace him when we stopped for a coffee at Newport Pagnell. That old chap was Johnny Whiteley and he greeted Andy like long lost kin.

I first encountered Andy Harland over 50 years ago in schools rugby league in Bradford. He was a feisty, abrasive scrum-half who attended St Blaise RC School, which he is the first to admit he couldn't escape from fast enough. He was delighted to enter the adult world of work and spent some time as a roofer before serving his apprenticeship in plumbing. Albert Fearnley was a major influence on Andy's early days in the game. Albert coached him in the Bradford Northern Colts team and remained in contact with him for many years after. Andy met Andrea when they were teenagers and it was his father-in-law to be who convinced the young half-back to throw in his lot with Dudley Hill. So began two enduring love affairs.

His talent was such that professional clubs courted Harland and he played for both Bramley and Halifax between 1975 and 1980. He told me that his greatest thrill from this era was that he played in teams with two all-time greats of the game in Arthur Keegan and Neil Fox. A burgeoning career in the professional game was cut short when he suffered a serious Achilles injury that threatened to end his playing days which necessitated a lengthy period of rehabilitation. Eventually Andy fought his way back to fitness and returned to Dudley Hill.

Andy Harland and Dave Jones (Courtesy Dave Jones)

Sadly, tragedy was to strike the club and I know that the episode in the club's history left a mark on Andy which still endures to this day. Neil Hunt was a promising teenage player when he was killed in a match following a horrendous neck injury. The event had a devastating impact on everyone in their community and eventually it was decided that the ground should be named in honour of the youngster who had been so tragically lost. Andy still stays in touch with the family and any future successes and achievements were dedicated to Neil's memory.

The mid-1980s saw Dudley Hill win successive promotions through the various Pennine Leagues and they were admitted to the inaugural Slalom Lager National League. But their finest hour occurred in 1984. On a hot, sunny May Bank Holiday weekend, they met the mighty Mysons club from Humberside and defeated the much-fancied favourites to win the prestigious trophy they would celebrate those many years later in their very own silver anniversary. Other honours followed in the form of the Pennine Cup, the Yorkshire County Cup and the Pennine Premier Division championship.

In 1986, Dudley Hill made club history when they qualified for the Rugby League Challenge Cup. Everyone was delighted when they drew Hull FC at the Boulevard. The Humberside club boasted such luminaries as Garry Schofield, Steve 'Knocker' Norton, Trevor Skerrett and Dane O'Hara in their ranks and this would be a great opportunity for the men from Dudley Hill to test themselves against the game's elites. Andy recalls that the weather for the trip down the M62 for the evening match was dire and the team bus had to make its way through snow and gales which put the fixture in doubt. When they finally arrived and hurriedly changed, the amateurs did themselves proud. Andy gave his opposite number Fred Au Koi a torrid time and scored a well-deserved try in his Man-of-the-Match performance. Although defeated 38–10, the Bradford side were cheered off the field by the faithful in the Threepenny Stand.

In the 1987–88 season, Andy gained his first taste as a coach when he became assistant to Tony Fisher when the granite hard Welshman became first team coach prior to departing to manage Bramley. Andy then took on the main job in a caretaker capacity. In 1989 he stood down to allow former Keighley and Bradford Northern centre Peter Roe to take up the reins before he moved on to Halifax. Andy again stepped into the breach. He eventually graduated to the administrative side of the club, serving on the Committee before assuming the mantle of President and subsequently he was recognised with Honorary Life Membership.

Andy has a long association with rugby league in Australia and New Zealand. In 1993, he was head coach to the Great Britain Young Lions Under–19 side to visit the Antipodes having led them in two tests against France. In 1995, Andy became the Bradford Development Officer, funded jointly by Bradford Council and the Bulls. In that same year I was honoured to join him on the Bradford Schools U–11s coaching staff to the team who played in the Wembley curtain raiser against Warrington in the Steve Mullaney Memorial Match. The game is played annually directly before the Challenge Cup Final and is named in commemoration of Steve who played in the fixture for Wakefield in 1980. The little lad who appeared on Grandstand breaking into tears having scored a dazzling solo, side-stepping try, was the nephew of Featherstone legend Terry Mullaney. Tragically, Steve was killed when he was knocked over by a car on his way home from school the following year. It was the experience of a lifetime for the lads involved who can count themselves among players like Phil Clarke and Kevin Sinfield to have represented their city's teams in this unique fixture.

Andy played a pivotal role in developing the game in the city's schools and amateur clubs which saw the emergence of future stars like Leon Pryce and John Bateman. In that first year in post, he also acted as Liaison Officer to the England World Cup team. The following year Andy was rewarded by being appointed as the Yorkshire Schools coach and became a Life Member of Yorkshire Schools Association. For several years he organised the Champion Schools competition to decide which lucky youngsters would get to grace the Wembley turf in the annual curtain raiser.

A new challenge came his way when he joined the RFL staff in 1998. Andy has served the game in a variety of administrative roles and became RFL National Development Manager in 2008. Rather than operating behind the scenes, he has been keen to don his tracksuit to serve in the coaching role in which he has always been happiest. As well as acting as Liaison Manager to ensure that touring teams from the other side of the world get the most from visiting these isles, he has led 23 overseas tours. He has taken charge of Young Lions tours and Open Age sides as well as leading British Army teams abroad. Over the years Andy Harland has visited Australasia, South Africa, Canada, the USA and Lebanon, giving the lucky participants once in a lifetime adventures and experiences which others could only imagine.

We live in the age of 'the influencer'. These on-line sages and self-appointed experts make a lucrative living by telling us lesser beings which skinny lattes to drink or how to decorate our homes with the latest fads and new-fangled gadgets. They inform us how we can 'live our best lives' or be 'the best version of ourselves'. You can call me old fashioned (and many do!) but to me it is people like Andy Harland who can really deem themselves 'influencers'. He has *influenced* the lives of countless youngsters for the better and no doubt kept many who might have strayed from the straight and narrow on the right side of the law. I have witnessed Andy's special gift in applied psychology in his dealings with players.

He is not just a rugby coach, but also a life mentor. Andy can connect with the most difficult to reach youngsters. He can empathise with the disengaged as he understands how the education system can feel like a straitjacket as he too felt constrained in his early years. Rugby league has been his best teacher and he is a true self-starter. He has studied and contributed to areas as diverse as child safeguarding, counselling and listening and management and development planning. He exemplifies what the American President Franklin D. Roosevelt said that, "It is better to be faithful than famous." He also reminds me that the greatest gift that rugby league has given to my life is very simple. It is ***friendship***.

41. 1969 – "I was there!"

That great Welsh bard, Max Boyce, revelled in wrapping himself in the snug, soothing, comfort blanket of nostalgia to obscure the harsh realities of the present, as he recalled the halcyon days of Welsh rugby dominance with the proud proclamation – "Roeddwn i yno – I was there!" Well, so it is with me as I look back to 1969. My own personal landmark event in the year, which saw out the swinging sixties and beckoned in the – whatever the 1970s were, was that I moved to secondary school. But this is not what makes the year stand out in my memory. Certainly, it was historic – for the first moon landing, for Concorde's maiden test flight and for John and Yoko doffing off in Amsterdam and jumping into bed for world peace. Yet none of these events competed in my thoughts to make this the year I would boast to my grandchildren, "*I was there!*" Perhaps we hold hard to memories because, in a rapidly changing world, they remain constant and anchor us in some reassuring way. I often wish I could rewind the past and press the pause button for a short time. Someone once said, "memories sometimes sneak out of my eyes and down my cheeks." This would certainly be true for me as I recall two Saturdays in May of that year. And I **was** there – on two consecutive Saturdays which live forever in my mind but as Winnie the Pooh said, "We didn't realise we were making memories. We were just having fun."

Early on the morning of 17 May 1969, my father and I took the half mile walk on Halifax Road from our home to Odsal Stadium. It was a journey we made together many times, but our business that day had nothing to do with my beloved Northern. We were off to Wembley to see Castleford take on a star-studded Salford side in the Challenge Cup Final. Our part in the competition had ended weeks previously at the very first hurdle of the race, whose culmination we had come to witness, when we were heavily beaten at Dewsbury 21–7. It was my first trip to the hallowed turf and my head was racing in barely imaginable paroxysms of anticipated delight. My mum had stuffed my tartan duffle bag with more plastic boxes than you might witness at half a dozen Tupperware parties, each containing industrial quantities of sarnies and comestibles to sustain us in our exertions! We boarded the Wallace Arnold Coach and headed for something called (apparently) the M1.

On reflection, I believe I get my nostalgic gene from the old man. The etymology of 'nostalgia' after all derives from the Greek 'nagos' pertaining to 'returning' or 'homecoming'. This being so and him being an exiled Welshman, it all fits. But as well as having a yearning for the past, he was also a man who marvelled at technological innovation. The M1 blew him away. It made him respond in the same way I saw him react to colour television and to the engineering in a Terry's Chocolate Orange. Dad just stared into the middle distance and then in hushed tones, almost without realising he was emitting sounds he would tut three times and whisper repeatedly, "well, well, well," much as I imagine Uncle Bryn might in *Gavin and Stacey*.

Suffice to say, Wembley exceeded my expectations, yet only fragments of memory remain: walking down Wembley Way eating half a Swiss roll which had been torn into two by my old man like two adolescent mates shunning culinary niceties, the outlandish homemade favours and placards boasting 'Classy Cas' or proposing 'Watkins for PM!' Then there was the *colour*, having only witnessed all of this previously on the small screen in monochrome. And the major sense to be assailed was the sound of it all. The cacophonous beat of the military band, the singing and the roar of 97,939 delirious voices giving full vent to the sheer unconfined delight in living. I retained two permanent mementoes which were large posters of both teams which adorned my bedroom walls for many years before Olivia Newton John's shimmering allure dictated that Hardisty, Hesketh, Hepworth, Hartley and their like were rolled up and consigned to the cupboard to make way for her fragrant delights.

I recently rewatched the game on YouTube for the very first time. They say that memories of our early years always seem to be bathed in sunlight. Well on this occasion mine were not as I recalled it rained before kick-off. Watching the grainy footage, I noticed how precarious it was for Salford's Ron Hill in trying to create a mound of hallowed mud from which to launch an early penalty. It reminded me of my fumbling efforts to effect a kick on Bridlington beach with its shifting sands. What struck me most was the sheer ferocity of the tackling and yet not a single replacement was made. The four-tackle rule dictated that no one died with the ball. It was attritional, borderline brutal at times and yes even though the conditions were greasy, the sides attempted to play expansive football as bodies flew at one another in Kamikaze fashion.

Colin Dixon combined raw power and aggression, with the soft touch of a maker of fine porcelain pots with ball in hand yet the claws of a dockyard stevedore in the tackle. Chris Hesketh eclipsed even Dai Watkins with his illusive silken breaks. Dennis Hartley was even more immense than I remembered, but Mal Reilly stood head and shoulders above the rest. I recalled seeing a teenage tearaway, bounding about with Tigger-like energy, wreaking havoc against Bradford Northern at Wheldon Road some years earlier and dad predicting greatness in the future for the blonde back-rower. What I witnessed in his Lance Todd performance that day confirmed the old man's earlier judgement was spot on. At half-time the Red Devils narrowly held sway with two penalties from Welsh loose-forward, Ron Hill, playing against his former club, to a 40 yard solo try by Castleford's winger Chris Howe.

Long before the tragedies of Valley Parade and Hillsborough and the Taylor Report, standing was the order of the day. We arrived in the stadium in a timely fashion so as to gain a good vantage point standing near the front at the scoreboard end of the stadium opposite the dressing rooms. The two decisive Castleford tries in the second half were both scored only yards from where we stood. These 55 years on, the picture in my mind's eye of Cas' second try was pretty accurate as I rewatched Malcolm Reilly receive the ball outside the 25-yard line. I recalled how he charged forward and flipped the Salford scrum-half Jack Brennan over his shoulder, rodeo style, before handing the ball on to Alan Hardisty who knew exactly where to be in support to sail regally beneath the posts without a finger being laid on him.

I was delighted at how closely my own mental image of the episode corresponded with the footage. What I ate for breakfast yesterday is less clear. In the final minute, Castleford prop, Johnny Ward, having tackled, scrummaged and carried non-stop for the full duration took the ball forward from acting half and with the deceptive prowess that would have done Tommy Cooper proud, handed the ball one handed to Keith Hepworth, the other half of the 'H Bombs', to seal the deal 11–6.

We travelled back immediately after the game, up that magical strip of tarmac which had so beguiled my father's imagination earlier. Unlike later experiences of visits to the Twin

Towers in maturer years, we were in no need of alcoholic stimulation, being high on the intoxicating memories of the day. Sadly, when we disembarked the coach back at Odsal, a sombre spokesman revealed that earlier that day Joe Phillips, the club Secretary and co-saviour of our club with Trevor Foster in 1964, had suddenly and unexpectedly passed away. Talk about in the midst of life...

Back in the day, when the season's competitions were allowed to reach a natural crescendo, Wembley was only the first course in a sumptuous banquet of rugby league which marked the climax of the domestic season. The week following Wembley marked the date of the Championship Final played, back then, between the top 16 clubs in the competition. The final was a moveable feast in that it could be played at a number of the larger rugby league grounds, Station Road, Fartown, Central Park or Headingley, in this end of season extravaganza. Dad and I would generally watch it on telly as we never reached the heady heights of being involved so didn't feel we should intrude on the private affairs of the game's elites. But in 1969, the stars were aligned and the rugby Gods shone down on me because the final was to be played at Odsal. Little pleading was necessary to get dad to stump up for tickets. Talk about all your birthdays coming at once – oh, happy days! The game would be fought out between the Challenge Cup holders and a Leeds side who had suffered the adversity of losing their coach Jack Nelson, who died suddenly on Christmas Day and was replaced by Joe Warham.

So once more, on Saturday 24 May 1969, "I was there!" and again the sun failed to shine. Indeed, the weather in the Odsal bowl that day made the previous week in the capital appear positively balmy! Cats and dogs would be putting it mildly. So if we were anticipating some free flowing, festival rugby we were to be disappointed. However, those of us who preferred a little more X-rated, gory stuff, would, thanks to the elements, be right in our element. All the ingredients for a slug-fest were in place. Pundits believed that Leeds held the aces in the backs whereas, Castleford's mongrel pack, fashioned in the image of their coach Derek 'Rocky' Turner, would be too physical for the pampered pedigree pouches from Headingley.

Like trash talk before a heavyweight boxing clash, these opinions in the press were fuel to the fire. Bill Ramsey, writing in *Leeds Rhinos: Match of My Life* some years later explained, "All the time I was at Headingley, I kept hearing the Leeds pack was soft and couldn't match the bigger, harder ones." Since they didn't come much bigger and harder than Hartley, Reilly and company then we were about to find out if the scribes were correct. The referee for the occasion was Billy Thompson, respected throughout rugby league, but with a reputation of allowing players to sort issues out among themselves, and who had a degree of tolerance for the more physical approach to the game.

Remarkably, despite the ferocity of the Wembley encounter, Castleford were able to field an unchanged starting XIII with only one change on the bench as Trevor Bedford came in for Dennis Harris who had not been called on in the Challenge Cup Final. Leeds had one major concern in their ranks as during the semi-final, their lynch-pin scrum half Barry Seabourne, who was so important in his role in those days of the four-tackle rule, was carrying an injury. In the semi-final win over Salford, he was forced to leave the fray four times with a dislocated shoulder. Miraculously he took the field down the Odsal steps for the game as the two sides alighted side by side, like a yellow and blue waterfall descending onto Trevor Foster's "little piece of heaven on earth."

I recall the early encounters were tense with both sides registering points and the score stood 7–5 to Castleford after a quarter of an hour. Then tempers flared. There are always two sides to a dispute, whether it be playground rows, minor domestic squabbles or seemingly intractable global conflicts and in all cases the vexed question is – who started it? Each side invariably blames the other and so it was at Odsal on this occasion. The touchline began to resemble the famous painting from the Crimea, *Hospital Ward at Scutari*. Mick Clark, the Leeds prop, reappeared having left the field, with his head swathed in bandages and a scrum cap, Seabourne's shoulder gave in, Keith Hepworth was stretchered off and Mal Reilly was sparked out and apparently came round sitting alone in the communal bath.

Harry Edgar recalled the battle in the *Rugby League Journal* (Autumn 2022, Number 80) and quoted Ken Dalby, a former Leeds manager who, writing in 1984, likened proceedings to "…a High Noon showdown, with players gunning for each other and Sheriff Thompson striving manfully to maintain law and order." Writing with commendable eloquence he summed up the situation: "Nor did Hepworth's return cool bestial passions, for flair and finesse were cynically sacrificed on the altar of blind barbaric brutality…"

On the odd occasion on which a rugby game broke out amongst the fighting, there was a trademark Hardisty interception try and a drop-goal from Bill Ramsey and the score stood at 14–11 to Castleford with the sands of time all but dry. Then, miraculously, the unflappable Bev Risman made a langiud, loping break down the left touchline. From our position in the stand opposite the players' steps we had a perfect view. As the teacher from Bradford Grammar School drew level with our vantage point on the 25, without breaking step, he threaded a grubber kick of slide rule precision across the saturated turf for John Atkinson to gather and score in the corner. Then with the pressure of the world on his shoulders, Risman knocked over the conversion with that wonderful, toe-on, metronomic style of his, with the follow through which would have done the Tiller Girls proud at the London Palladium! Leeds had emerged victorious 16–14. The changing rooms must have resembled field dressing stations in Flanders.

Oscar Wilde said, "Memory is the diary we all carry about with us." I hold these treasures with me always, of two consecutive Saturdays which exemplify how lucky I was to have been indulged in my passion for the game, spent with someone, whose memory still sometimes sneaks down my cheek. So to paraphrase Max Boyce:

When I'm old, and my hair turns grey
And they put me in a chair -
I'll tell my great grandchildren
That their **hen daid** was there.
Then they'll ask to hear the story,
Of that wild and wet May day,
When I went up to Odsal and
I saw Bev Risman play.

More rugby league books from London League Publications Ltd

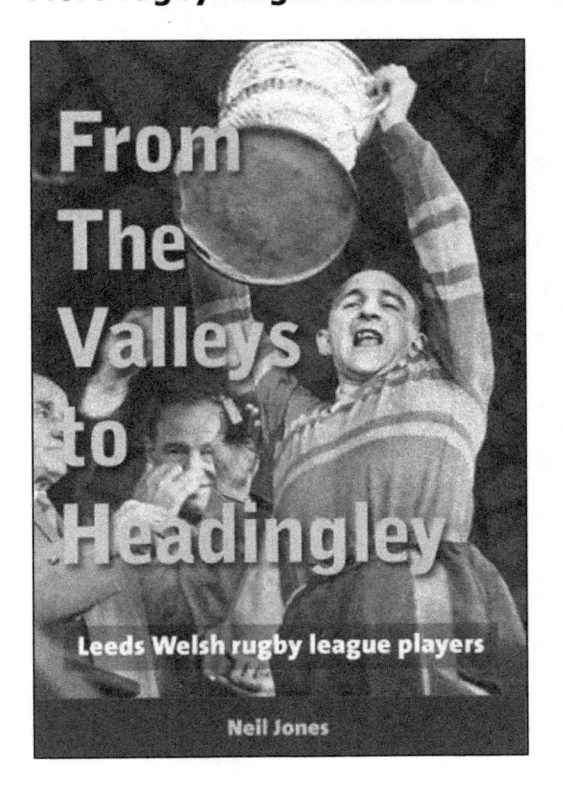

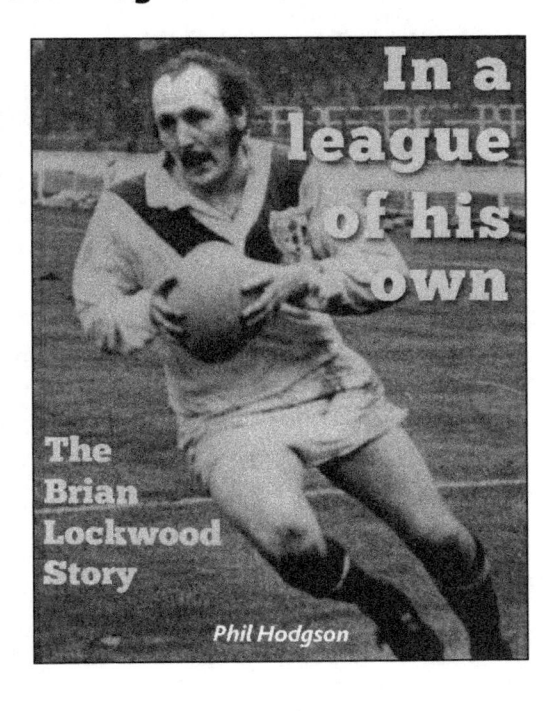

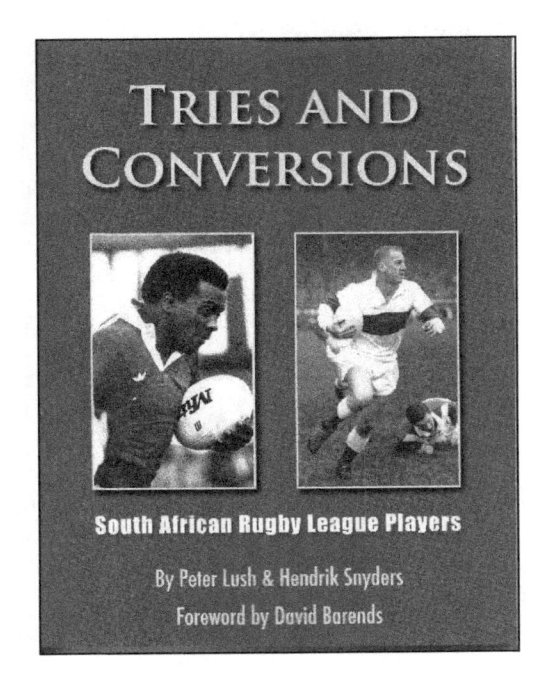

From The Valleys to Headingley
Leeds Welsh rugby league players
Neil Jones

In a league of his own
The Brian Lockwood Story
Phil Hodgson

Ahead of his time
Roy Francis and Rugby League
Peter Lush

Tries and Conversions
South African Rugby League Players
By Peter Lush & Hendrik Snyders
Foreword by David Barends

Our books are available from our website, www.llpshop.co.uk

Most titles are also available on Amazon, AbeBooks and EBay. Some books are also available on Amazon Kindle. They can also be ordered from any bookshop.

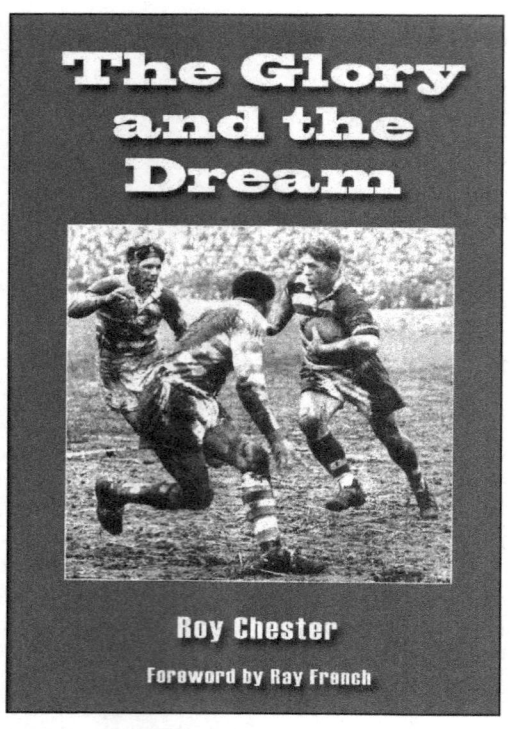

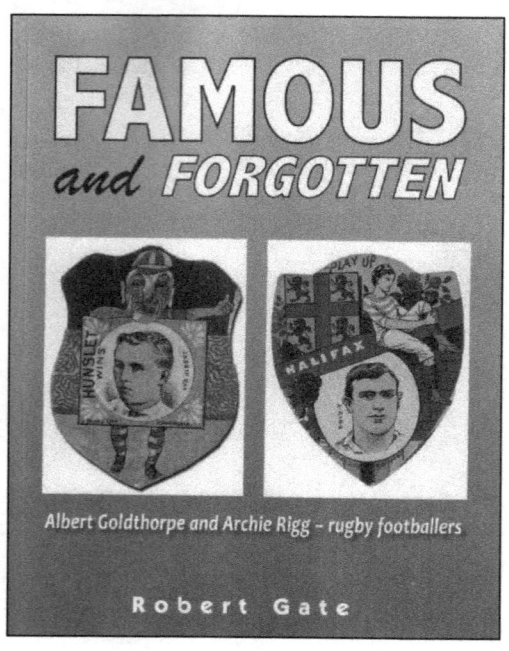